Computer Science with Python

Textbook - XI
(As per CBSE Syllabus CODE 083)

Sarika Kaushal

www.bpbonline.com

FIRST EDITION 2022

ISBN: 978-93-5551-140-9

REPRINT 2023

LIMITS OF LIABILITY AND DISCLAIMER OF WARRANTY

The information contained in this book is true to correct and the best of author's and publisher's knowledge. The author has made every effort to ensure the accuracy of these publications, but publisher cannot be held responsible for any loss or damage arising from any information in this book.

All trademarks referred to in the book are acknowledged as properties of their respective owners but BPB Publications cannot guarantee the accuracy of this information.

CBSE is in no way connected with this book. This Book is written solely for the benefit and guidance of students appearing of CBSE Examination.

Distributors:

BPB PUBLICATIONS
20, Ansari Road, Darya Ganj
New Delhi-110002
Ph: 23254990/23254991

MICRO MEDIA
Shop No. 5, Mahendra Chambers,
150 DN Rd. Next to Capital Cinema,
V.T. (C.S.T.) Station, MUMBAI-400 001
Ph: 22078296/22078297

DECCAN AGENCIES
4-3-329, Bank Street,
Hyderabad-500195
Ph: 24756967/24756400

BPB BOOK CENTRE
376 Old Lajpat Rai Market,
Delhi-110006
Ph: 23861747

To View Complete BPB Publications Catalogue Scan the QR Code:

Published by Manish Jain for BPB Publications, 20 Ansari Road, Darya Ganj, New Delhi-110002 and Printed by him at Manipal Technologies Limited, Manipal

www.bpbonline.com

Dedicated to

My Parents
My Husband Dr Vimal Kaushal
My children Aviral & Rahul

About the Author

Sarika Kaushal is a Postgraduate in Computer Science and a Senior PGT in a reputed school of Delhi with an experience of 23+ years of teaching. She has been conducting various workshops on IT Skills. She is a Master Trainer with the AIEF (All India Educators Forum). She is an Adobe Creative Educator and a Google Certified Educator. She has written many books on the Computer Science curriculum for all classes. She is also the recipient of the Most Creative Educationist Award 2020 from Educlouds.

Acknowledgement

There are a few people I want to thank for the continued and ongoing support they have given me during the writing of this book. First and foremost, I would like to thank my parents for continuously encouraging me for writing the book — I could have never completed this book without their support.

My gratitude also goes to the team at BPB Publication (including Surbhi and Anugraha) for being supportive enough to provide me quite a long time to finish the first part of the book and also allow me to publish the book in multiple parts, since image processing, being a vast and very active area of research, it was impossible to deep-dive into different class of problems in a single book, especially by not making it too voluminous.

Preface

Python is an easy to code Object Oriented programming language introduced by CBSE for grade XI and XII. This book covers the curriculum as per the newly introduced pattern of Term1 and Term2. The concepts are explained in an easy to understand language with a lot of examples. The examples also include the type of questions that are frequently asked by the Board in their annual examination. Real time examples are taken wherever needed to make students connect and relate with the situation to make them understand the concept.

This book is divided into two subsections called Term1 and Term2. Term1 includes 9 chapters with explanations of each topic in detail. Since the Term1 is MCQ based, there are ample number of questions provided to make the concepts clear. Term2 has 6 chapters. Each chapter has good amount of questions for hands on as well as for written pratice.

The following Learning Outcomes are kept in mind as suggested by the CBSE:

1. Develop basic computational thinking
2. Explain and use data types
3. Appreciate the notion of algorithm
4. Develop a basic understanding of computer systems - architecture, operating system and cloud computing
5. Explain cyber ethics, cyber safety and cybercrime
6. Understand the value of technology in societies along with consideration of gender and disability issues

Coloured Images

Please follow the link to download the
Coloured Images of the book:

https://rebrand.ly/9b2f34

We have code bundles from our rich catalogue of books and videos available at **https://github.com/bpbpublications**. Check them out!

Errata

We take immense pride in our work at BPB Publications and follow best practices to ensure the accuracy of our content to provide with an indulging reading experience to our subscribers. Our readers are our mirrors, and we use their inputs to reflect and improve upon human errors, if any, that may have occurred during the publishing processes involved. To let us maintain the quality and help us reach out to any readers who might be having difficulties due to any unforeseen errors, please write to us at :

errata@bpbonline.com

Your support, suggestions and feedbacks are highly appreciated by the BPB Publications' Family.

Piracy

If you come across any illegal copies of our works in any form on the internet, we would be grateful if you would provide us with the location address or website name. Please contact us at **business@bpbonline.com** with a link to the material.

If you are interested in becoming an author

If there is a topic that you have expertise in, and you are interested in either writing or contributing to a book, please visit **www.bpbonline.com**. We have worked with thousands of developers and tech professionals, just like you, to help them share their insights with the global tech community. You can make a general application, apply for a specific hot topic that we are recruiting an author for, or submit your own idea.

Reviews

Please leave a review. Once you have read and used this book, why not leave a review on the site that you purchased it from? Potential readers can then see and use your unbiased opinion to make purchase decisions. We at BPB can understand what you think about our products, and our authors can see your feedback on their book. Thank you!

For more information about BPB, please visit **www.bpbonline.com**.

Contents

1 Basic Computer Organization

Introduction

In the current scenario, when everything has become automated, starting from a toy to a 'smart' Robot, it is an absolute necessity to have computer knowledge. Computers are used in various fields starting from basic data entry for organizing the work to handle high-tech machines. Whether in business or in companies, schools, or colleges, computers are used for various operations. New technological tools are getting developed day by day to help students learn better. We are able to access the information globally and quickly as the technology has made things convenient and easy for all of us. Whether we want to get updated by what's happening around the world or to know the cricket score or to book airline tickets, things are just a click away. As technology continues to advance, computers have become a part of everyday life. Since the technology has influenced our life in a big way, it is more so important to keep ourselves aware and updated. The first step towards it is to understand the term 'Computer' and its basic organization'.

What is a Computer?

A computer in simple language is a machine which takes data in the form of input, processes it based on the given instructions and generates the output. We provide **Data** to the computer, which is unprocessed. Data can be text, numbers, images, video or audio. The final result generated is processed and hence it is called as **Information**. Information in other words is meaningful data. The series of instructions which we provide to the computer is called a **Program.**

To understand how computer works, let us see a basic layout diagram, also called as IPO (Input Process Output) Cycle :

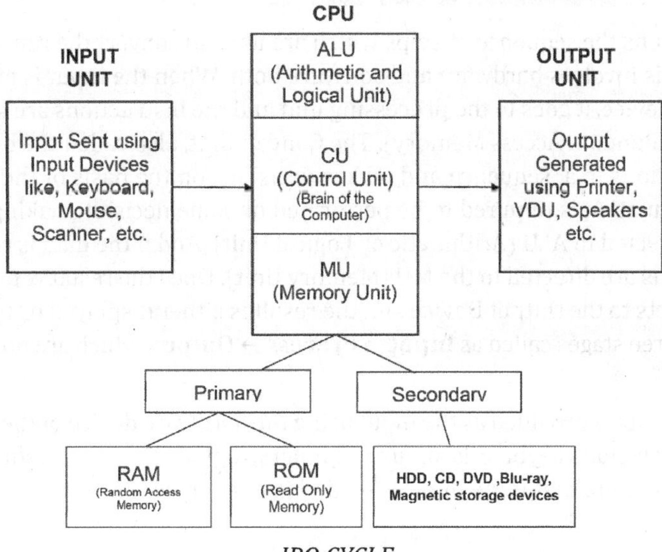

IPO CYCLE

IPO Cycle

There are two main components of Computer, namely, Hardware and Software. The physical component of the computer which we can touch is called **hardware**. This component includes input devices, output devices, system unit, storage devices, and communications devices (It enables information to and from one or more computers or mobile devices). **Software** on the other hand is the set of instructions stored as a program that governs the operation of a computer system and makes the hardware run.

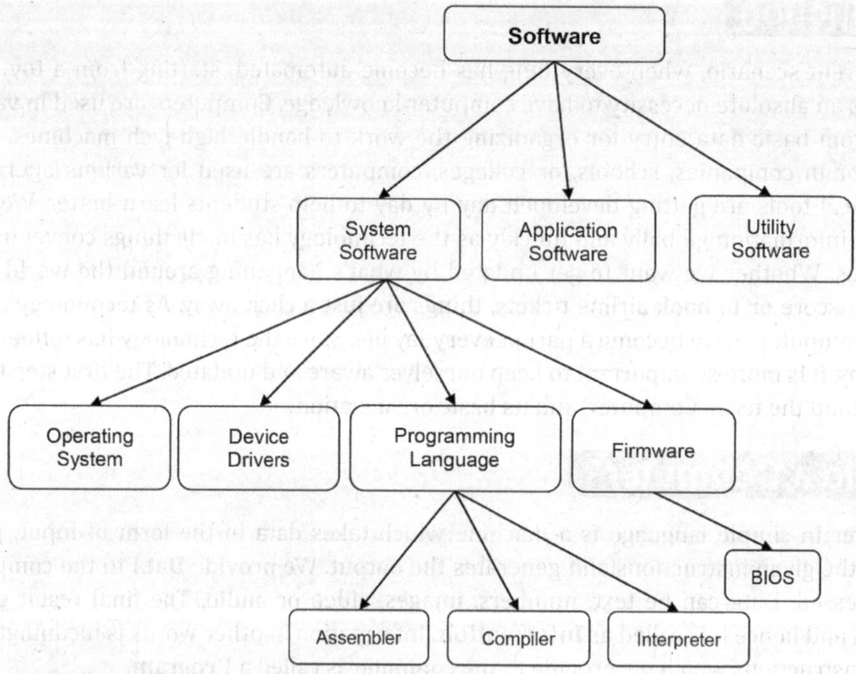

Computer's Hardware Component

The IPO Cycle explains the sequence of steps which are used to convert the raw data into meaningful information and this involves hardware and software both. When the input is given to the computer through the input device, it goes to the processing unit and the instructions are stored temporarily in the memory (RAM-Random Access Memory). The Control Unit, also called the brain of the computer, fetches the instructions in a sequence and makes decisions on the basis of the task performed. For example, if the calculation is required to be performed or some decision making is needed, then the instructions are directed to ALU (Arithmetic or Logical Unit). And if the data is required to be stored, then the instructions are directed to the MU (Memory Unit). Once the result is processed, the Control Unit further redirects to the Output Device and the result is either displayed or printed. Thus, the IPO Cycle undergoes three stages called as **Input → Process → Output**, which are now explained in detail below:

1. Input: The raw data is provided as the input using the hardware device of the computer. Examples of input devices include keyboards, mouse, scanners, digital cameras, joysticks, microphones etc. It is important to note that if the input provided is not correct or appropriate then the result or

output generated will also be incorrect and hence the concept "Garbage in – Garbage out". We will see few input devices using which we can provide the data to the computer in various ways:

a. Keyboard : Keyboard is the most common and widely used input device. The different types of keys available on the keyboard are Alphabet keys, Function keys (F1, F2, F3) , Numeric keys , Arrow keys, Command keys (insert, delete, home, end, page up/down). You can input Text, numbers and instructions into the computer using a keyboard. Most keyboards use a QWERTY key layout. This name comes from the first six letters on the top row of the alphabet keys. *Do you know that The QWERTY layout was devised and created in the early 1870s by Christopher Latham Sholes.*

   Various keyboards are available in the market, like **Ergonomic Keyboards** (which are designed to reduce strain on the body from typing), **USB Keyboards** (which connects to your PC using a small device called a dongle, which you plug into your laptop's USB ports), **Magic Keyboards** (which are Bluetooth-enabled keyboards connect to Mac computers automatically), **Gaming Keyboards** (which are designed for avid PC gamers, offering extra durable and the quickest key response times for split-second action), **Membrane Keyboards** (which are designed without space between the individual keys and the keys are pressure-sensitive, with the different characters outlined on a flat surface.)

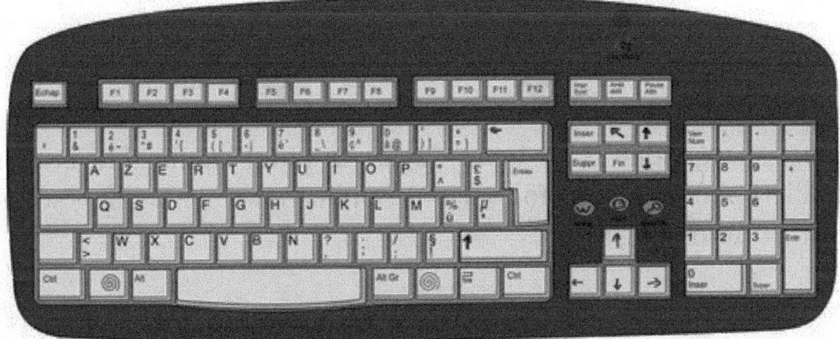

b. Mouse : This input device is used to send the signal to the computer using the cursor which points at a particular application and hence it is also called as a pointing device. The left button on the mouse is used to select and open an application program while the right mouse button is generally used to access the properties of the application program. Today various types of mouse are available in the market, like wired, wireless, Bluetooth, trackball, optical, laser, USB, Gaming, Vertical etc.

c. Scanners : It takes the input from the paper (which has an image or text) and converts it into digital data. The scanned data can be edited. There are many different types of scanners available. Some of them are **Flatbed scanners** (which has a flat surface on which we can lay down the documents to be scanned), Handheld scanners, **Sheet-fed scanners** (They are like small portable printers where we can move the document to be scanned but the scan head is fixed), **Photo scanners** (They are usually small in size and are used to scan pictures. The scanned images are of high resolution), **Drum scanners** (Used by publishing industry for high end image scanning)

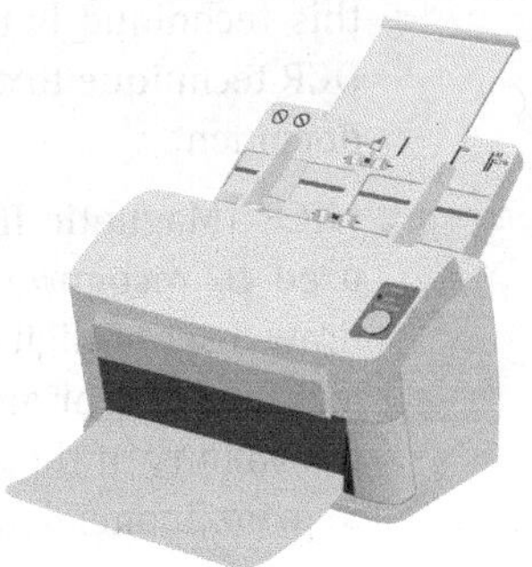

d. Digital cameras : They are used to capture pictures and can be transferred to the computer as digital data for editing or sharing. They use an image sensor chip to capture the image

e. Joystick: Just like mouse it is also a pointing device which is used to control the cursor/pointer on the screen. It is a stick having a spherical ball at its both lower and upper ends. The lower spherical ball moves in a socket. The joystick can be moved in all directions. They are used to give a better gaming experience.

f. Microphones: Microphone is an input device to input sound that is then stored in digital form. The microphone is used for various applications like adding sound to a multimedia presentation or for mixing music.

f. OCR (Optical Character Recognition) : This input device is used to read the text by optically scanning it character by character and then converting the characters into computer readable code. The scanned text can be handwritten, printed or typed. It is used in various areas, like bank statements, business cards, digital receipts etc. The best example where this technique is used is in Google doc. Google doc uses OCR technique to convert either a pdf or an image to a text document.

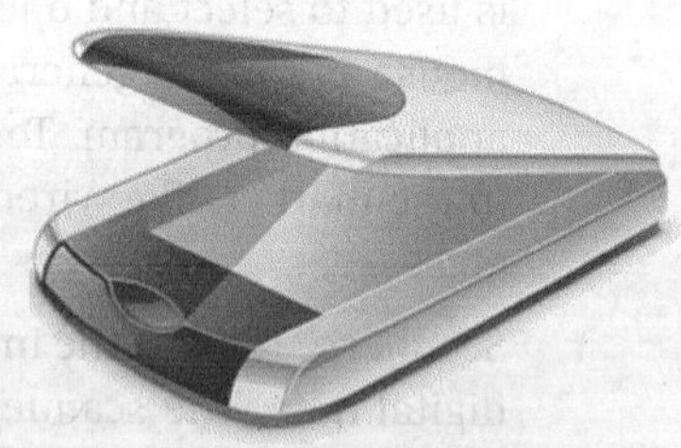

g. MICR (Magnetic Ink Character Recognition): This input device is used to recognize characters by using magnetic ink or toner to draw a set of digital numbers. This technology is used to verify the legitimacy or originality of the document. Banks use MICR to verify the validity of the authorized cheques. This technology is also used to print financial forms, credit card invoices, and rebate coupons.

h. Barcode Reader : A barcode consists of bars and spaces and is a machine-readable representation of numbers and characters. To read the barcode an optical scanner called Barcode reader is used, which uses laser light to read a barcode symbol and then provide an electrical output to a computer via a decoder and cable. The decoder recognizes the type of barcode symbol and translates the bar and space content and transmits data to a computer in a human readable format. We see the barcode readers commonly in shopping malls.

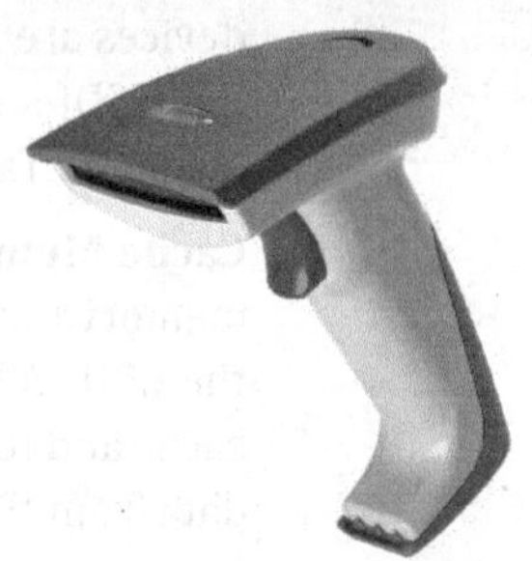

This is the feeding of collected data, raw and sieved data for processing. If the input is not given properly or entered wrong, then the result will be adversely affected. This is because software follows the rule of " Utmost care should be taken to provide the right data and minimum errors in data entry. The quality of input will determine the quality of output. An input device is a piece of computer hardware equipment used to provide data and control signals to an information processing system such as a computer or information appliance.

2. **Processing:** Once the data is taken from the input device, it is directed for processing. Since the data taken is raw, it is converted into meaningful information using the Central Processing Unit, also called the brain of the computer. The CPU has three important parts, MU (Memory Unit), CU (Control Unit) and the ALU (Arithmetic and Logical Unit).

   a. When the input is given, it goes to the Memory Unit. There are two types of memory in the computer, Primary and Secondary. The input from the input device gets stored in the primary memory (RAM) of the computer. The computer system cannot work without the primary memory.

   i. **Primary memory** is the computer's main memory without which it cannot function. Primary Memory consists of RAM (Random Access Memory) and ROM (Read Only Memory).

   1. **RAM** or Random Access memory is a volatile memory, which stores the data temporarily and the data is erased when the computer reboots or shuts down. The amount of RAM limits how large and how many programs and data files you can have open at once. The data stored in RAM is used by the CPU of the computer for processing the information.

   2. **ROM** or Read Only Memory is a non-volatile memory, which stores the instructions permanently and are not affected by the system rebooting or shut down. ROM contains instructions which are required to boot, i.e. what computer should do when it's switched on (like loading the desktop). The instructions of self-check, like all required hardware are properly working or not etc. are also stored in ROM. Initially, the instructions written in ROM were not allowed to get modified, but now ROM is available as EEPROM chip (Electrically Erasable Programmable ROM), where the motherboard includes special circuitry that allows the "permanent" contents of the chip to be updated if needed.

   ii. **Secondary Memory:** This memory is used to store large data for a longer period of time. It is also called the Auxiliary memory or the Backup memory. Secondary memory is cheaper compared to primary memory and the data is stored permanently in Secondary Memory even when the power of the computer is switched off. Commonly used secondary storage devices are HDD (Hard Disk Drive), CD (Compact Disk), DVD(Digital Versatile Disc) Blue Ray, SSD(solid-state drive) , Flash Drive, Optical Drive, USB (Universal Serial Bus) Drive, Magnetic Tapes etc. The computer can work without a secondary storage device.

iii. **Cache Memory:** It is a high-speed memory which stores frequently used data from the memory for fast access. It's a memory between the Primary memory of the computer and the CPU. When the processor needs to either read or write the data, it first checks the cache and if only the data is not found, then the cache allocates a new entry and copies the data from the main memory. This is done to make the processing faster.

b. The most important part of the CPU is the **Control Unit**. This unit doesn't do actual processing but it is responsible for controlling all the operations required for processing. Once the input gets stored in the primary memory, it is the responsibility of the Control Unit to fetch the instruction one by one and direct then to the required unit. If the instructions involve any decision making or any calculations, then it is directed to the ALU. If the instruction tells to store the data, then it is redirected to the MU and if the final result is required to be displayed or printed, then it is sent to the Output Unit. All this happens through the Control Unit (CU)

c. Arithmetic and Logical Unit : This area of the IPO cycle is used to perform either arithmetic/ mathematical operations or Logical operations. Logical operations include decision making, comparing, merging of data etc. For example, if we need to find the sum of two numbers A and B, then A+B will involve addition, which is a mathematical operation but if we need to check whether the sum is an even number or an odd number, then decision making is done. And this is a logical operation. Both are taken care by the ALU of the Computer.

3. **Output** – This is the last step of the data processing cycle as the processed data is delivered in the form of information/ results in this step. Once the result or output is received, it is either saved in a file or is redirected to display or printed. Following are the few examples of the output devices:

a. VDU (Visual Display Unit) : Commonly known as a monitor, this output device is used to display the processed information. Different types of Monitors are used starting from Desktop Monitors (CRT - Cathode-ray tube) to Liquid Crystal Displays (LCDs) to LED (light-emitting diodes)

b. Printer : They are used to print text, images on paper. Most commonly used printers are inkjet and LaserJet which we use in our homes. Other printers are dot matrix, LED, 3D printers, Daisy wheel, Drum Printer etc. Apart from printing the documents, all in one printers can also be used to scan documents and send and receive faxes too.

c. Headphones: This output device is used to listen to audio, when connected to the computer. There are many types of headphones available in the market, like, Bluetooth headphones, On-Ear Headphones. Over-Ear Headphones. In-Ear Headphones. Earbuds, Noise-Cancelling Headphones etc.

d. Speakers: It is a commonly used output device which takes input from the sound card of the computer or any such audio device and generates audio by converting electromagnetic waves to sound waves. The sound produced by speakers is defined by frequency and amplitude. The frequency determines how high or low the pitch of the sound is while amplitude is determined by the change in air pressure created by the speakers' sound waves. Some of the commonly used speakers are multimedia speakers, portable speakers, internal speakers etc.

e. Projector: This output device is used to project an image on a larger area. They are available in various shapes and sizes and can be portable or mounted. They are commonly used in classrooms. Laboratories, auditoriums etc. Some projectors support Wi-Fi and Bluetooth also.

Computer's Software Component

The series of instructions given to the computer which direct the hardware of the computer to respond is called as a software. Depending upon the operations performed, there are different types of software. Three important software categories are :

1. System software 2. Application software 3. Utility software

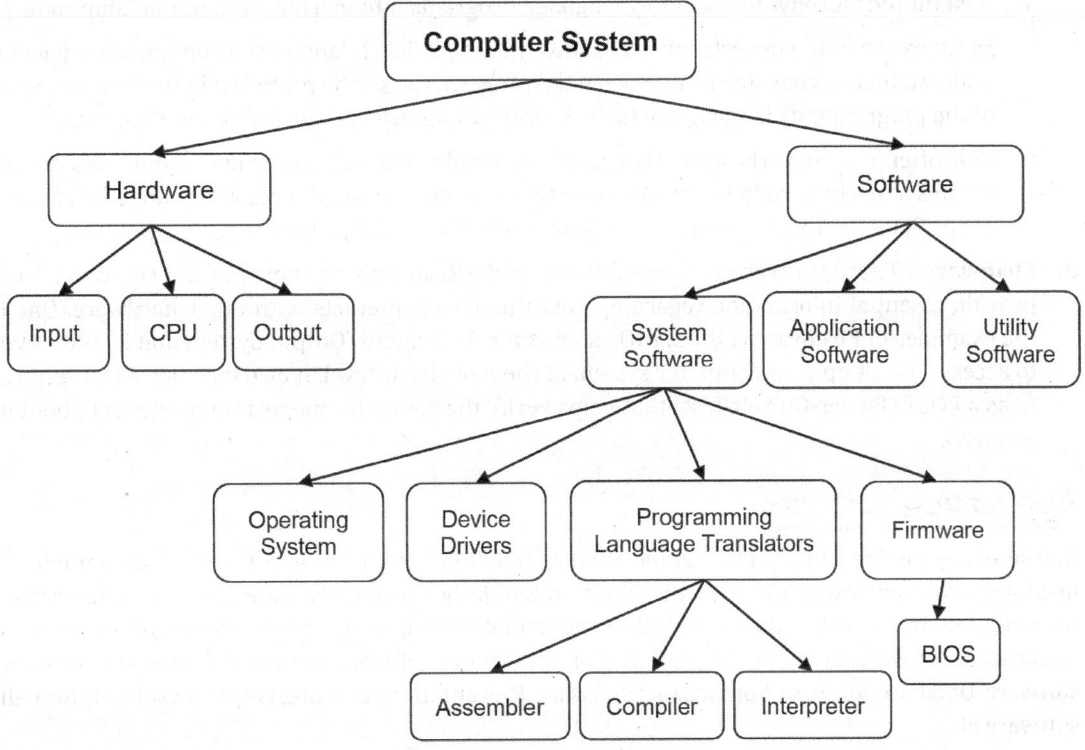

System software

The series of instructions which are used to control the operation of the computer and make its hardware run are called System software. Depending upon the task to be performed, the systems software are further categorized as:

a. **Operation System :** It is the most common and important example of System software as it provides the platform using which the user interacts with the computer system. It is an interface between the computer and the user as it converts low level language to high level language and vice-versa and controls system resources. Some of the common examples of operating system are

- Mac OS
- MS Windows
- Ubuntu
- Unix
- Linux

b. **Device Drivers:** To control the hardware attached to the computer, the system software used is called as device drivers. They contain group of files which allow the hardware of the computer to communicate with the operating system. Today's operating systems have a lot of generic drivers that allow hardware to work at a basic level without needing drivers or software. However, if that device has features unknown to the operating system, it will not work without drivers. Some of the devices which need drivers are HDD, mouse, keyboard, monitor, RAM etc.

c. **Programming Language Translators :** They are also used to convert high level program or user understandable code to machine understandable code or low level program. A program which is written by the programmer in a high level language is known as a source program. The source program is converted into machine level instruction for execution. This converted program (in the machine language) is known as an object program. The types of the translators are :

- **Assembler :** It converts assembly language programs into machine understandable code.
- **Interpreter :** It converts or translates the high level language programs to machine understandable code line by line when the program runs. Interpreted code runs slower. Some of the programming languages which use interpreter are python, JavaScript, Ruby etc.
- **Compiler :** It converts user understandable code into machine code in one session and creates a machine code file, which is further executed to see the result. Compiled code runs faster. Some of the programming languages which use interpreter are C, C++, Java etc.

d. **Firmware :** These software are stored in the ROM(Read Only Memory) of the computer. They provide essential information regarding how the device interacts with other hardware. One of the examples of Firmware is BIOS. BIOS stands for Basic Input/Output System and it allows you to access and set up your computer system at the most basic level. It also includes a test referred to as a POST (Power-On Self-Test) that helps verify the computer meets requirements to boot up properly.

Application software

The software used to run a specific application or function is application software. For example, we need a specific software to browse the internet. Similarly specific software is required to create a presentation or to create a database. All the apps that we see on our smartphones are examples of application software. Some of the examples of application software are Word processors, Graphics software, Database software, Spreadsheet software, Presentation software, Web browsers, Multimedia software etc.

To create presentations, we use application software like MS PowerPoint, Google Slide. Similarly , for creating or editing drawings/pictures on the computer we use paint brush, photoshop etc.

Utility software

Utility software is used to enhance the maintenance of the computer. In other words, it does the housekeeping task for the computer. This means that the computer can run without the utility software but with the utility software, the performance of the computer definitely gets better. Examples are Firewalls or ***Antivirus software, Disk Cleaner-*** which can remove unnecessary files and data, ***Disk Defragmenter-*** which helps to access files quickly thus enhancing the performance of the computer, ***Backup software-*** which can make copies of all information stored on a disk and restore the data when needed.

Mobile Operating System

The way the operating system manages the resources of the computer, similar way the OS also manages the applications stored on the mobile phone. So the function of the mobile operating system is to define the way the mobile will respond to features and functions of the apps installed on it. The mobile operating system manages the hardware and makes it possible for smartphones, tablets etc. to run the apps and other programs in a user-friendly way. The operating system is specific to the mobile. Some of the common mobile OS are:

iOS

It is Apple's very own operating system and is available for apple products like, iPod, iPad, iPhone, and Apple Watch. It is a secure operating system but it cannot be used for any other devices

Android OS

This operating system is owned by Google. It's based on Linux and is an open source software specially designed for touchscreen devices, which includes mobile, tablets etc.

BlackBerry OS

The BlackBerry OS is a proprietary mobile operating system developed by Research In Motion for use on the company's popular BlackBerry handheld devices. The BlackBerry platform is popular with corporate users. It is well-liked for its enhanced security.

Symbian OS (NOKIA)

Symbian is a mobile operating system (OS) for mobile phones that offers a high-level of integration with communication and personal information management (PIM) functionality. Some of the key features of this OS is that it allows impressive battery life and has lower hardware requirements.

Memory Unit

It is the unit required to represent and measure the data which we store in the computer. It is measured in bits, bytes, Megabytes, Gigabytes, Terabytes, Petabytes and so on.

- Bit: It's the smallest unit to measure the data stored in the computer. As we know that the data in the computer is stored in binary or low-level language (language of 0 and 1), so a bit can be either 0 or 1.
- Byte: A byte contains 8 bits. So if the data occupies 8 bits of memory in the computer, then its equivalent to 1 Byte. It is also the fundamental unit to measure the data in the computer . Similarly, if it occupies 16 bits (8+8 bits), then it occupies 2 bytes, 24 bits (8 X 3), then 3 bytes and so on.
- Kilobyte (KB): 1 KB=1024 Bytes (2^{10} bytes)
- Megabyte (MB): 1 MB=1024 Kilobyte (2^{20} bytes)
- Gigabyte (GB): 1 GB=1024 Megabyte (2^{30} bytes)
- Terabyte (TB): 1 TB=1024 Gigabyte (2^{40} bytes)
- Petabyte (TB): 1 TB=1024 Terabyte (2^{50} bytes)

After Petabyte, the memory unit is exabyte, then zettabyte and yottabyte.

Table for quick Revision

Bit	1 Byte	1 Kilobyte	1 Megabyte	1 Gigabyte	1 Terabyte	1 Petabyte
0 or 1	8 bits	1024 Bytes	1024 KB	1024 MB	1024 GB	1024 TB
			10242 Bytes	1024^2 KB	1024^2 MB	1024^2 GB
				1024^3 Bytes	1024^3 KB	1024^3 MB
					1024^4 Bytes	1024^4 KB
						1024^5 Bytes

Quick Revision

Components of Computer System

1. Input Unit
2. Central Processing Unit
   a. MU (memory Unit)
      i. Primary Memory
         1. RAM
         2. ROM
      ii. Secondary Memory
   b. CU (Control Unit)
   c. ALU Arithmetic and Logical Unit)
3. Output Unit

RAM	ROM
Random Access memory	Read Only Memory
Volatile	Non Volatile
Data can be read, modified or deleted	Data in ROM is permanent
Its speed is high	Its speed is comparatively slower.

Compiler	Interpreter
Converts the high level language program into machine code as a whole.	Converts the program into machine code line by line
Compiler displays all errors and warnings at the compilation time. So you need to fix the errors before executing.	The interpreter reads a single statement and shows the error if any. You must correct the error to interpret the next line.
After successful compilation, the compiler creates an object file, which is executed.	No intermediate file is created. The source code is directed executed line by line
Compiled code run faster	Interpreted code run slower

System Software	Application Software	Utility Software
It's an interface between the user and the computer	It is used to run a specific application	It is used to enhance the performance of the computer.
System software is must to run the computer.	Computer can work without application software	Though computers can work without utility software but without the utilities it would be a lot harder for users to manage and keep their computers running optimally.
It runs independently	Application software cannot run independently. It needs system software to run	Utility software is a part of system software
Examples are Operating system, Assembler, Compiler, Interpreter etc.	Examples are word processor, web browser, media player etc.	Examples are Disk defragmenter, Antivirus etc.

- The series of instructions given to the computer which direct the hardware of the computer to respond is called software.
- Three important software categories are:
    - System software
    - Application software
    - Utility software
- The series of instructions which are used to control the operation of the computer and make its hardware run are called System software.
- Operation System is the most common and important example of System software as it provides the platform using which the user interacts with the computer system.
- To control the hardware attached to the computer, the system software used is called device drivers.
- Programming Language Translators are also used to convert high level program or user understandable code to machine understandable code or low level program.
- A program which is written by the programmer in a high level language is known as a source program.
- The source program is converted into machine level instruction for execution. This converted program (in the machine language) is known as an object program.
- Assembler converts assembly language programs into machine understandable code.
- Interpreter converts or translates the high level language programs to machine understandable code line by line when the program runs.
- Compiler converts user understandable code into machine code in one session and creates a machine code file, which is further executed to see the result
- Firmware software is stored in the ROM (Read Only Memory) of the computer.

- The software used to run a specific application or function is application software.
- Utility software is used to enhance the maintenance of the computer. In other words it does the housekeeping task for the computer.
- The way the operating system manages the resources of the computer, similar way the OS also manages the applications stored on the mobile phone. So the function of the mobile operating system is to define the way the mobile will respond to features and functions of the apps installed on it.
- Some of the common mobile OS are:
  - iOS
  - Android OS
  - BlackBerry OS
  - Symbian OS (NOKIA)

? EXERCISE

Multiple Choice Questions

1. Basic architecture of computer was developed by:

   a. Blaise Pascal b. Charles Babbage c. Konrad Zuse d. John Von Neumann

2. __________ allows simultaneous write and read operations.

   a. RAM b. ROM c. EROM d. PROM

3. _________ is not considered as a peripheral device.

   a. CPU b. Keyboard c. Monitor d. Mouse

4. ________ computer memory is fastest.

   a. Register b. Hard disk c. RAM d. ROM

5. ________ operations are performed by the ALU.

   a. Data manipulation b. Exponential
   c. Square root d. All of the above

6. _________ format is used to store data.

   a. Decimal b. Octal c. Binary d. Hexadecimal

7. ________ memory of the computer is used to speed up the computer processing?

   a. RAM b. ROM c. Cache memory d. Secondary memory

8. Components of a computer are connected to each other by:

   a. Computer parts b. Computer architecture
   c. Computer hardware d. Computer software

9. The address in the main memory is called as:

   a. Logical address b. Physical address
   c. Memory address d. Computer address

10. _______ memory unit communicates directly with the CPU.

    a. Main b. Secondary c. Auxiliary d. Cache

11. The collection of 8-bits is:

    a. Byte b. Bit c. Nibbe d. Word

12. Computer stores its data in memory in the form:

    a. Decimal b. Binary c. Octal d. Hexadecimal

13. ______ is equal to 4 bits.

    a. Byte b. Kilobyte c. Nibble d. Record

14. EEPROM stands for:

    a. Electrically Erasable and Programmable Read-Only Memory
    b. Electronically Erasable and Programmable Read-Only Memory
    c. Electrically Enabled and Programmable Read-Only Memory
    d. Electrically Enabled and Programmable Random-Only Memory

15. The _______ is the computational center of the CPU.

    a. Registers b. ALU c. Memory d. Control unit

16. CPU stands for

    a. Central Program Unit b. Control Processing Unit
    c. Central Processing Unit d. Control Program Unit

17. Mouse is an _____ device

    a. Processing b. Output c. Display d. Input

18. IPO stands for

    a. Internet Programs Output b. Input Program Output
    c. Intelligent Processing Output d. Input Processing Output

19. The physical component of a computer which we can see and touch is known as _____

    a. Software b. Hardware c. Data d. Information

20. _____ is an example of a Software

    a. Monitor b. USB c. CD d. Microsoft Word

Fill in the blanks

1. A computer in simple language is a machine which takes data in the form of _________, processes it based on the given instructions and generates the **output**.
2. The physical component of the computer which we can touch is called _________.

3. __________ is the set of instructions stored as a program that governs the operation of a computer system and makes the hardware run.
4. The __________ Cycle explains the sequence of steps which are used to convert the raw data into meaningful information and this involves hardware and software both.
5. The __________ is also called the **brain of the computer.**
6. The raw data is provided as the input using the __________ device of the computer.
7. Data is taken from the input device; it is directed for __________.
8. There are __________ types of memory in the computer, **Primary** and **Secondary.**
9. __________ **Memory** is used to store large data for a longer period of time.
10. __________ **Memory** is a high speed memory which stores frequently used data from the memory for fast access.
11. **Arithmetic and Logical Unit** is used to perform either arithmetic/mathematical operations or __________ operations.
12. __________ is the unit required to represent and measure the data which we store in the computer.
13. __________ is the smallest unit to measure the data stored in the computer.
14. A __________ contains 8 bits.
15. __________ can be text, numbers, images, video or audio.

State whether the following statements are true or false

1. IPO is Input Process Output Cycle.
2. There are three main components of Computer.
3. Software is the set of instructions stored as a program that governs the operation of a computer system and makes the hardware run.
4. The different types of keys available on the Mouse are Alphabet keys, Function keys (F1, F2, F3), Numeric keys, Arrow keys, Command keys (Insert, delete, home, end, page up/down).
5. Mouse is used to send the signal to the computer using the cursor which points at a particular application and hence it is also called as a pointing device.
6. Joystick is an input device to input sound that is stored in digital form.
7. A barcode consists of bars and spaces and is a machine-readable representation of numbers and characters.
8. The CPU has three important parts, MU (Memory Unit), CU (Control Unit) and the ALU (Arithmetic and Logical Unit).
9. Auxiliary memory is the computer's main memory without which it cannot function.
10. ROM or Read Only Memory is a non-volatile memory, which stores the instructions permanently and are not affected by the system rebooting or shut down.
11. Memory Unit. is responsible for controlling all the operations required for processing.
12. VDU (Visual Display Unit) is commonly known as a monitor, and is used to display the processed information.

13. Speaker is commonly used output device which takes input from the sound card of the computer or any such audio device and generates audio by converting electromagnetic waves to sound waves.
14. Memory Unit is the unit required to represent and measure the data which we store in the computer.
15. If the data occupies 16 bits of memory in the computer, then its equivalent to 1 Byte.

Short Questions

1. What is a Computer?
2. Define the term Data.
3. What is program?
4. Define IPO cycle.
5. What does hardware comprise of?
6. What is the full form of RAM and ROM.
7. Name the computer's hardware component.
8. Define the input unit and give two example.
9. Define the Output unit and give two example.
10. Name the types of ROM.

Long Questions

1. Explain the components of CPU.
2. Differentiate among primary memory and secondary memory.
3. Write a short note on cache memory.
4. Explain the function of Arithmetic and Logical Unit.
5. What is the use of speaker.
6. Explain the types of Memory unit.
7. Differentiate among RAM and ROM.
8. Explain the types of ROM.
9. Differentiate among VDU and projector.
10. Explain Auxiliary memory.

Answer:

Multiple choice questions

1. d	2. a	3. a	4. a	5. d	6. c	7. c	8. b
9. b	10. a	11. a	12. b	13. c	14. a	15. b	16. c
17. d	18. d	19. b	20. d				

Fill in the blanks

1. input	2. hardware	3. Software	4. IPO	5. Control Unit
6. hardware	7. processing	8. two	9. Secondary	10. Cache
11. Logical	12. Memory unit	13. Bit	14. byte	15. Data

State whether the following statements are true or false.

1. True	2. False	3. True	4. False	5. True
6. False	7. True	8. True	9. False	10. True
11. False	12. True	13. True	14. True	15. False

2 Boolean Algebra

Introduction

We know that the data stored in the computer is in the form of binary language 0 and 1 or True and False signals where 0 is False and 1 is True. So how is an expression solved when we provide the input signals in the form of 0's and 1's and in what form the result will be generated? In 1954, George Boole invented the concept of Boolean logic, which is a core concept of Boolean Algebra and a branch of mathematics. Boolean logic can be used to describe the manipulation and processing of binary information. Digital electronic circuits and microprocessors based systems are made using Gates which are formed using the boolean logic.

Boolean Variable and Boolean Expression

The expression which takes the input in the form of boolean variables and generates boolean result is called a *Boolean expression.* The input in a boolean expression is given in the form of 0 or 1 through a variable, which is called as a *Boolean variable.*

For example, if X,Y and Z are three boolean variables, such that they accept input in the form of 0 or 1, then the expression formed from them would be a boolean expression, like

`X+Y.Z`

Or

`X.Y+Z'`

Or

`X.(Y'+Z)`

Truth Table

The binary inputs and the output of the boolean expression is displayed using a table called a Truth Table. Truth table helps us to understand the behaviour of a boolean expression of a given logic circuit. Truth table allows us to take all the possible combinations of input possible in a given expression and its resultant output.

The possible number of input combinations provided in a boolean expression is based on the total no of variables in that expression and that is 2^N, where N represents total no of variables.

For example, a boolean expression with 1 variable X will have 2^1 inputs and thus its truth table will be as follows:

X
0
1

While the total number of inputs provided by two boolean variables in a boolean expression would be 2^2=4. Its truth table will appear like this:

X	Y
0	0
0	1
1	0
1	1

Similarly for three variables, the possible number of inputs would be $2^3 = 8$

X	Y	Z
0	0	0
0	0	1
0	1	0
0	1	1
1	0	0
1	0	1
1	1	0
1	1	1

And so on...

Simple rules to remember to create a Truth table for given sets of input.

1. The total number of inputs will be based on the number of variables in a boolean expression. The inputs will be 2^N, where N denotes the number of boolean variables.
2. We always write the input values in the table from right to left.
3. The right most boolean variable will have alternate 0 and 1 , starting from 0.
4. The next variable will have a series of two zeroes and two ones and so on.
5. The next variable will have a series of four zeroes and four ones and so on.
6. And now can guess the input for the next variable? Yes it will be a series of eight zeroes and eight ones and so on.

Can you fill the Truth table for four boolean variables?

A	B	C	D

A	B	C	D

Boolean Operators

The operators used in boolean algebra are called Boolean operators. The three operators using which the boolean expression is formed are AND/OR/NOT

AND operator

This operator when used with boolean variables will generate the result True if all the inputs are True or 1 else it will be False or 0. AND operation is expressed using '.' or '^'

X	Y	X.Y (or X^Y)
0	0	0
0	1	0
1	0	0
1	1	1

OR operator

It generates the final result of a boolean expression True if either one input or all the inputs are True or 1 else it will be False or 0. OR operation is expressed using '+' or 'V'

X	Y	X+Y (or X∨Y)
0	0	0
0	1	1
1	0	1
1	1	1

NOT operator

It reverses the result of the input by negating its value by making True to False (or 1 to 0) and False to True(or 0 to 1). NOT operation is expressed '~' or '''

X	~X (or X')
0	1
1	0

Quick Recap

Operator	Symbol	Input		Output
AND	(.) or (^)	X	Y	X.Y
		0	0	0
		0	1	0
		1	0	0
		1	1	1
OR	(+) or (v)	X	Y	X+Y
		0	0	0
		0	1	1
		1	0	1
		1	1	1
NOT	(') or (~)	X		X'
		0		1
		1		0

Logic Gates

To carry out the logical operations where single or multiple binary inputs generate one binary output, logic gates are used. In other words, logic gates are electronic circuits which generate a boolean output based on the boolean inputs provided by the boolean variables. The different logical gates are AND, OR, NOT, NOR, NAND, XOR.

AND Gate

This gate will achieve the output 1/True if all the inputs are 1 or True else the output will be False.

A	B	A.B
0	0	0
0	1	0
1	0	0
1	1	1

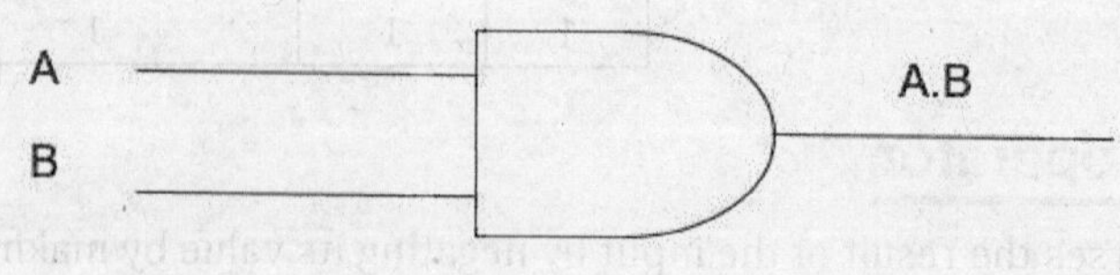

OR Gate

This gate will achieve the output 1/True if either one or all the inputs are 1 or True else the output will be False

A	B	A+B
0	0	0
0	1	1
1	0	1
1	1	1

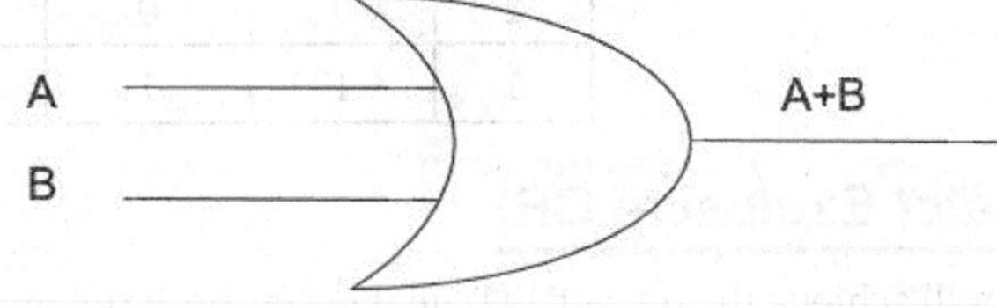

NOT Gate

This gate gives the complement of the input provided. If the input is True or 1, the resultant complement would be 0 or False and vice versa.

A	A'
0	1
1	0

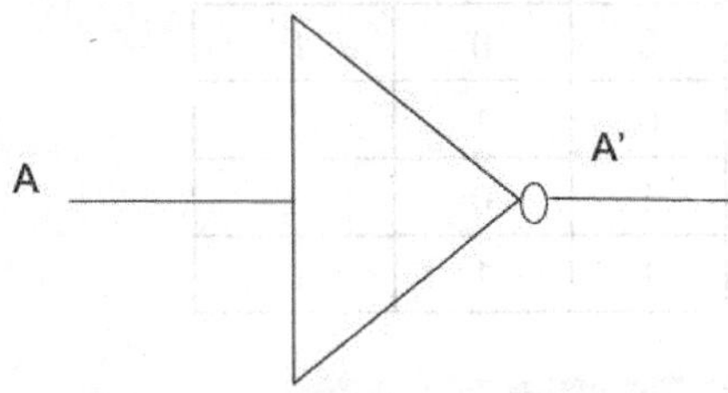

Universal Gate (NOR, NAND)

NOR and NAND are known as universal gates as any boolean expression can be created or converted into only "NAND' or only 'NOR Gates, which we will learn in the next section.

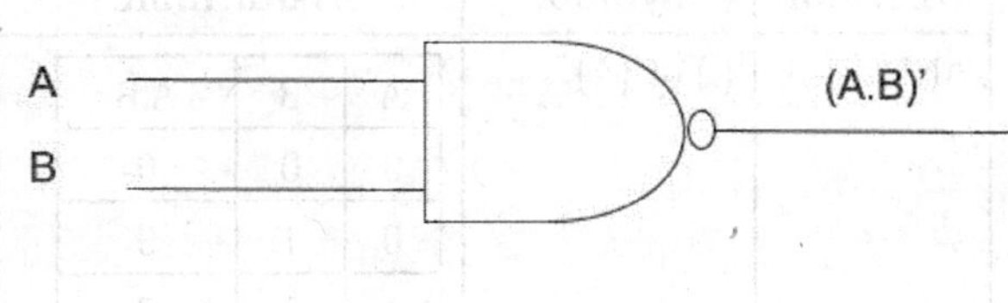

NOR Gate (Not-of OR)

As the name suggests, it gives the complement of the result of the OR gate and thus the name NOR

A	B	(A+B)	(A+B)'
0	0	0	1
0	1	1	0
1	0	1	0
1	1	1	0

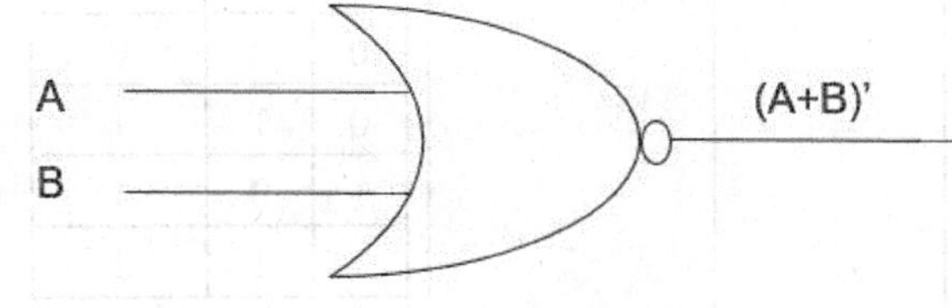

NAND Gate(Not-of-AND)

Just like NOR gate, NAND gate gives the complement of the AND Gate, i.e. Not of AND and hence the name.

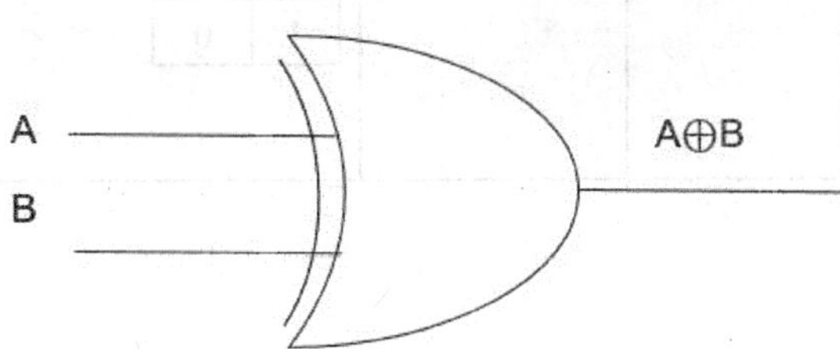

A	B	A.B	(A.B)'
0	0	0	1
0	1	0	1
1	0	0	1
1	1	1	0

XOR Gate(Exclusive OR)

This gate will achieve the output 1/True if either both the inputs are different. With the same inputs (whether True or False), the result will be False or 0. It is denoted by the symbol ⊕

A	B	A⊕B
0	0	0
0	1	1
1	0	1
1	1	0

Quick Recap

<table>
<tr><th>Operator</th><th>Symbol</th><th>Truth Table</th><th>Logic Gate</th></tr>
<tr><td>AND</td><td>(.) or (^)</td><td>A B A.B
0 0 0
0 1 0
1 0 0
1 1 1</td><td>A
B
A.B</td></tr>
<tr><td>OR</td><td>(+) or ()</td><td>A B A+B
0 0 0
0 1 1
1 0 1
1 1 1</td><td>A
B
A+B</td></tr>
<tr><td>NOT</td><td>(') or (~)</td><td>A A'
0 1
1 0</td><td>A
A'</td></tr>
</table>

<table>
<tr><th>Operator</th><th>Symbol</th><th>Truth Table</th><th>Logic Gate</th></tr>
<tr><td>NOR</td><td></td><td>

A	B	(A+B)'
0	0	1
0	1	0
1	0	0
1	1	0

</td><td>A
B
(A+B)'</td></tr>
<tr><td>NAND</td><td></td><td>

A	B	(A.B)'
0	0	1
0	1	1
1	0	1
1	1	0

</td><td>A
B
(A.B)'</td></tr>
<tr><td>XOR</td><td>⊕</td><td>

A	B	A⊕B
0	0	0
0	1	1
1	0	1
1	1	0

</td><td>A
B
A⊕B</td></tr>
</table>

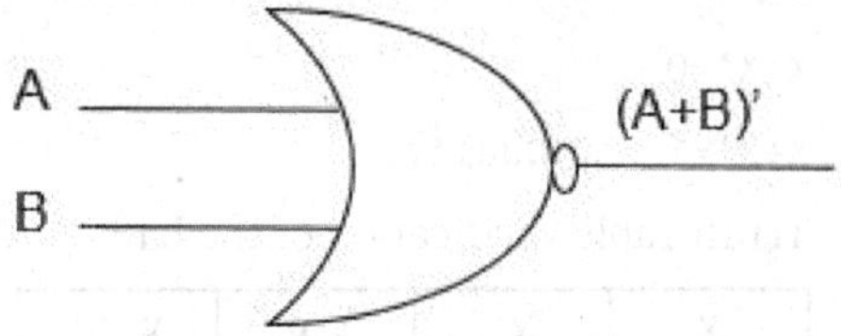

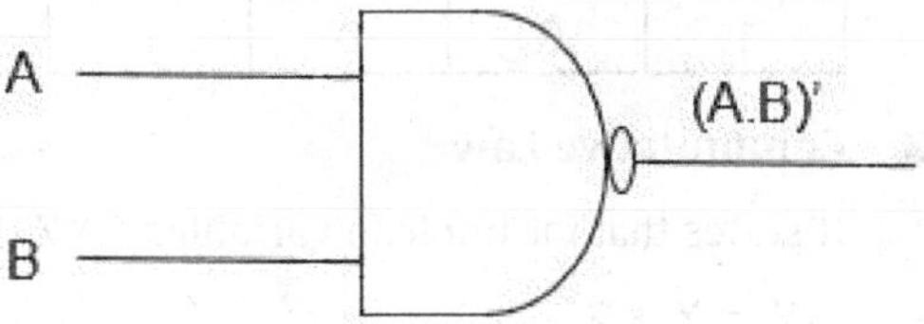

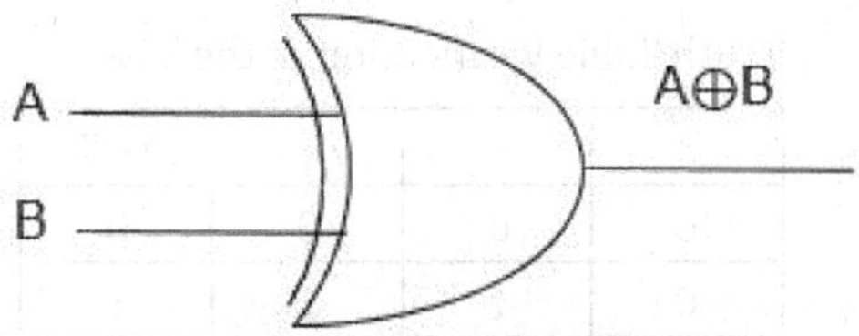

Logic Circuits

Now we know that the Logic circuits are made using the logic gates based on the given boolean expression. But these boolean expressions can further be simplified using certain laws and rules. Let us study few important Laws along with their Truth table Verification

Postulates of Boolean Algebra

1. **Identity Law**

   Its states that for a boolean variable X, the following holds True

   ```
   X+0=X
   X.1=X (by Duality)
   ```

   Truth Table Verification

X	0	X+0
0	0	0
1	0	1

X	1	X.1
0	1	0
1	1	1

2. **Complement Law**

It states that the AND of a boolean variable and its complement is always 0.

```
X.X'=0
X+X'=1 (by Duality)
```

Truth Table Verification of the Law

X	X'	X.X'	X+X'
0	1	0	1
1	0	0	1

3. **Commutative Law**

It states that for boolean variables X,Y,Z the following holds True:

```
X+Y = Y + X
X.Y=Y.X (by Duality)
```

Truth Table Verification of the Law

X	Y	X+Y	Y+X
0	0	0	0
0	1	1	1
1	0	1	1
1	1	1	1

4. **Associative Law**

It states that for boolean variables X,Y,Z the following holds True:

```
X+(Y+Z) = (X+Y)+Z   → Law 1
X.(Y.Z)=(X.Y).Z     → Law 2 (By Duality)
```

Truth Table Verification of the Law

X	Y	Z	(Y+Z)	X+(Y+Z)	(X+Y)	(X+Y)+Z
0	0	0	0	0	0	0
0	0	1	1	1	0	1
0	1	0	1	1	1	1
0	1	1	1	1	1	1
1	0	0	0	1	1	1
1	0	1	1	1	1	1
1	1	0	1	1	1	1
1	1	1	1	1	1	1

5. **Distributive Law**

It states that for boolean variables X,Y,Z the following holds True:

```
X.(Y+Z) = X.Y + X.Z  → Law 1
X+Y.Z = (X+Y).(X+Z)  → Law 2 (By Duality)
```

Truth Table Verification of the Law 1

X	Y	Z	(Y+Z)	X.(Y+Z)	X.Y	X.Z	X.Y+X.Z
0	0	0	0	0	0	0	0
0	0	1	1	0	0	0	0
0	1	0	1	0	0	0	0
0	1	1	1	0	0	0	0
1	0	0	0	0	0	0	0
1	0	1	1	1	0	1	1
1	1	0	1	1	1	0	1
1	1	1	1	1	1	1	1

Can you do the Truth Table Verification of the Law 2?

X	Y	Z	Y.Z	X+Y.Z	X+Y	X+Z	(X+Y).(X+Z)
0	0	0					
0	0	1					
0	1	0					
0	1	1					
1	0	0					
1	0	1					
1	1	0					
1	1	1					

6. **Duality Principle**

It states that any boolean expression derived using the boolean laws remain unaffected, if we

A. Change the all AND operations to OR or vice versa and

B. Change all 0's with 1 or vice versa.

7. **Complement of Complement**

It states that the complement to complement of a boolean variable is same as the boolean variable. This means that:

```
X=((X)')'
```

Truth Table Verification

X	X'	(X')'
0	1	0
1	0	1

Logic Circuit

While converting the given boolean expression into logic gate, we need to remember that the priority is given to NOT, then AND and then OR (if no brackets are given)

Let us take few examples which help us understand how to draw the logic gate from the given Boolean expression:

A+B'C

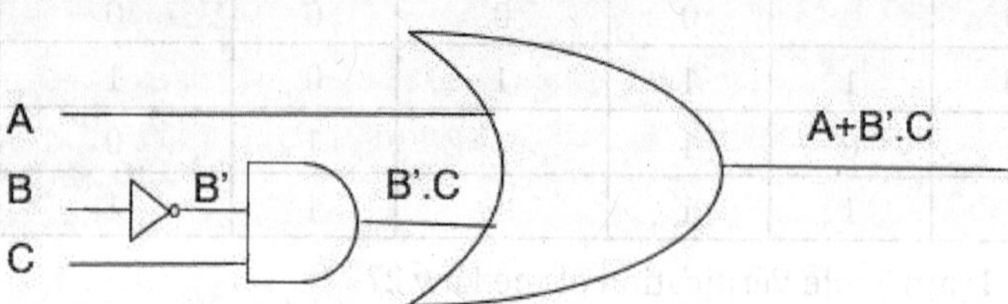

X.Y+Z

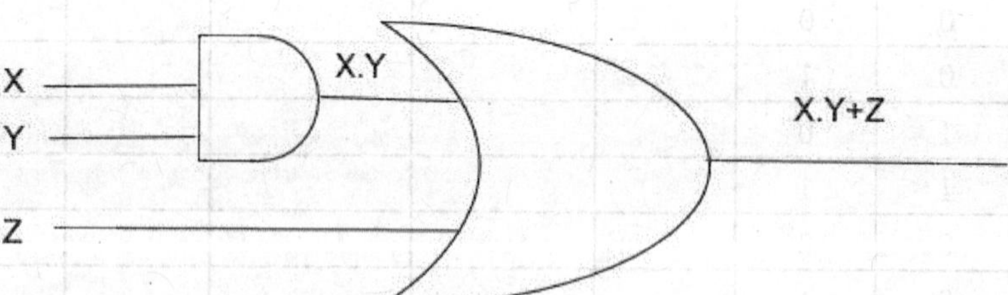

X'.(Y+Z)

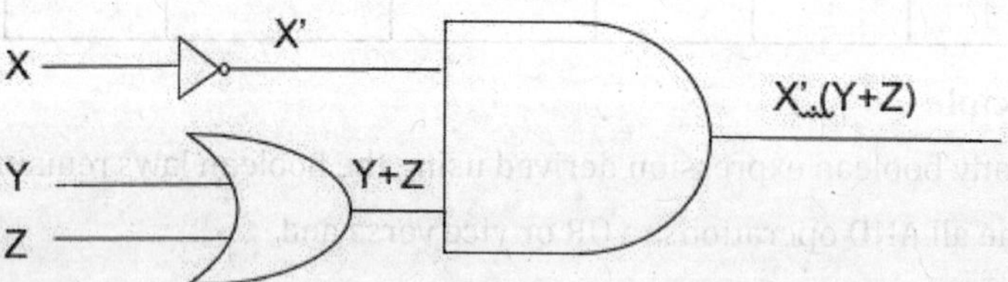

De Morgan's Law

It states that for boolean variables A1, A2, A3.....An, the complement of the product of all the terms is equal to the sum of the complement of each term.

```
(A+B)'=A'.B' → Law 1

(A.B)'=A'+B' → Law 2 (By Duality)
```

Similarly, for n Boolean Variables

`(A1+A2+A3+......An)'=A1'.A2'.A3'......An'`

`(A1.A2.A3.......An)'=A1'+A2'+A3'+......An'`

Truth Table Verification of De Morgan's Law 1

A	B	(A+B)	(A+B)'	A'	B'	A'.B'
0	0	0	1	1	1	1
0	1	1	0	1	0	0
1	0	1	0	0	1	0
1	1	1	0	0	0	0

Truth Table Verification of De Morgan's Law 2

A	B	(A.B)	(A.B)'	A'	B'	A'+B'
0	0	0	1	1	1	1
0	1	0	1	1	0	1
1	0	0	1	0	1	1
1	1	1	0	0	0	0

Application of De Morgan's Law

We use this law to convert the given boolean expression into alternative gates, where we can design the logic circuit using only the universal gates, like only NOR or only NAND. Let us take an example to understand the application of De Morgan's Law:

To convert the given Boolean expression using NAND gate

A+B'.C

(applying complement to complement)

((A+B'.C)')'

Applying De Morgan's Law 1 (X+Y)'=X'.Y' , by considering X as A and B'.C as Y

=> (A'.(B'.C)')'

Logic Circuit

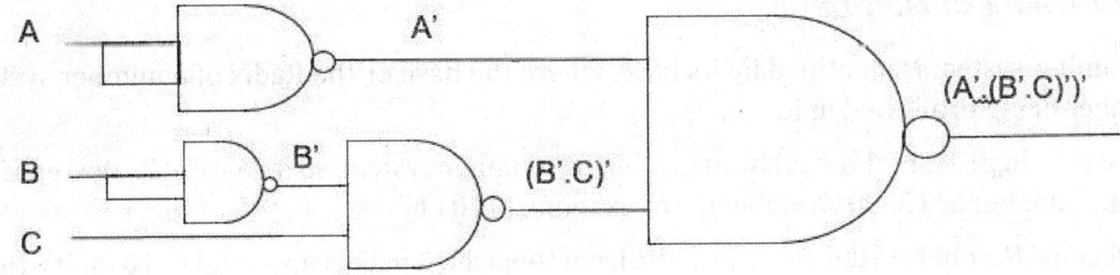

To convert the given Boolean expression using NOR gate

A+B'.C

(applying complement to complement)

A+((B'.C)')'

Applying De Morgan's Law 1 (X.Y)'=X'+Y' , by considering X as B' and Y as C

=> A+((B')'+(C)')'

=> A+(B+C')'

=>((A+(B+C')')')'

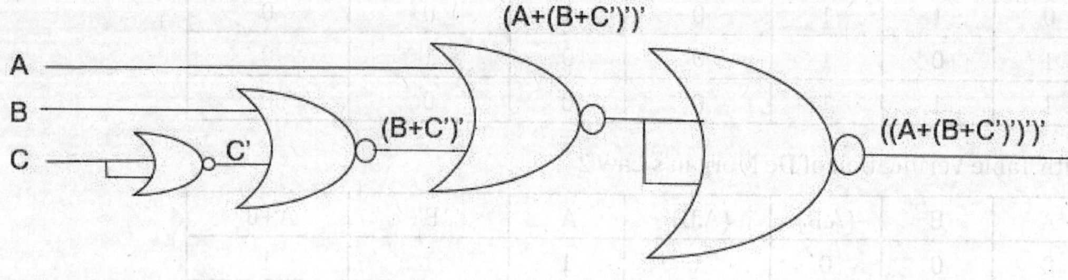

Number System

When we send data to the computer through the programs we write , we use numeric as well as alphanumeric data, both. But the data is not stored as it is in the computer. Rather, every input given to the computer gets converted into numbers. This means that the computer understands only numbers and thus every data provided to the computer, be it text or audio or video gets converted into the digital form. Computer's architecture supports many different types of numbers and thus to represent the data in various digital formats as per computer architecture the technique of Number System is Provided. So, the Number system helps us to understand how data is represented in various formats. The following number systems are supported by the computer architecture:

1. Decimal Number system
2. Binary Number System
3. Octal Number System
4. Hexadecimal Number System

In this section we will learn in detail about the above number systems and how one number system can be converted into another.

Base or Radix of Number System

Every number system is identified by its base, where the base or the Radix of a number system tells the number of digits allowed in it.

1. Since two digits 0 and 1 are allowed in a Binary number system, so its base is 2. We represent the Binary number as $(BinaryNumber)_{2..}$ For example $(11011)_2$
2. In Decimal Number system, we use digits from 0-9, which makes up a total of 10 digits. Hence the base of a decimal number system is 10. For example $(128901)_{10}$ is a representation of a decimal number.
3. In Octal Number System the digits allowed are 0-7, which means a total of 8 digits. So the Octal number is identified by Base 8. Example $(65723)_8$.

4. In hexadecimal Number system, there are 16 alphanumeric values allowed, which are 0-9 and then A-F, which means (0,1,2,3,4,5,6,7,8,9,A,B,C,D,E,F) total of 16 digits. Hence the base is 16. Example $(AB12)_{16}$

Decimal Number System

The features of this number system are as follows:

1. Its base is 10 as the digits allowed are 0 to 9.
2. We use this number system to send the data to the computer.

Let us see how a decimal number is expanded in mathematics:

$(261)_{10} = 10^2 \text{ X } 2 + 10^1 \text{ X } 6 + 10^0 \text{ X } 1$

We will apply the same methodology to convert Binary, Octal and Hexadecimal to Decimal.

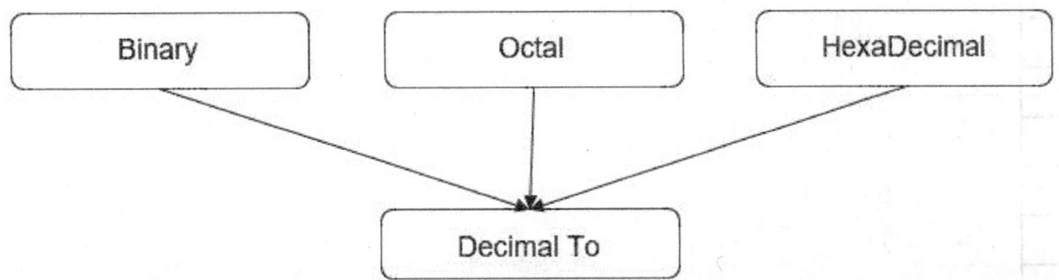

Binary to Decimal: Take the base of Binary with the power of the number's position starting from power 0 going in increasing order in the direction from right to left and multiply with the binary number at the given position..

$(1011101)_2 = (?)_{10}$

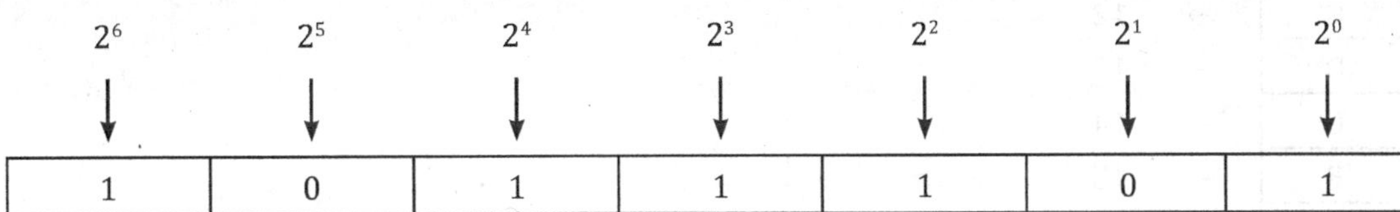

2^6	2^5	2^4	2^3	2^2	2^1	2^0
1	0	1	1	1	0	1

$=2^6\text{X}1 + 2^5\text{X}0 + 2^4\text{X}1 + 2^3\text{X}1 + 2^2\text{X}1 + 2^1\text{X}0 + 2^0\text{X}1$

$=64+0+16+8+4+0+1$

$=93$

$\Rightarrow (1011101)_2 = (93)_{10}$

Octal to Decimal: Take the base of Octal with the power of the number's position starting from power 0 going in increasing order in the direction from right to left and multiply with the octal number at the given position.

$(124)_8 = (?)_{10}$

8^2	8^1	8^0
1	2	4

$=8^2X1 + 8^1X2 + 8^0X4$

=64+16+4

=>84

$=>(124)_8=(84)_{10}$

HexaDecimal to Decimal: Take the base of Hexadecimal with the power of the number's position starting from power 0 going in increasing order in the direction from right to left and multiply with the hexadecimal number at the given position... Here one important thing has to be remembered while converting into decimal. The digits and alphabets allowed are (0-9) and (A-F). The numeric representation for A is taken as 10, B as 11 and so on, while doing the base conversion.

Hex		Decimal
0	→	0
1	→	1
2	→	2
3	→	3
4	→	4
5	→	5
6	→	6
7	→	7
8	→	8
9	→	9
A	→	10
B	→	11
C	→	12
D	→	13
E	→	14
F	→	15

$(7AB)_{16}=(?)_{10}$

16^2	16^1	16^0
↓	↓	↓
7	A	B

$=16^2X7 + 16^1XA + 16^0XB$

=256X7 + 16X10 + 1X11

=1792+160+11

=1963

$=>(7AB)_8=(1963)_{10}$

Now let us see how we can convert Decimal Number to Binary, Octal and Hexadecimal:

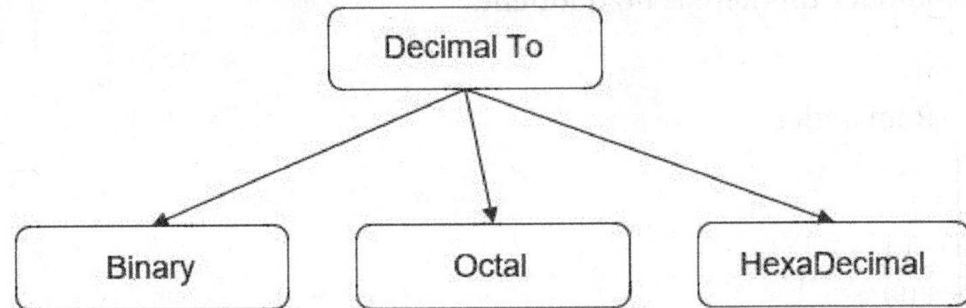

Decimal to Binary : Divide the Decimal no by the base of binary number, i.e. 2 and keep taking the remainder till the quotient becomes zero.

$(123)_{10}=(?)_2$

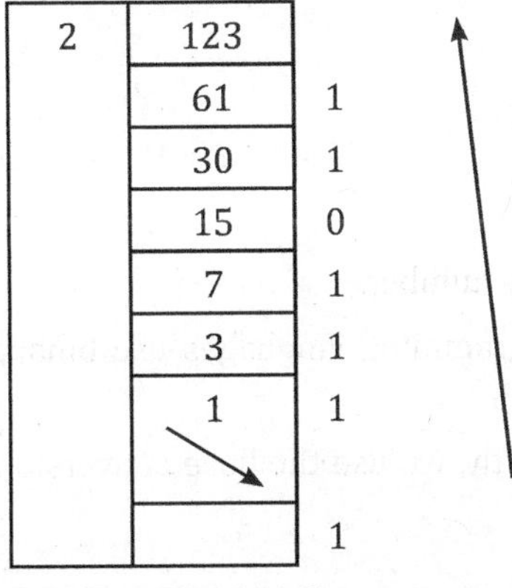

$(123)_{10}=(1111011)_2$

Can you recheck whether the answer generated is correct or not by converting the binary number to decimal using the method we learned in the previous section?

$(1111011)_2=(?)_{10}$

Decimal to Octal : Divide the Decimal no by the base of Octal number, i.e. 8 and keep taking the remainder till there is no quotient.

$(123)_{10}=(?)_8$

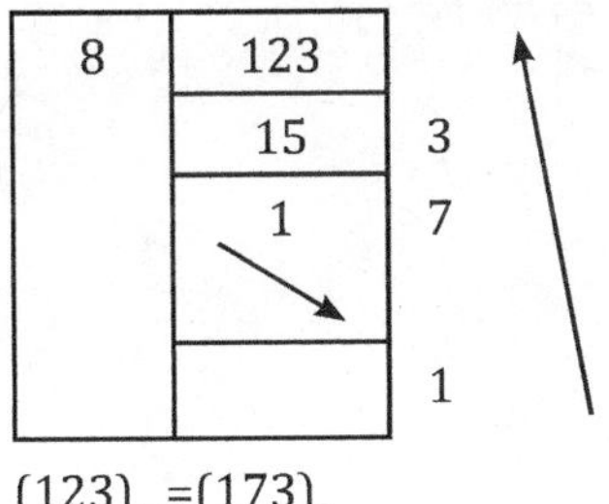

$(123)_{10}=(173)_8$

Decimal to HexaDecimal : Divide the Decimal no by the base of Hexadecimal number, i.e. 16 and keep taking the remainder till there is no quotient.

$(123)_{10}=(?)_{16}$

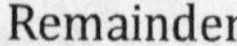

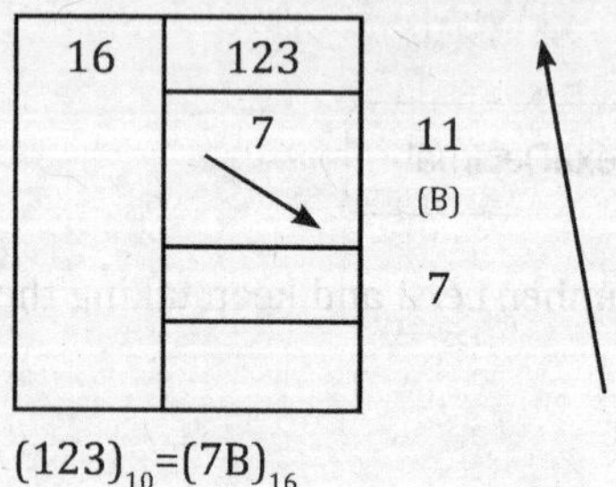

$(123)_{10}=(7B)_{16}$

Binary Number System

Following are the features of Binary number system:

1. Its base is 2 as the digits allowed are 0 and 1.
2. A single binary digit takes 1 bit.
3. 1101 is a four-bit binary number while 101101 is a six bit binary number.
4. We use binary number system in computer applications. Programming languages use binary number system.
5. For converting Binary into Octal or Hexadecimal numbers directly, we use the base conversion table.

Base conversion table for Binary to Octal and Vice-versa

Since Octal number has the base 8 (which is 2^3), each octal digit occupies 3 bits, which are taken from the table shown below. This table is nothing but the binary representation of the decimal number from 0-7 in three bits. Extreme right column has alternate 0-1, then the second column will have alternatively two 0's and two 1's and the first column will have group of four 0's and four 1's

0	0	0	→	0 (2^2X0+2^1X0+2^0X0=0)
0	0	1	→	1 (2^2X0+2^1X0+2^0X1=1)
0	1	0	→	2(2^2X0+2^1X1+2^0X0=2)
0	1	1	→	3(2^2X0+2^1X1+2^0X1=3)
1	0	0	→	4(2^2X1+2^1X0+2^0X0=4)
1	0	1	→	5(2^2X1+2^1X0+2^0X1=5)
1	1	0	→	6(2^2X1+2^1X1+2^0X0=6)
1	1	1	→	7(2^2X1+2^1X1+2^0X1=7)

Example 1

$(125)_8=(?)_2$

Referring to the base conversion table

1	2	5
001	010	101

So the answer is :

$(125)_8=(001\ 010\ 101)_2$

Example 2

$(10100101)_2=(?)_8$

Make a group of three digits from right to left. In case you are short of digits on extreme left then add preceding 0, as shown in this example.

Referring to the base conversion table after making the group:

(10100101)

010	100	101
2	4	5

So the answer is :

$(10100101)_2=(245)_8$

Base conversion table for Binary to Hexadecimal and Vice-versa

Since the Hexadecimal number has the base 16 (which is 2^4), each hexadecimal digit occupies 4 bits, which are taken from the table shown below. This table is nothing but the binary representation of the decimal number from 0-9 in four bits. Extreme right column has alternate 0-1, then the second column will have alternatively two 0's and two 1's, third column will have group of four 0's and four 1's and finally the extreme left column will have sequence of eight 0's and eight 1's

0	0	0	0	→	0 (2^3X0+2^2X0+2^1X0+2^0X0=0)
0	0	0	1	→	1 (2^3X0+2^2X0+2^1X0+2^0X1=1)
0	0	1	0	→	2(2^3X0+2^2X0+2^1X1+2^0X0=2)
0	0	1	1	→	3(2^3X0+2^2X0+2^1X1+2^0X1=3)
0	1	0	0	→	4(2^3X0+2^2X1+2^1X0+2^0X0=4)
0	1	0	1	→	5(2^3X0+2^2X1+2^1X0+2^0X1=5)
0	1	1	0	→	6(2^3X0+2^2X1+2^1X1+2^0X0=6)
0	1	1	1	→	7(2^3X0+2^2X1+2^1X1+2^0X1=7)
1	0	0	0	→	8(2^3X1+2^2X0+2^1X0+2^0X0=8)
1	0	0	1	→	9(2^3X1+2^2X0+2^1X0+2^0X1=9)
1	0	1	0	→	A(2^3X1+2^2X0+2^1X1+2^0X0=10)
1	0	1	1	→	B(2^3X1+2^2X0+2^1X1+2^0X1=11)
1	1	0	0	→	C(2^3X1+2^2X1+2^1X0+2^0X0=12)
1	1	0	1	→	D(2^3X1+2^2X1+2^1X0+2^0X1=13)

1	1	1	0	→	$E(2^3X1+2^2X1+2^1X1+2^0X0=14)$
1	1	1	1	→	$F(2^3X1+2^2X1+2^1X1+2^0X1=15)$

Example 1

$(ABC9)_{16}=(?)_2$

Referring to the base conversion table

A	B	C	9
1010	1011	1100	1001

So the answer is :

$(ABC9)_{16}=(1010101111001001)_2$

Example 2

$(1010100101)_2=(?)_{16}$

Make a group of four digits from right to left. In case you are short of digits on extreme left then add preceding 0, as shown in this example.

Referring to the base conversion table after making the group:

(001010100101)

0010	1010	0101
2	A	5

So the answer is :

$(1010100101)_2=(2A5)_{16}$

Note:

To convert Octal to Hexadecimal number, you can Convert Octal→ Binary and then Binary→ Hexadecimal.

Things to Remember

1. To convert a Decimal number to any other number system, divide the decimal number by the base of the number to be converted and take the remainder in the reverse order from bottom to top.
2. To convert any number to the Decimal number system, take the sum of power of the base of the number(to be converted) as per its position and multiply with the digit at that given position.
3. To convert Binary to Octal or Hexadecimal to Binary or vice versa, use the base conversion table.
4. To convert Octal to Hexadecimal, convert it first to Binary and then convert Binary to Hexadecimal. Do the same while converting hexadecimal to Octal.

Features of Octal Number System are as follows:

1. The base of Octal number is 8 as it allows numbers from 0-7
2. Computer programmers use the Octal number system as it is easier to work with it because they are shorter and easy to remember.

Features of Hexadecimal Number System are as follows:

1. The base of hexadecimal number is 16 as it allows numbers from 0-9 and alphabets from A-F
2. We use hexadecimal number system to define the memory location in the computer.
3. They are easy to convert to binary
4. They are used to represent colours where the format used is for three basic colors, Red, Green and Blue as #RRGGBB

Binary addition

Addition in the binary number system is much easier than in the decimal number system as there are only few rules to remember.

Rules

1. 0+0→ 0
2. 0+1→ 1
3. 1+0→ 1
4. 1+1→ 0 with carry 1
5. (1+1)+1→ (0 with carry 1) + 1→ 1 with carry 1

Let us take few examples to understand how Binary addition works

Example 1

```
 1    1
   1 0 0 1 1
+  1 1 0 1 0
----------------------------
 1 0 1 1 0 1
```

Example 2

```
 1    1
   1 1 0 0 1
+  1 1 0 1 0
----------------------------
 1 1 0 0 1 1
```

We can check the answer of the above Binary addition by converting binary number into decimal, using this quick method:

32	16	8	4	2	1
(2^5)	(2^4)	(2^3)	(2^2)	(2^1)	(2^0)

(Add the numbers where the position value is 1)

```
    1  0  0  1  1  →  16+2+1=19
 +  1  1  0  1  0  →  16+8+2=26
------------------------------------------------------------
 1 0  1  1  0  1      32+8+4+1=45
----------------------------------
```

Summary

- In 1954, George Boole invented the concept of Boolean logic, which is a core concept of Boolean Algebra and a branch of mathematics. Boolean logic can be used to describe the manipulation and processing of binary information.
- Digital electronic circuits and microprocessors based systems are made using Gates which are formed using the Boolean logic.
- The expression which takes the input in the form of boolean variables and generates boolean result is called a Boolean expression. The input in a boolean expression is given in the form of 0 or 1 through a variable, which is called as a Boolean variable.
- The binary inputs and the output of the boolean expression is displayed using a table called a Truth Table. Truth table helps us to understand the behaviour of a boolean expression of a given logic circuit.
- The operators used in boolean algebra are called Boolean operators. The three operators using which the boolean expression is formed are AND/OR/NOT.
- AND operator when used with boolean variables will generate the result True if all the inputs are True or 1 else it will be False or 0. AND operation is expressed using '.' or '^'
- OR operator generates the final result of a boolean expression True if either one input or all the inputs are True or 1 else it will be False or 0. OR operation is expressed using '+' or 'V'
- NOT operator reverses the result of the input by negating its value by making True to False (or 1 to 0) and False to True (or 0 to 1). NOT operation is expressed '~' or '''
- To carry out the logical operations where single or multiple binary inputs generate one binary output, logic gates are used. In other words, logic gates are electronic circuits which generate a boolean output based on the boolean inputs provided by the boolean variables. The different logical gates are AND, OR, NOT, NOR, NAND, XOR.
- AND gate will achieve the output 1/True if all the inputs are 1 or True else the output will be False.
- OR gate will achieve the output 1/True if either one or all the inputs are 1 or True else the output will be False
- NOT gate gives the complement of the input provided. If the input is True or 1, the resultant complement would be 0 or False and vice versa.

- NOR and NAND are known as universal gates as any boolean expression can be created or converted into only "NAND' or only 'NOR Gates, which we will learn in the next section.
- Just like NOR gate, NAND gate gives the complement of the AND Gate, i.e. Not of AND and hence the name.
- XOR gate will achieve the output 1/True if either both the inputs are different. With the same inputs (whether True or False), the result will be False or 0. It is denoted by the symbol ⊕.
- Logic circuits are made by using the logic gates based on the given boolean expression.
- Identity Law states that for a boolean variable X, the following holds True.
    - X+0=X
    - X.1=X (by Duality)
- Complement Law

  Complement Law states that the AND of a boolean variable and its complement is always 0.
    - X.X'=0
    - X+X'=1 (by Duality)
- Commutative Law states that for boolean variables X,Y,Z the following holds True:
    - X+Y = Y + X
    - X.Y=Y.X (by Duality)
- Associative Law states that for boolean variables X,Y,Z the following holds True:
    - X+(Y+Z) = (X+Y)+Z → Law 1
    - X.(Y.Z)=(X.Y).Z → Law 2 (By Duality)
- Distributive Law states that for boolean variables X,Y,Z the following holds True:
    - X.(Y+Z) = X.Y + X.Z → Law 1
    - X+Y.Z = (X+Y).(X+Z) → Law 2 (By Duality)
- Duality Principle states that any boolean expression derived using the boolean laws remain unaffected, if we
    - Change the all AND operations to OR or vice versa and
    - Change all 0's with 1 or vice versa.
- Complement of Complement states that the complement to complement of a boolean variable is same as the boolean variable. This means that:
    - X=((X)')'
- De Morgan's Law states that for boolean variables A1, A2, A3.....An, the complement of the product of all the terms is equal to the sum of the complement of each term.
    - (A+B)'=A'.B' → Law 1
    - (A.B)'=A'+B' → Law 2 (By Duality)

? EXERCISE

Multiple Choice Questions

1. To implement the Boolean functions __________ is used.
   a. Logical notations b. Arithmetic logics
   c. Logic gates d. Expressions
2. Inversion of single bit input to a single bit output can be done by using __________
   a. NOT gate b. NOR gate c. AND gate d. NAND gate
3. A __________ is a Boolean variable.
   a. Literal b. String c. Keyword d. Identifier
4. (X+Y`)(X+Z) can be represented by __________
   a. (X+Y`Z) b. (Y+X`) c. XY` d. (X+Z`)
5. A __________ value is represented by a Boolean expression.
   a. Positive b. Boolean c. Recursive d. Negative
6. Which of the following is/are the universal logic gates?
   a. OR and NOR b. AND c. NAND and NOR d. NOT
7. __________ operator reverses the truth value of the operation.
   a. AND b. OR c. NOT d. NAND
8. __________ operator returns true, if all the sub-conditions are true.
   a. NAND b. OR c. NOT d. AND
9. __________ operator returns true, if any of the sub-condition is true.
   a. AND b. OR c. NOT d. NAND
10. __________ logical operator does not allow us to combine two or more conditions?
    a. AND b. OR c. NOT d. NAND
11. The inputs of a NAND gate are connected together. The resulting circuit is __________
    a. OR gate b. AND gate c. NOT gate d. NAND gate
12. The NOR gate is OR gate followed by __________
    a. OR gate b. AND gate c. NOT gate d. NAND gate
13. Digital circuit can be made by the repeated use of __________
    a. OR gates b. NOT gates c. NAND gates d. AND gate
14. When an input signal 1 is applied to a NOT gate, the output is __________.
    a. 0 b. 1 c. Either 0 & 1 d. None of the above
15. In Boolean algebra, the bar sign (-) indicates __________
    a. OR operation b. AND operation c. NOT operation d. NAND operation

Fill in the blanks

1. _________ invented the concept of Boolean logic.
2. Boolean logic can be used to describe the manipulation and processing of _________ information.
3. Digital electronic circuits and microprocessors based systems are made by using _________ which are formed using the Boolean logic.
4. The expression which takes the input in the form of boolean variables and generates boolean result is called a _________.
5. The input in a boolean expression is given in the form of 0 or 1 through a variable, which is called as a _________.
6. The binary inputs and the output of the boolean expression is displayed using a table called a _________.
7. The operators used in boolean algebra are called _________.
8. The three operators using which the boolean expression is formed are _________.
9. _________ operator when used with boolean variables will generate the result True if all the inputs are True.
10. _________ operator generates the final result of a boolean expression True if either one input or all the inputs are True.
11. _________ operator reverses the result of the input by negating its value by making True to False (or 1 to 0) and False to True (or 0 to 1).
12. _________ are electronic circuits which generate a boolean output based on the boolean inputs provided by the boolean variables.
13. _________ gate will achieve the output 1/True if all the inputs are 1 or True else the output will be False.
14. _________ gate will achieve the output 1/True if either one or all the inputs are 1 or True else the output will be False
15. _________ gate gives the complement of the input provided.

State whether the following statements are true or false

1. If the input is True or 1, the resultant complement would be 0 or False and vice versa.
2. NOR and NAND are known as universal gates.
3. Like NOR gate, NAND gate gives the complement of the OR Gate, i.e. Not of AND and hence the name.
4. XOR gate is denoted by the symbol ⊕.
5. Logic circuits are made by using the logic gates based on the given boolean expression.
6. Complement Law states that the OR of a boolean variable and its complement is always 0.
7. Commutative Law states that for boolean variables X,Y,Z the X+Y = X + Y.

8. Duality Principle states that any boolean expression derived using the boolean laws remain unaffected, if we change the all AND operations to OR or vice versa.
9. Complement of Complement states that the complement to complement of a boolean variable is not the same as the boolean variable.
10. De Morgan's Law states that for boolean variables A1, A2, A3.....An, the complement of the product of all the terms is not equal to the sum of the complement of each term.
11. Digital electronic circuits and microprocessors based systems are made using Gates which are formed using Boolean logic.
12. The expression which takes the input in the form of boolean variables and generates a boolean result is called a Boolean expression.
13. The input in a boolean expression is given in the form of 0 or 1 through a variable, which is called a Boolean variable.
14. The binary inputs and the output of the boolean expression is displayed using a table called a Truth Table.
15. Truth table helps us to understand the behaviour of a boolean expression of a given logic circuit.

Short Questions

1. Define the term boolean variable.
2. What is a boolean expression?
3. What does truth table represent?
4. Write any two rules to remember to create a Truth table for given sets of input.
5. What is boolean operators?
6. Differentiate among the AND, OR, NOT operator.
7. Define the term Logic gate.
8. Name the universal gate.
9. How does NOR Gate (Not-of OR) works.
10. Define the term Logic circuit.

Long Questions

1. Explain the Identity Law
2. Write a short note on Complement Law.
3. Differentiate among states that the three Boolean operators.
4. What does Commutative Law states?
5. Explain the Associative Law
6. Differentiate among the Associative law and Distributive Law
7. Draw the Truth Table Verification of the Law 1.

8. Write a short note on Duality Principle.
9. Explain the meaning of Complement of Complement.
10. Design the logic circuit of X.Y+Z.

Answer:

Multiple choice questions

1. c	2. a	3. a	4. a	5. b	6. c	7. a	8. d
9. b	10. c	11. c	12. c	13. c	14. a	15. c	

Fill in the blanks

1. George Boole	2. binary	3. Gates	4. Boolean expression
5. Boolean variable	6. Truth Table	7. Boolean operators	8. AND/OR/NOT
9. AND	10. OR	11. NOT	12. Logic gates
13. AND	14. OR	15. NOT	

State whether the following statements are true or false.

1. True	2. True	3. False	4. True	5. True
6. False	7. False	8. True	9. False	10. False
11. True	12. True	13. True	14. True	15. True

3 Encoding Schemes

Introduction

When we deal with the digital data in terms of sending or receiving information through our programs or the applications, we are not restricted to use a specific language. Today people use various languages to work on the computer but every key we press on the keyboard is encoded and provided a unique code so that it can be converted into binary language. The process of converting the keys we press on the keyboard into their equivalent code is called ***encoding***. The code for a particular character remains same for all keyboards. For example, if we press 'a', its equivalent code is 97. Similarly the code for 'A' is 65. If we press a character in the Arabic language, then its equivalent code will be different. All this is possible due to the different encoding schemes. In this chapter, we will study some of the commonly used encoding schemes.

1. ASCII : It stands for American Standard Code for Information Interchange. It was published in 1963. It uses 7 bits to represent a character. But it uses 8 bits of memory to store the character. The total number of characters which are represented using this encoding system is 2^7= 128 (from 0-127). UNIX file systems use ASCII codes. ASCII character set includes:

   a. Lower (a-z) having ASCII code from 97-122 and uppercase(A-Z) alphabets from 65-90

   b. Digits (0-9) having ASCII code from 48-57

   c. Control characters (which you cannot print, like Esc, Null, Tab etc.)

   d. Special Characters

   One of the limitations of ASCII is the limitation of representing the character sets for several different language structures.

Dec	Hex	Oct	Binary	Char	Dec	Hex	Oct	Binary	Char	Dec	Hex	Oct	Binary	Char	Dec	Hex	Oct	Binary	Char
0	00	000	0000000	NUL (null character)	32	20	040	0100000	space	64	40	100	1000000	@	96	60	140	1100000	`
1	01	001	0000001	SOH (start of header)	33	21	041	0100001	!	65	41	101	1000001	A	97	61	141	1100001	a
2	02	002	0000010	STX (start of text)	34	22	042	0100010	"	66	42	102	1000010	B	98	62	142	1100010	b
3	03	003	0000011	ETX (end of text)	35	23	043	0100011	#	67	43	103	1000011	C	99	63	143	1100011	c
4	04	004	0000100	EOT (end of transmission)	36	24	044	0100100	$	68	44	104	1000100	D	100	64	144	1100100	d
5	05	005	0000101	ENQ (enquiry)	37	25	045	0100101	%	69	45	105	1000101	E	101	65	145	1100101	e
6	06	006	0000110	ACK (acknowledge)	38	26	046	0100110	&	70	46	106	1000110	F	102	66	146	1100110	f
7	07	007	0000111	BEL (bell (ring))	39	27	047	0100111	'	71	47	107	1000111	G	103	67	147	1100111	g
8	08	010	0001000	BS (backspace)	40	28	050	0101000	(	72	48	110	1001000	H	104	68	150	1101000	h
9	09	011	0001001	HT (horizontal tab)	41	29	051	0101001	)	73	49	111	1001001	I	105	69	151	1101001	i
10	0A	012	0001010	LF (line feed)	42	2A	052	0101010	*	74	4A	112	1001010	J	106	6A	152	1101010	j
11	0B	013	0001011	VT (vertical tab)	43	2B	053	0101011	+	75	4B	113	1001011	K	107	6B	153	1101011	k
12	0C	014	0001100	FF (form feed)	44	2C	054	0101100	,	76	4C	114	1001100	L	108	6C	154	1101100	l
13	0D	015	0001101	CR (carriage return)	45	2D	055	0101101	-	77	4D	115	1001101	M	109	6D	155	1101101	m
14	0E	016	0001110	SO (shift out)	46	2E	056	0101110	.	78	4E	116	1001110	N	110	6E	156	1101110	n
15	0F	017	0001111	SI (shift in)	47	2F	057	0101111	/	79	4F	117	1001111	O	111	6F	157	1101111	o
16	10	020	0010000	DLE (data link escape)	48	30	060	0110000	0	80	50	120	1010000	P	112	70	160	1110000	p
17	11	021	0010001	DC1 (device control 1)	49	31	061	0110001	1	81	51	121	1010001	Q	113	71	161	1110001	q
18	12	022	0010010	DC2 (device control 2)	50	32	062	0110010	2	82	52	122	1010010	R	114	72	162	1110010	r
19	13	023	0010011	DC3 (device control 3)	51	33	063	0110011	3	83	53	123	1010011	S	115	73	163	1110011	s
20	14	024	0010100	DC4 (device control 4)	52	34	064	0110100	4	84	54	124	1010100	T	116	74	164	1110100	t
21	15	025	0010101	NAK (negative acknowledge)	53	35	065	0110101	5	85	55	125	1010101	U	117	75	165	1110101	u
22	16	026	0010110	SYN (synchronize)	54	36	066	0110110	6	86	56	126	1010110	V	118	76	166	1110110	v
23	17	027	0010111	ETB (end transmission block)	55	37	067	0110111	7	87	57	127	1010111	W	119	77	167	1110111	w
24	18	030	0011000	CAN (cancel)	56	38	070	0111000	8	88	58	130	1011000	X	120	78	170	1111000	x
25	19	031	0011001	EM (end of medium)	57	39	071	0111001	9	89	59	131	1011001	Y	121	79	171	1111001	y
26	1A	032	0011010	SUB (substitute)	58	3A	072	0111010	:	90	5A	132	1011010	Z	122	7A	172	1111010	z
27	1B	033	0011011	ESC (escape)	59	3B	073	0111011	;	91	5B	133	1011011	[	123	7B	173	1111011	{
28	1C	034	0011100	FS (file separator)	60	3C	074	0111100	<	92	5C	134	1011100	\	124	7C	174	1111100	|
29	1D	035	0011101	GS (group separator)	61	3D	075	0111101	=	93	5D	135	1011101	]	125	7D	175	1111101	}
30	1E	036	0011110	RS (record separator)	62	3E	076	0111110	>	94	5E	136	1011110	^	126	7E	176	1111110	~
31	1F	037	0011111	US (unit separator)	63	3F	077	0111111	?	95	5F	137	1011111	_	127	7F	177	1111111	DEL

Extension of ASCII is called extended ASCII, which uses 8 bits to represent a character and thus uses extra 128 characters in it, from 128-255. The extra characters represent characters from foreign languages and special symbols for drawing pictures.

128	Ç	144	É	160	á	176	░	193	┴	209	╤	225	ß	241	±
129	ü	145	æ	161	í	177	▒	194	┬	210	╥	226	Γ	242	≥
130	é	146	Æ	162	ó	178	▓	195	├	211	╙	227	π	243	≤
131	â	147	ô	163	ú	179	│	196	─	212	╘	228	Σ	244	⌠
132	ä	148	ö	164	ñ	180	┤	197	┼	213	╒	229	σ	245	⌡
133	à	149	ò	165	Ñ	181	╡	198	╞	214	╓	230	µ	246	÷
134	å	150	û	166	ª	182	╢	199	╟	215	╫	231	τ	247	≈
135	ç	151	ù	167	º	183	╖	200	╚	216	╪	232	Φ	248	°
136	ê	152	_	168	¿	184	╕	201	╔	217	┘	233	Θ	249	·
137	ë	153	Ö	169	_	185	╣	202	╩	218	┌	234	Ω	250	·
138	è	154	Ü	170	¬	186	║	203	╦	219	█	235	δ	251	√
139	ï	156	£	171	½	187	╗	204	╠	220	▄	236	∞	252	_
140	î	157	¥	172	¼	188	╝	205	═	221	▌	237	φ	253	²
141	ì	158	_	173	¡	189	╜	206	╬	222	▐	238	ε	254	■
142	Ä	159	ƒ	174	«	190	╛	207	╧	223	▀	239	∩	255	
143	Å	192	└	175	»	191	┐	208	╨	224	α	240	≡		

2. UNICODE: The problem with the ASCII code is that it does not encode characters from other scripts, such as Arabic or Greek.

   Unicode was created to allow more character sets than ASCII. Unicode contains the alphabets of almost all known languages, as diverse as Japanese, Chinese, Greek, Cyrillic, Canadian Aboriginal, and Arabic. It was originally a 16-bit character set, but in 1995, with Unicode 2.0, it became 32 bits. The Unicode standard defines Unicode Transformation Formats(UTF). There are several encoding schemes that can represent Unicode, including UCS-2, UCS-4, UTF-2, UTF-4, UTF-8, UTF-16, and UTF-32 but the most commonly used encodings are UTF-8 and UTF-16. The first 65535 characters in Unicode cover most of the common languages. Unicode character sets are grouped in scripts which include Latin, Korean, Greek languages etc.

   Companies like Apple, Hewlett-Packard, IBM, Microsoft use Unicode

3. UTF8: UTF-8 stands for "Unicode Transformation Format - 8 bits. UTF-8 encoding follows the UTF character set. It uses 8-bit binary numbers to represent a character. Since the value of character A in the UTF character set is decimal 65 (or hexadecimal 41), UTF-8 encoding encodes character A to 01000001 which is the binary equivalent of decimal value 65. UTA-8 is backward compatible with ASCII and since it uses 1 byte to encode every character, the encoded file size which has characters in ASCII character set would be the same as the file size which would have been encoded using ASCII. Any character not in ASCII takes up two or more bytes in UTF-8. UTF-8 is adopted very well in WWW due to its size and space efficiency. This is due to the reason that the web pages have text files which contain characters generally not outside the ASCII character set, so not much load in terms of size on the network. UTF8 is a variable length encoding system.

4. UTF32: UTF32 is a fixed length encoding system which uses 4 bytes per character. This means that for simple English text, it would take 4 times more size than what it would have taken with UTF-8 encoding system.

5. ISCII : It stands for Indian Script code for Information Interchange. It was established as a standard by the Bureau of Indian Standards in 1991. It is an 8 bit encoding system used to encode Indian scripts which includes Devanagari, Gujarati, Kannada etc. It consists of 256 characters where the first 128 characters are the same as the ASCII codes while the rest characters from 128-255 are the characters of different Indian languages.

   Most of the characters of the Indian language are derived from the Brahmi script. The advantage of ISCII is that its character set is easy to understand and translation from one language to another is easy. We need a special keyboard for ISCII characters. Character encoding for Devanagari, Punjabi, Gujarati, Oriya, Bengali, Assamese, Telugu, Kannada, Malayalam, Tamil and Roman scripts has been standardized by the ISCII.

Difference between ASCII and UNICODE

ASCII	UNICODE
ASCII supports 128 characters while the Extended ASCII supports 256 characters	As per The Unicode Consortium, Unicode presently supports 143,859 characters
DOS and UNIX support ASCII	Most operating systems, databases, programming languages and Web browsers currently support Unicode.
ASCII used 8 bits to store a character where	A disadvantage of the Unicode Standard is the amount of memory required by UTF-16 and UTF-32.
ASCII code uses English language characters.	It can store characters from more than one language
Requires/uses less storage space	Takes more storage space

Difference between UTF-8/UTF-16/UTF-32

UTF-8	UTF-16	UTF-32
It is a variable length encoding system	It is a variable length encoding system	It is a fixed length encoding system
An encoded character takes between 1 and 4 bytes.	It requires either 16 or 32 bits to encode a character	It always requires 32 bits to encode a character.
UTF-8 file containing only ASCII characters has the same encoding as an ASCII file so it is backward compatible with ASCII.	UTF-16 encoding is not compatible with ASCII	Even an English character will occupy 4 bytes of memory. So it takes a lot of memory.

Operating System

Operating System is an interface between the user and the computer as its main job is to manage the hardware of the computer, make other applications run and to convert high level language (user understandable language) into low level language (or Binary language or computer understandable language) and vice versa. Examples of Operating Systems are Microsoft Windows (Windows 10, Windows 8, Windows 7, Windows Vista, and Windows XP), Apple's macOS, Google's OS, BlackBerry Tablet OS, Unix and Linux.

Need for an operating system

Will the computer run without an Operating System? The answer is Yes but it will merely be a box which will not understand how to communicate with various parts or programs of the computer. In other words a computer won't be of any use without an operating system. So why is an operating system required? The operating System allows you to do the following :

1. **Interface:** Using the operating system, the programs are able to communicate with the hardware of the computer. When we send instruction to the computer through the program we write they, interact with various parts of the computer which includes the central Processing Unit, Memory unit, Arithmetic and logical unit. All this is possible because of the operating system because it helps the various parts of the computer to coordinate with each other. So whenever the user sends the instruction in user understandable language or high level language, the operating system converts it into low level language or machine understandable language (or binary language, language is 0 and 1) and vice versa.
2. **Device Management:** The operating system also helps various programs to run on different hardware platforms as it acts as an interface between the Software and Hardware.
3. **Multitasking:** We can run multiple programs at the same time as the operating system allows multitasking.
4. **Memory Management:** The operating system also helps in memory management. This means then when the data is provided to the computer, it is the job of the operating system to decide which application data will be stored where and will occupy how much memory.
5. **Resource Management:** The operating system controls input-output resources of the computer and allocates them to the users or programs as per their requirement.

Types of Operating Systems

- **Batch Operating System :** There are certain tasks of similar type which can be 'batched' or combined together to speed up the process and the execution time. The job in the batch are picked up one by one, sorted as per the similar needs and executed. The example is the Banking Management System. This type of OS doesn't interact with the computer.
- **Multitasking/Time Sharing OS:** When there are multiple applications required to be run by single or multiple users, or when multiple resources are required to be shared, then the CPU time is divided among all the users on scheduled basis. This is done by the Time Sharing Operating System. It is also known as Multitasking Operating System. The Operating System allocates a set of time to each user. When this time expires, it passes control to the next user on the system. Time taken by each task to get executed is called the quantum. Example of such operating systems are Unix, Linux, Windows NT etc.
- **Multiprocessing OS:** These Operating systems are capable of processing multiple tasks. This is possible due to multiple processors being used in a single computer. The OS divides the task into many subtasks and they are further redirected to the different Central Processing Units. This

OS is used when we need high execution speed for a process. They are expensive due to large architecture. Examples are Solaris, Digital UNIX, Windows NT, SunOS Version 4, IOS etc.

- **Real Time OS:** A Real Time OS is the one which manages the time and resources of a CPU by splitting the given application into multiple tasks and runs the most important task first. It keeps on switching between the tasks giving an impression of running multiple programs simultaneously. A real-time operating system must have well-defined, fixed time constraints, otherwise the system will fail. This OS splits and prioritizes the application task and runs the highest priority task that is ready first. It is a time-bound system that can be defined as fixed time constraints. Some of the examples are air traffic control and medical systems.
- **Distributed OS:** Computers over the network also communicate to perform a given task. The system where independent computers over the network appear as a single system to the user in spite of being separate are called distributed systems. This means that the processors of these multiple computers work together to work on a real time application. Processors communicate with each other through various communication lines (like high-speed buses or telephone lines). Distributed OS has various advantages, like, failure of one system will not affect the rest of the systems. Moreover, the speed of the application execution is very fast and thus provides better service to the customers. Good example of this OS is the Online examination system where a single question paper is distributed among all the systems(computers) and can accessed independently.
- **Network OS:** A network operating system (NOS) is an operating system that manages hardware of the computers over the network and provides services to the Application software. The Network Operating Systems can distribute their tasks and functions amongst connected nodes in the network, which enhances the system overall performance. The NOS manages multiple requests (inputs) concurrently and provides the security necessary in a multiuser environment. Popular network operating systems are Novell Netware, Windows NT/2000, Linux, Sun Solaris, UNIX etc.
- **Mobile OS:** As the name suggests, this software is specifically designed to run applications on your mobile phone. Some of the commonly used mobile OS are iPhone's OS, Apple iOS, Google's Android etc.

Some of the important functions of Operating System are:-

1. Process management:- Since multiple applications can run at a time on our computer, it is the duty of the operating system to synchronize between various applications, allocate resources so that the data can be shared. Tasks like creation, scheduling and termination of processes are managed by the operating system for faster execution of multiple processes.
2. Memory management:- Every program/application running on the computer needs memory for storing the data. It is the operating system which is responsible for allocation and deallocation of memory for these programs.
3. File management:- We work on and store various types of files on our computer. The operation system is responsible for not only creating files but also storing them at specific locations, renaming them, sharing and protecting the files. Similarly, it also manages fast retrieval of files when searching is done.
4. Device Management:- Device management keeps track of all devices which includes I/O, storage devices and other networking devices etc. The operating system allocates and deallocates the devices to the processes as and when needed. It needs device drivers (which are programs to

control the device and make them respond to I/O processes) to run the I/O devices. The OS stores, registers and uses these drivers as per the requirement of the program.

5. Security:- Since the data stored on our computer is vulnerable to malware threats, the operating system security allows different applications and programs to perform required tasks and stop unauthorized interference by installing updated antivirus software, providing specific privileges to files etc.

Cloud Computing

Cloud computing is the evolution in the field of information technology where delivery of on-demand computing services is done over the internet. In simple terms, cloud computing means storing and accessing data and applications over the Internet instead of your computer's local hard drive. The concept of maximizing resource utilization by sharing is the foundation of cloud. Companies can rent hardware as well as software and can access anything from application to storage from the service provider. This helps the companies to avoid the extra cost of purchasing and further maintaining them.

Many companies like Google, Microsoft are delivering cloud based services.

Benefits of Cloud Computing:

1. Cost : No extra money is to be spent for purchasing the hardware and software as everything is handled online.
2. Security : Cloud service providers provide technologies to ensure that the data is safe and secure.
3. Speed : Most of the cloud services are not only easily available but are very fast too as the resources are easily accessible by clicking a mouse button.
4. Performance : Cloud service providers keep themselves updated and upgrade themselves regularly which results in good performance.
5. Reliability : The data stored in the cloud can be recovered under some disaster circumstance like system crashing.

Main characteristics of Cloud computing are:

1. On demand service : You don't need to go anywhere physically. As and when there is a requirement, you can access the applications through the browser.
2. Resource pooling : The same services like, storage, networking capabilities, software can be used by multiple users
3. Broad Network access : The service can be accessed from PCs, Mobile, Laptops etc. using the Application Program Interface (API).
4. Rapid Elasticity: As and when the expansion of the services required, it can be done without any complexity.

Types of Cloud Computing

There are a variety of Cloud Computing available depending upon the service demanded and the solution expected. The three types of cloud computing are public, private and hybrid.

Public Cloud is the one where the services like server and storage are provided by a third-party cloud service provider. The entire infrastructure is owned as well as maintained by these providers. Such service supports multiple customers and is suited for less confidential information. The services provided by them can be accessed using the browser. The customers have to pay as per the usage for the CPU cycles, storage or bandwidth they consume. Examples are Gmail services provided by Google. Its resources are shared by millions of people worldwide

Private Cloud is the one which is used exclusively by a business or a company as per their need and requirement. The maintenance is done by third party providers on the private network of the company and the company's IT department is held responsible for the cost and accountability of managing the private cloud. The cloud is set up on the company's onsite data center. The customization is done as per the requirement of the company. Moreover such service is comparatively made more secure using the company firewalls and internal hosting so that the sensitive data is safe. Such service is costly. Examples are Banking systems or Hospitals

Hybrid Cloud is the combination of Private and Public cloud. More flexibility is provided to the business as the data can be moved between public and private cloud. More sensitive data can be kept on the private cloud while the non-sensitive data can be on the public cloud. For example in the Banking system, the details of the customers can be stored on the private cloud while the bank's policy details can be on public cloud. Hybrid cloud is cost effective, flexible and secure.

The services themselves have long been referred to as Software as a Service (SaaS). The datacenter hardware and software is what we will call a Cloud. When a Cloud is made available in a pay-as-you-go manner to the general public, we call it a Public Cloud; the service being sold is Utility Computing. We use the term Private Cloud to refer to internal datacenters of a business or other organization, not made available to the general public. Thus, Cloud Computing is the sum of SaaS and Utility Computing, but does not include Private Clouds.

Cloud Service Models

Once a cloud is established, how its cloud computing services are deployed in terms of business models can differ depending on requirements. These services include providing software applications, programming platforms, data-storage or computing infrastructure. Cloud computing services include Hardware, Software and Data Services. There are three types of models depending upon the requirement of the customer. They are:-

- Software as a Service (SaaS)
- Platform as a Service (PaaS)
- Infrastructure as a Service (IaaS)

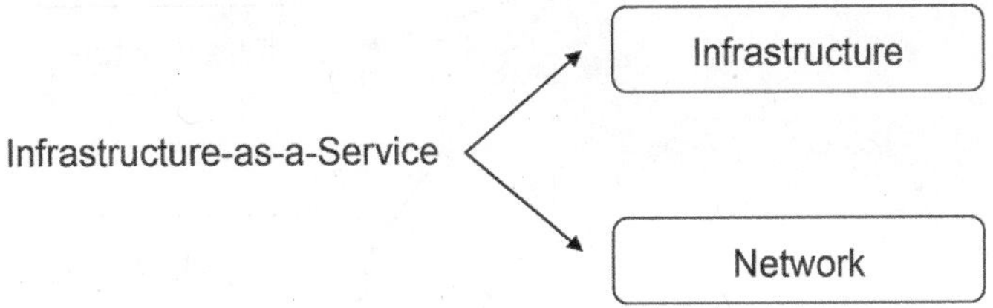

Infrastructure as a Service (IaaS)

The first type of model provided by the cloud service provider includes computational resources (hardware), software, servers, data storage, and communication. These services come under Infrastructure as a service (IaaS). So as the name suggests, it provides the infrastructure for developing your web app/website. In this case, they host users applications and handle tasks including system maintenance, backup and planning. The customers pay as per their usage of the services. It is also called Hardware as a service. More customer efforts are required in terms of technical knowledge as only infrastructure support is given by the service provider. It is popular between developers and researchers. The companies which provide IaaS are Amazon, Microsoft, Red Hat. Netflix rents Amazon cloud to host the various streaming applications.

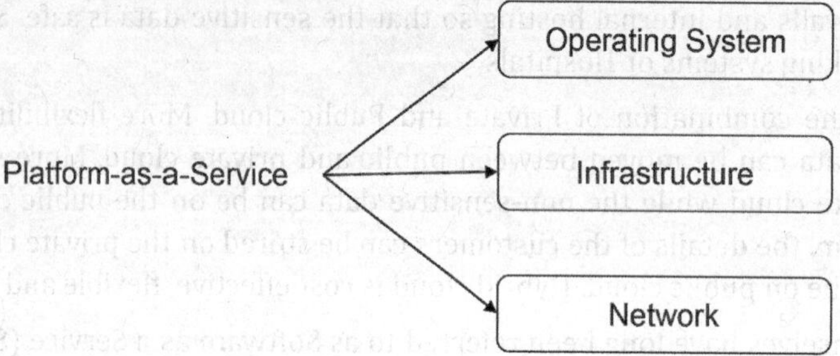

Platform as a Service (PaaS)

The second model after IaaS is Platform as a Service, where business development can happen which saves both time and resources. The solutions provided by the service provider include virtualized servers, databases and operating systems. The money to be spent on the hardware can be avoided and it helps in easy collaboration too. PaaS provides tools for web development as so the basic knowledge of the subject to setup is needed. PaaS is used by the developers and provides a runtime environment for applications, development and deployment tools. Examples of PaaS service providers are Google App Engine and Microsoft Azure.

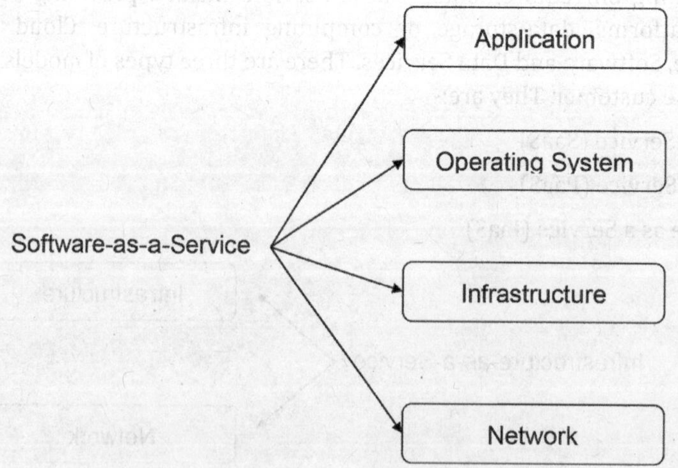

Software as a Service (SaaS)

The third and final model of the cloud is Software-as-a-Service, or SaaS. It is sometimes referred to as on-demand software. Any application hosted on a remote server that can be accessed over the Internet using a web browser is considered a SaaS. It represents the capability provided to the consumer to use the provider's applications running on a cloud infrastructure. The applications are accessible from various client devices through an interface such as a web browser. This model hosts the software and makes it available to the client to be used by the end-user. It is popular between consumer and company. Examples are M.S office web, Facebook and google apps.

Software as a Service (SaaS)	Platform as a Service (PaaS)	Infrastructure as a Service (IaaS)
Used by End users	Used by Developers	Used by Network architect and system administrators
It provides everything like Software, Infrastructure, Network and Application	Provide tools for web development	Provide Space for web development
Technical knowledge not required	Basic setup knowledge required.	Technical knowledge required.
Not very Expensive	Expensive	Very Expensive
Not very flexible	This model is flexible with limitations	This model is very flexible

Blockchain technology

Blockchain is a transparent money exchange system that defines the way transactions are done. It is a database of records of transactions which is distributed, and which is validated and maintained by a network of computers around the world. It is also referred to as digital gold. Instead of a single central authority such as a bank, the records are supervised by a large community and no individual person has control over it and no one can go back and change or erase a transaction history.

Artificial Intelligence (AI)

You all must be aware of smart devices like Alexa, Siri, Microsoft cortana etc. Why they are called smart is due to the reason that they understand what you say when you talk to them and respond accordingly. When you say, 'Hey Alexa play the song......', the song is immediately searched and played. Does that mean that the machine has become intelligent and has started thinking the way we do?

AI is a branch of science which enables machines to behave and respond intelligently to a given task or a situation, the way humans do.

AI allows machines to do tasks quickly, modify the operations based on given situations and automate the things.

We all know that machines understand the language of 0 and 1 (also called binary language). Whatever input we provide to the computer is converted into the machine understandable language. We can provide the input to the computer through speech, visuals, text etc. Artificial Intelligence is a huge branch which makes machines intelligent by providing the data using various modes of inputs and then making predictions on the basis of the real time data.

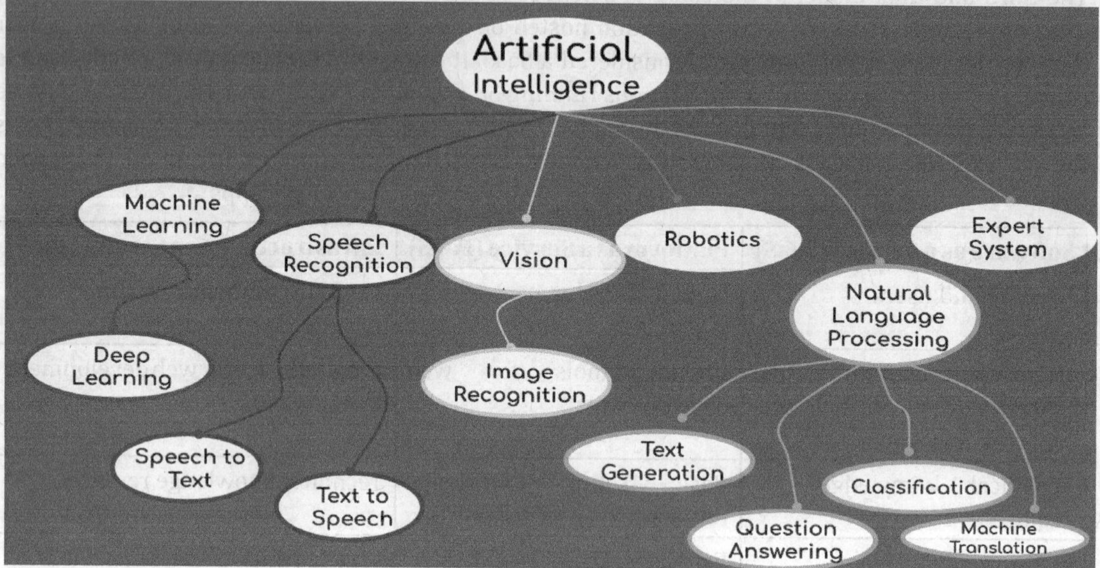

Today AI is used in almost all fields, like:

- Finance industry
- Education Industry
- Healthcare Industry
- Insurance Industry etc.

As per the New Education policy also, there will be more emphasis on coding and AI due to the following reasons:

- Coding helps children learn to problem solve
- Coding enhances thinking ability in a child.
- Computer programming teaches children to experiment and gives them the confidence to be creative.
- Coding is more about teaching children how to think differently.
- Coding helps children learn how to have fun with math.
- Children should become innovative, adaptive, build problem solving and logical reasoning skills
- Mathematics is essential due to its role in numerous upcoming fields and it requires computational thinking.
- Will raise awareness on issues of privacy, laws, standards associated with data handling and data protection.
- AI will add value to existing curriculum as its multidisciplinary nature will help to make connections between different subjects.
- AI based software can be developed and used by students to track their growth in school learning years and to improve learning experience.

Machine Learning (ML)

As mentioned above, AI is a huge branch which has many subsets and one such subset is Machine Learning.

Machine Learning is a branch of Artificial Intelligence which allows machines to learn from the data stored in the computer or on cloud.

As the data grows, the predictions made by the model become more accurate. Machine learning works for specific domains based on the designed algorithms. For example, teaching machines to identify fruits correctly. If the data is limited, then a machine may predict a tomato as an apple as both are red in color. So as we grow the data with all possibilities of an apple which includes color, dimensions etc., the machine model will become more accurate.

Some of the applications of machine learning are Google search algorithms, Facebook auto friend tagging suggestions, Netflix suggestions etc.

Internet of Things (IoT)

You must have heard of smart devices, like smart lights which can be controlled using your mobile. Car ACs can be switched on before you reach your car to get a comfortable temperature. All these devices which can be connected to the internet and allow collection and sharing of data is called the Internet of Things (IoT). The otherwise dumb devices are made intelligent by using sensors, software and technology and thus allowing them to communicate with the real time data. The IoT has brought the power of the internet, data processing and analytics to the real world of physical objects.

As per Wikipedia, the term IoT was coined by Kevin Ashton of P&G in 1999.

Note: You can check few interesting AI based experiments at the given links

https://mysteryanimal.withgoogle.com/ (MYSTERY ANIMAL)

https://mixlab.withgoogle.com/ (MIX LAB)

https://teachablemachine.withgoogle.com/ (TEACHABLE MACHINE)

https://quickdraw.withgoogle.com/ (QUICK DRAW)

https://experiments.withgoogle.com/ai/ai-duet/view/ (PIANO WITH RESPONSE)

https://shadowart.withgoogle.com/?lang=en-us (SHADOW ART)

https://www.autodraw.com/

Summary

1. The process of converting the keys we press on the keyboard into their equivalent code is called encoding.
2. ASCII stands for American Standard Code for Information Interchange.
3. Unicode contains the alphabets of almost all known languages. UTF8: UTF-8 stands for "Unicode Transformation Format - 8 bits. UTF32 is a fixed length encoding system which uses 4 bytes per character.
4. ISCII stands for Indian Script code for Information Interchange.

5. Operating System is an interface between the user and the computer as its main job is to manage the hardware of the computer, make other applications run and to convert high level language (user understandable language) into low level language (or Binary language or computer understandable language) and vice versa.
6. Examples of Operating Systems are Microsoft Windows (Windows 10, Windows 8, Windows 7, Windows Vista, and Windows XP), Apple's macOS, Google's OS, BlackBerry Tablet OS, Unix and Linux.
7. The operating system also helps various programs to run on different hardware platforms as it acts as an interface between the Software and Hardware.
8. We can run multiple programs at the same time as the operating system allows multitasking.
9. Memory Management means then when the data is provided to the computer, it is the job of the operating system to decide which application data will be stored where and will occupy how much memory.
10. Resource Management controls input-output resources of the computer and allocates them to the users or programs as per their requirement.
11. Types of Operating Systems
    - Batch Operating System
    - Multitasking/Time Sharing OS
    - Multiprocessing OS
    - Real Time OS
    - Distributed OS
    - Network OS
    - Mobile OS
12. Some of the important functions of Operating System are:
    - Process management
    - Memory management
    - File management
    - Device Management
    - Security
13. Cloud computing means storing and accessing data and applications over the Internet instead of your computer's local hard drive.
14. Benefits of Cloud computing are cost, speed, security, performance and reliability.
15. Different types of cloud computing are Public, Private and Hybrid Cloud.
16. There are three types of models depending upon the requirement of the customer, which are:-
    - Software as a Service (SaaS)
    - Platform as a Service (PaaS)
    - Infrastructure as a Service (IaaS)

17. Blockchain technology is a database of records of transactions which is distributed, and which is validated and maintained by a network of computers around the world.
18. AI is a branch of science which enables machines to behave and respond intelligently to a given task or a situation, the way humans do.
19. Machine Learning is a branch of Artificial Intelligence which allows machines to learn from the data stored in the computer or on cloud.
20. The devices which can be connected to the internet and allow collection and sharing of data is called the Internet of Things (IoT).

Multiple choice questions

1. Operating system is:
   a. collection of programs that manages hardware resources
   b. system service provider to the application programs
   c. interface between the hardware and application programs
   d. all of the above
2. To access the services of the operating system, the interface is provided by:
   a. System calls b. API
   c. Library d. Assembly instructions
3. Operating system can handle________ errors.
   a. power failure b. lack of paper in printer
   c. connection failure in the network d. all of the mentioned
4. Operating system is placed in:
   a. low memory b. high memory
   c. either low or high memory d. none of the mentioned
5. If case of a failure of a process, most operating system writes the error to:
   a. log file b. another running process
   c. new file d. Parent process
6. ________ is not a part of the operating system.
   a. Input/output control program b. Job control program
   c. Supervisor d. Performance monitor
7. Operating system is a collection of:
   a. Software routines b. Input-output devices
   c. Hardware components d. Software components
8. _______ is not an example of an operating system.
   a. UNIX b. MS-DOS c. CP/M d. PASCAL

9. ______ is the operating system which reads and reacts in terms of actual time.
   a. Real time system
   b. Time sharing system
   c. Quick response system
   d. Batch system
10. ________ software is used to simplify using of system software.
   a. Time sharing
   b. Multi-tasking
   c. Operating environment
   d. Spreadsheet
11. To access the services of operating system, the interface is provided by the:
   a. system calls
   b. API
   c. Library
   d. assembly instructions
12. ________ runs on computer hardware and serves as a platform for other system to run on
   a. Operating system
   b. Application system
   c. System software
   d. All of above
13. ______ is the layer of a computer system between the hardware and the user.
   a. Operating environment
   b. Operating system
   c. System environment
   d. None of these
14. Which is the first program run on a computer when the computer boots up?
   a. System software
   b. Operating system
   c. System operations
   d. None
15. Which of the following requires a device driver?
   a. Register
   b. Cache
   c. Main memory
   d. Disk
16. ASCII stands for..
   a. American Standard Code for Information Interchange
   b. Accurate Standard Code for Information Interchange
   c. American Suitable Code for Information Interchange
   d. American Standard Code for Inter Interchange
17. Which of the following encoding systems include Korean, Greek, Latin and many such languages?
   a. ASCII
   b. ISCII
   c. UNICODE
   d. PASCII
18. Which of the following is not the advantage of Cloud Computing?
   a. Speed
   b. Security
   c. Reusability
   d. Reliability
19. Which cloud service refers to internal datacenters of a business or other organization, not made available to the general public.
   a. Hybrid
   b. Hierarchical
   c. Private
   d. Public
20. Expanded form of PaaS is:
   a. Platform as a Service
   b. Poor as a Service
   c. Packet as a Server
   d. Packet as as Service
21. Which technology is referred to as digital gold?
   a. Brokerage Technology
   b. Blocking Technology
   c. Backward Technology
   d. Blockchain Technology

22. Alexa, Siri, Microsoft Cortana etc. are the examples of
 a. Augmented Reality
 b. Blockchain Technology
 c. Artificial Technology
 d. None of the above

Fill in the blanks

1. Operating System is an ____ between the user and the computer as its main job is to manage the hardware of the computer.
2. Using the operating system the programs are able to communicate with the ______ of the computer.
3. Whenever the user sends the instruction in user understandable language or high level language the operating system converts it into low level language or ______ understandable language.
4. The operating system also helps various programs to run on different hardware platforms as it acts as an interface between the _______ and Hardware.
5. We can run multiple programs at the same time as the operating system allows______.
6. Job of the operating system to decide which application data will be stored where and will occupy how much______.
7. The operating system controls ________ resources of the computer and allocates them to the users or programs as per their requirement.
8. Certain tasks of similar type can be ______ or combined together to speed up the process and the execution time.
9. Time Sharing Operating System is also known as _______ Operating System.
10. Time taken by each task to get executed is called the_____.
11. Multiprocessing Operating systems are capable of processing_____ tasks.
12. A ______ OS is the one which manages the time and resources of a CPU by splitting the given application into multiple tasks and runs the most important task first.
13. Computers over the network also ______ to perform a given task.
14. The system where independent computers over the network appear as a single system to the user in spite of being separate are called________.
15. A network operating system (NOS) is an operating system that manages hardware of the computers over the network and provides services to the ________ software.

State whether the following statements are true or false.

1. Mobile OS is specifically designed to run applications on your mobile phone.
2. Multiple applications can run at a time on our computer, it is the duty of the operating system to synchronize between various applications, allocate resources so that the data can be shared.
3. Tasks like creation, scheduling and termination of processes are not managed by the operating system for faster execution of multiple processes.
4. Every program/application running on the computer needs memory for storing the data.

5. We work on and store various types of files on our computer.
6. The operation system is responsible for only creating files but not with storing them at specific locations, renaming them, sharing and protecting the files.
7. Device management does not keep track of all devices which include I/O, storage devices and other networking devices etc.
8. The operating system allocates and deallocates the devices to the processes as and when needed.
9. Operating system needs device drivers to run the I/O devices.
10. Operating System is an interface between the user and the computer.
11. Using the operating system the programs are able to communicate with the hardware of the computer.
12. The operating system does not help various programs to run on different hardware platforms as it acts as an interface between the Software and Hardware.
13. We cannot run multiple programs at the same time as the operating system allows multitasking.
14. The operating system also helps in memory management.
15. It is the job of the operating system to decide which application data will be stored where and will occupy how much memory.

Short questions

1. Define the term operating system.
2. Write the main purpose of using an operating system.
3. Give any five examples of an operating system.
4. What is the need of an operating system?
5. Define the term device management.
6. What is multitasking?
7. What is memory management?
8. Write one difference between device management and memory management.
9. Define the term resource management.
10. Name the types of operating system.

Long questions

1. Explain batch operating system.
2. What's the main purpose of an OS? What are the different types of OS?
3. Write a short note on multitasking operating system.
4. Differentiate between multiprocessing OS and real time OS.
5. Write a short note on distributed OS.
6. Explain network OS.

7. Explain the functions of operating system.
8. Differentiate among process management and memory management.
9. Explain the function of operating system device management.
10. What are the benefits of a multiprocessor system?

Answer:

Multiple choice questions

1. d	2. a	3. d	4. c	5. a	6. d	7. a	8. d
9. a	10. a	11. a	12. a	13. b	14. b	15. d	

Fill in the blanks

1. interface	2. hardware	3. machine	4. software
5. multitasking	6. memory	7. input-output	8. batched
9. multitasking	10. quantum	11. multiple	12. real Time
13. communicate	14. distributed systems	15. application	

State whether the following statements are true or false

1. True	2. True	3. False	4. True	5. True
6. False	7. False	8. True	9. True	10. True
11. True	12. False	13. False	14. True	15. True

4 Problem Solving

Introduction to problem solving

There were times when for managing the records in the schools, offices, business there were piles of registers required to be maintained. For doing any kind of calculation, either manual mode was used or one had to rely on a calculator. There were possibilities of lack of accuracy and the work was tedious too. But in today's scenario things have been made convenient due to the automation in almost every field. Be it generating a report card of a child, or doing train/air reservations, online shopping of clothes or grocery, ordering food, accessing eBooks to study anytime and anywhere, the list is endless. But all these things were not made convenient just like that. The people identified the problems they were facing in different areas and started looking for the solution through computers to make the task execution quick and accurate. Problem solving thus is the key feature of computers. We use and need computers in almost every field for solving the problems in almost all areas.

Solving a problem requires many steps starting from identifying the actual need to breaking up the problem into small sub problems and then working towards getting the desired output for each sub problem and then doing the final compilation. Once it's done then we need to test whether we were able to achieve the result successfully or not. In this section we will study more about the concept of problem solving and its techniques.

Steps for problem solving

Suppose while working on your laptop or desktop, you face an issue of sudden shutdown. What will you do if the system is not able to boot? You will first try to find a problem. It could be because of the virus or there could be some problem in the IC of the computer or could be a problem in the power button. The possibilities are many. If we are not able to solve the issue ourselves then the next step we follow is to take the system to the service center where the technical person checks the machine, identifies the problem, rectifies it, tests your machine after rectification and once everything is checked, returns your machine. So in the process of problem solving, certain steps are followed to reach the desired result.

Same is the case when we need to do a task in computers. To perform a task, we need to follow some steps to achieve the required result and they are:

- Analyze the problem
- Develop an algorithm
- Write the Code
- Test the Code and Debug if any issue

Analyze the problem

Before we start to work it is very important to understand the issue we need to solve. If the issue is not clear then we can never reach the correct result. Suppose we want to find the sum of numbers. So the problem we need to solve is to do addition so that the sum can be generated. We also need to decide whether we want to find the sum of two numbers or more numbers.

Develop an algorithm

The next step is to know the requirements we need to solve the problem. This task is achieved when we design the process from the requirement to the final result in natural and simple to understand language. This is called an algorithm. So algorithms are the step-by-step procedure or set of rules needed to reach the desired result.

In continuation to the above problem, if we want to develop algorithm of finding sum of 2 numbers then the procedure we will follow will be:

a. We need to take one number

b. We need to take second number

c. We must add two numbers and store result in a temporary memory

d. We display the answer stored in the memory by extracting the result from it.

Write the Code

Once the algorithm is written we need to choose a programming language to write the program so that the steps of algorithms are understood by the computer and the result can be generated. Coding will be discussed in detail via Python Language in the later part of the chapter.

Test the Code and Debug if any issues

This is the final phase of problem solving, where the program written is checked by executing. If the result is successfully generated as per the requirement, then the code is successful. There can be possibilities where either the code doesn't run due to the incorrect syntax rules or the code executes but generates the incorrect result.

We must always remember the GIGO concept(Garbage in Garbage out) also. If we provide incorrect input, the result will always be incorrect.

There are a number of testing tools used by the companies to test the code developed. Some of the testing automation tools are Selenium, TestingWhiz, TestComplete, Ranorex etc.

Algorithm

Algorithms are the step-by-step procedure or set of rules needed to solve a given progroblem and reach the desired result. Before we start writing the algorithms we must have the answers of few questions like:

- Do I understand the questions? What type of input and output can the problem have?

- Are there multiple ways to solve the problem? If yes, then which one is most efficient?
- Will working be the same for all cases and inputs?
- If not then what exception should be included and how to handle them?

We must remember the following while writing an algorithm:

- The steps of the algorithm must be clear and precise. It should not be conflicting or ambiguous.
- Input and output should be defined precisely.
- The algorithm must be effective and should be able to run with minimum number of resources
- Algorithms should be able to work on any programming language.

There are two ways to write the algorithm:

1. Using Flowchart
2. Using Pseudo Code

Representation of algorithms using flowchart

Flowchart is a visual representation of algorithms. We use symbols to prepare flowchart. Following is the list of symbols used to prepare flowchart.

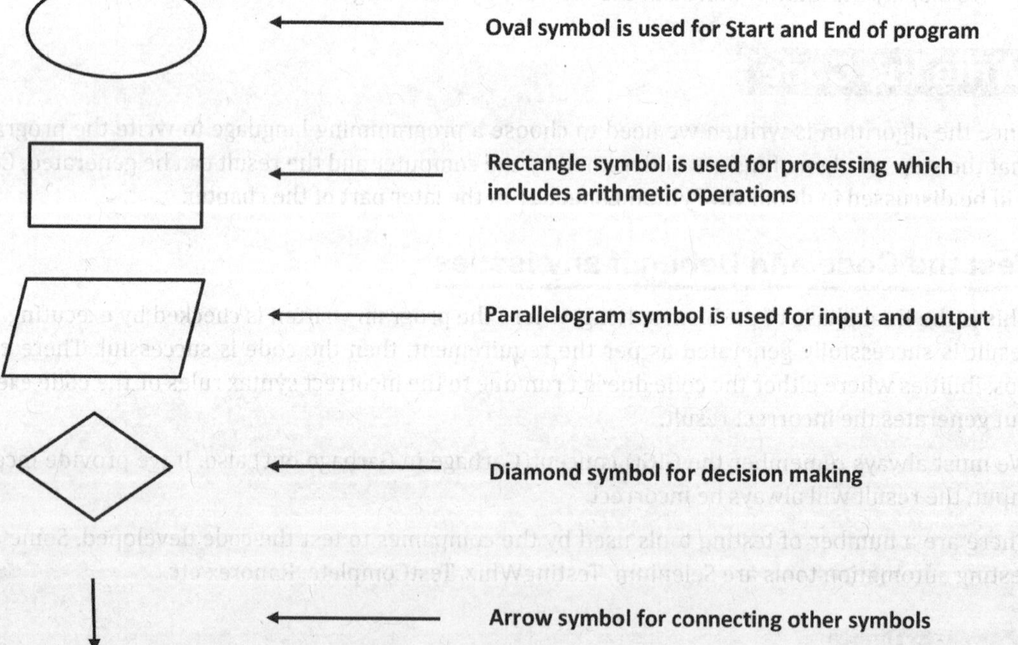

Let us take a few examples to understand how flowchart is made.

Example 1: Write an algorithm to accept two numbers and find their sum. Also draw the flowchart for the same.

Algorithm

1. Start the program
2. Accept number 1.
3. Accept number 2
4. Find the sum
5. Print the sum
6. Program ends

Flowchart

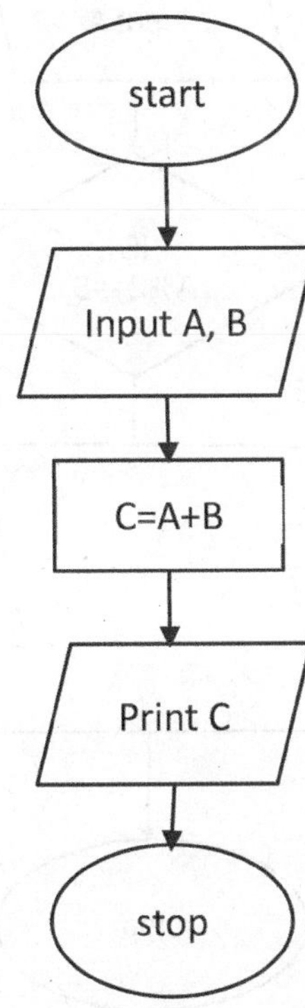

Example 2: Write an algorithm to accept a number and find whether it is an even number or odd. Also draw the flowchart for the same.

Algorithm

1. Start the program
2. Accept a number.
3. Check if it is divisible by 2. The remainder will be 0 if the number is divisible by 2.
4. If remainder is 0 print the number is "Even"
5. If remainder is not 0 print the number is "odd"
6. Program ends

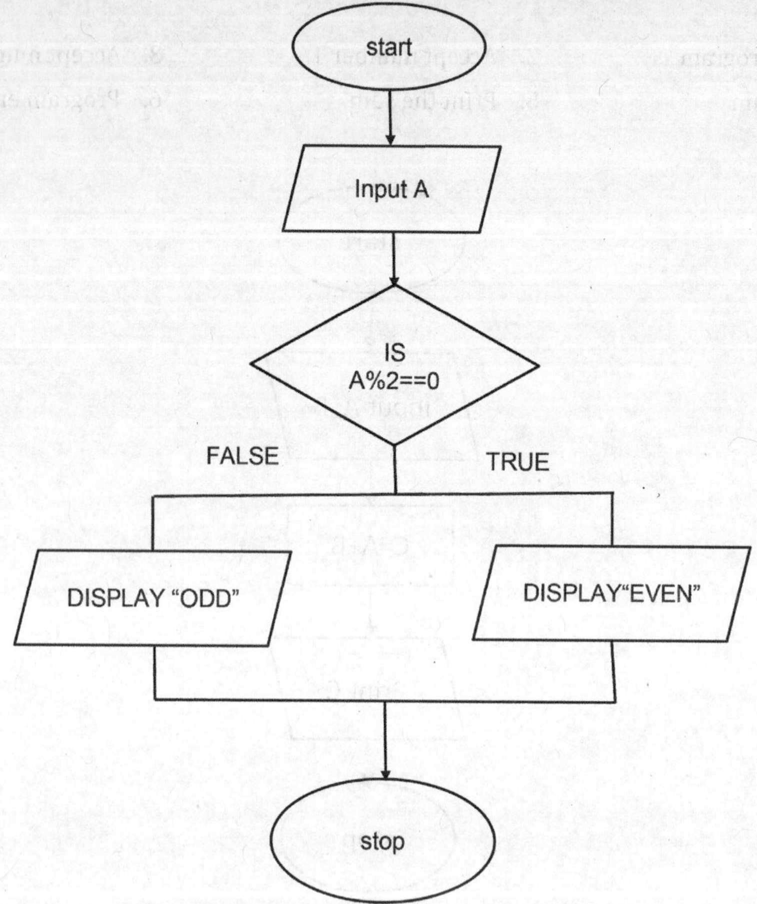

Representation of algorithms using pseudo code

Pseudocode is another way to represent algorithms. It's the informal way by which the programmers develop the algorithm. It is used for creating an outline or a rough draft of a program. It summarizes the flow of the program. Pseudocode is not an actual programming language. It uses short terms or simple English language syntaxes to write code for programs. The main advantage of writing a pseudocode is that it Improves the readability of the algorithm as it acts like a bridge between the program and the algorithm or flowchart.

Some of the keywords used in Pseudocode are :

- INPUT
- PRINT
- INCREMENT
- DECREMENT
- IF/ELSE
- WHILE
- TRUE/FALSE

Let us see the following examples to understand how to write Pseudocode and draw flowcharts.

Example 1

Write an algorithm using pseudocode and flowchart to accept a number and find whether it is an even number or odd.

Pseudocode

1. Input number A
2. If A MOD 2==0 then

    Print "EVEN"

    Else

    Print "ODD"

Flowchart

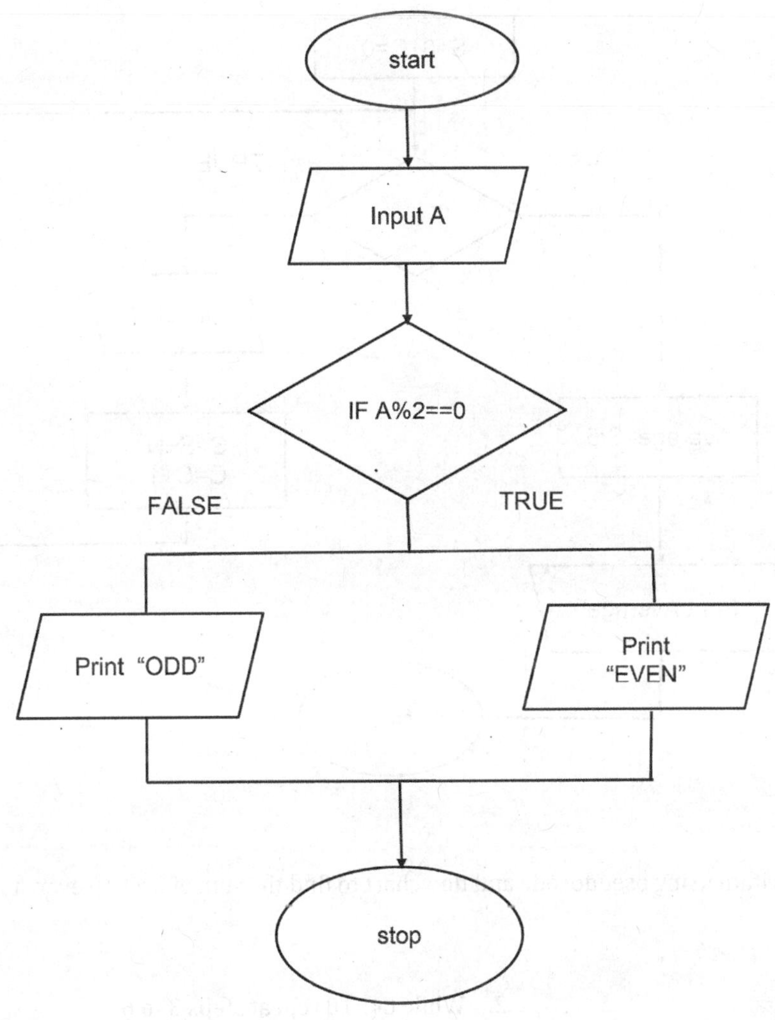

Example 2

Write an algorithm using pseudocode and flowchart to accept five numbers and find their average

Pseudocode

1. C=0 and S=0
2. While C<5 repeat steps 3 to 6

3. Input Number N
4. Compute S=S+N
5. Compute C=C+1
6. Go back to step 2
7. Compute Average = S/5
8. Print Average

Flowchart

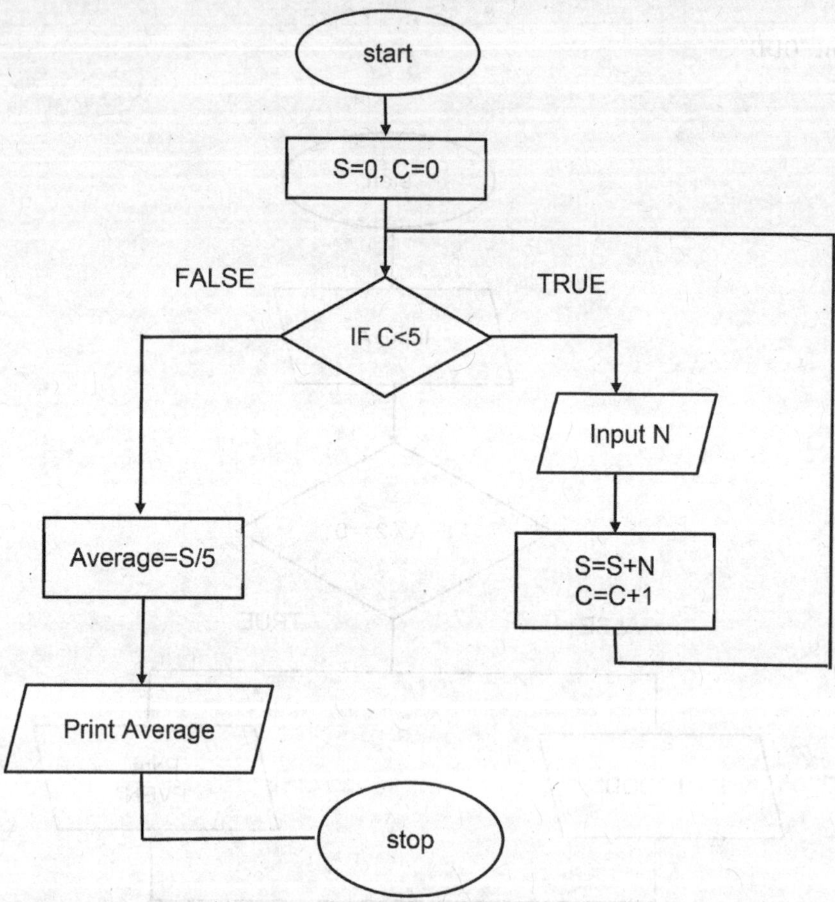

Example 3

Write an algorithm using pseudocode and flowchart to find the sum of first 10 even numbers starting from 2

Pseudocode

1. C=1 and S=0
2. While C<=10 repeat steps 3 to 6
3. Compute N=2*C
4. Compute S=S+N
5. Compute C=C+1
6. Go back to step 2
7. Print Sum

Flowchart

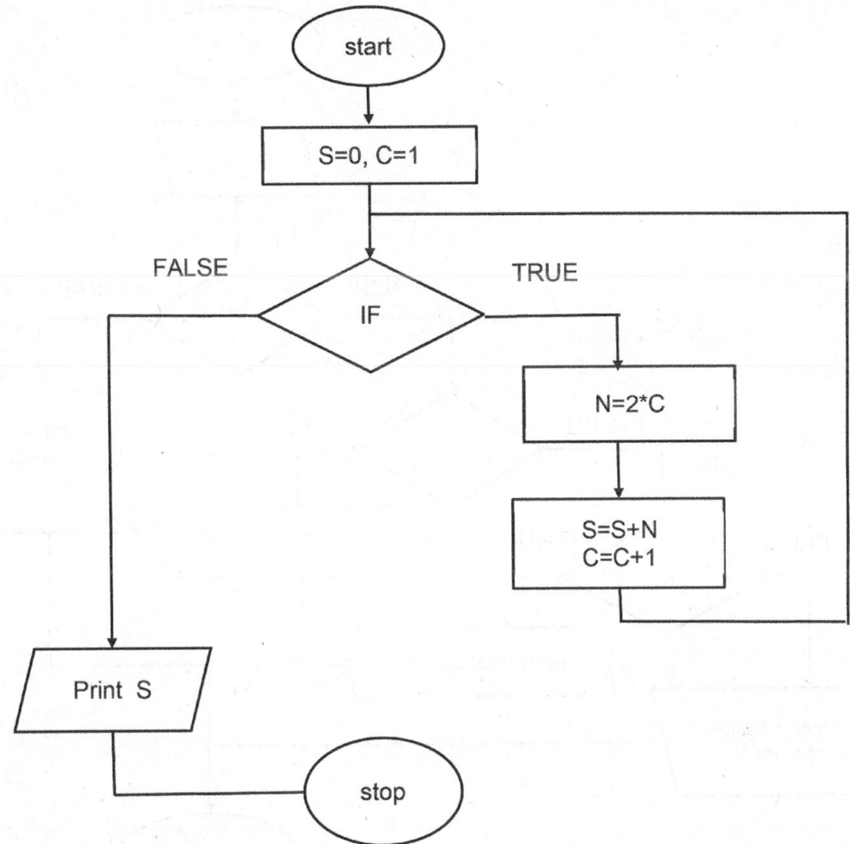

Example 4

Write an algorithm using pseudocode and flowchart to accept a number and find whether it is a multiple of 6 or just 3 or just 2 or the other number.

Pseudocode

1. Input number N
2. If N mod 6 ==0 then

    Print Its multiple of 6

    Else if N mod 3==0 then

    Print its multiple of just 3

    Else if N mod 2==0 then

    Print its multiple of 2

    Else

    Print Multiple of other number

Flowchart

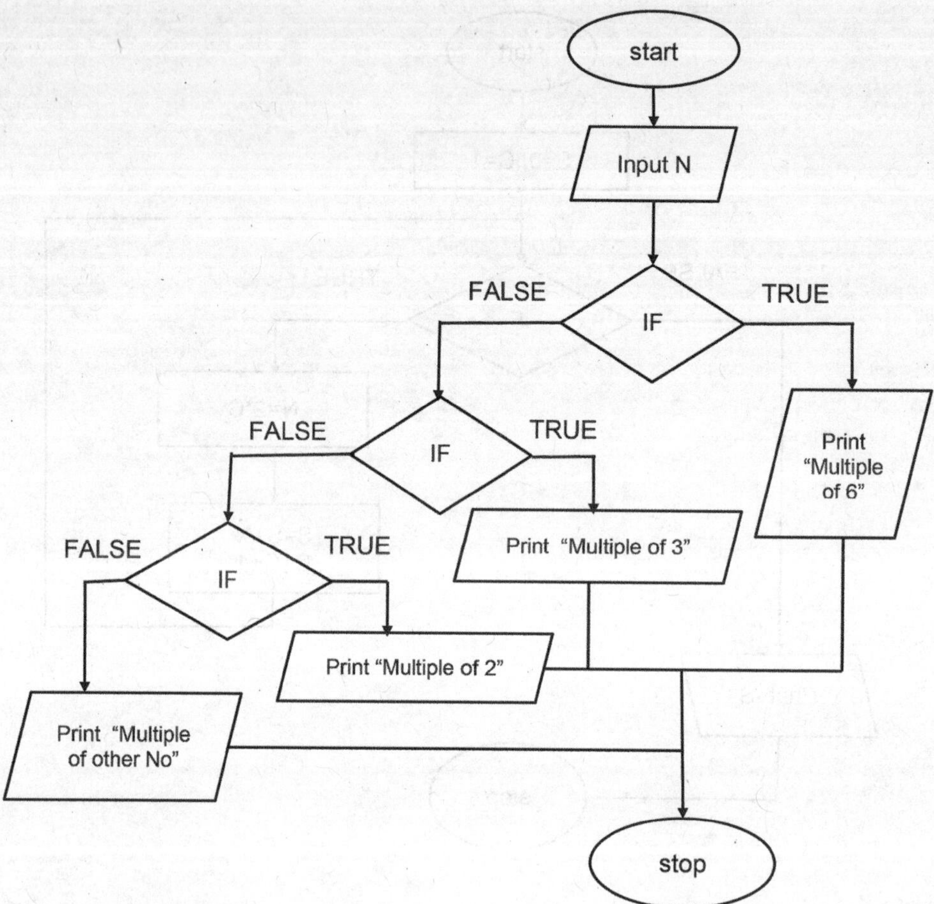

Decomposition

Sometimes the problem we want to work on is complex. By complex, it means it has a lot of sub options or sub functions to perform. So it is always better to break up the complex tasks into subtasks and work on them individually. This process of breaking large problems into small manageable small problems is called decomposition.

Take an example of a school management system. The tasks performed by the school are not just the result generation but also to manage the teachers records, transport details of students, fee details, teachers salary, time table details, hostel details.

When each sub task is taken individually, it's managed and handled properly. Moreover each sub task can be handled by the specific team of members who are specialized in their respective areas. These subtasks can later be combined to run a complete management system,

Summary

1. The steps for problem solving include Analyze the problem, Develop an algorithm, Write the Code, Test the Code and Debug if any issues
2. Algorithms are the step-by-step procedure or set of rules needed to solve a given progroblem and reach the desired result.
3. There are two ways to write the algorithm, Flowchart and Pseudo Code
4. Flowchart is a visual representation of algorithms.
5. Pseudocode is the informal way by which the programmers develop the algorithm.
6. Pseudocode improves the readability of the algorithm as it acts like a bridge between the program and the algorithm or flowchart.
7. The process of breaking large problems into small manageable small problems is called decomposition.
8. In flowchart
   a. The oval symbol is used for start/end of program
   b. The rectangle Symbol is used to represent arithmetic operations
   c. The parallelogram symbol is used when we need to accept value or display the output.
   d. Diamond symbol is used for making decisions
   e. An arrow symbol is used for connecting the other symbols

? EXERCISE

Multiple Choice Questions

1. Which of the following is not a step needed to solve a problem:

   A. Analyze the problem B. Develop an algorithm

   C. Copy the Code D. Test the Code and Debug if any issues

2. The step by step procedure or set of rules needed to solve a given progroblem and reach the desired result is called as:

   a. Coding b. Algorithm c. Output d. Testing

3. The symbol used to represent input or output is: (c)

   a. ⬭ b. ▭ c. ▱ d. ↓

4. The symbol which is used for connecting other symbols is: (d)

   a. ⬭ b. ▭ c. ▱ d. ↓

5. Arithmetic operations in a flowchart can be represented using the following symbol. (b)

   a. ⬭ b. ▭ c. ▱ d. ↓

6. Following is the flowchart which checks whether a number X is positive or negative. Choose the correct option in the order of the blank boxes

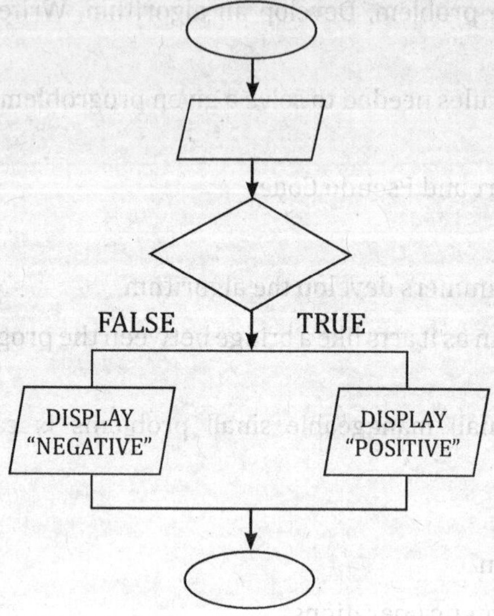

a. Input X, Is X>=0, Stop
b. Is X>=0, Stop, Input X
c. Stop, Input X, Is X>=0
d. Input X, Stop, Is X>=0

7. Which of the following is one of the ways to write the algorithm?

a. PseudoCode
b. Decomposition
c. Chart
d. None of the above

8 This process of breaking large problems into small manageable small problems is called

a. Analysis
b. Decomposition
c. Problem breaking
d. All the above

Subjective Questions

1. Write the steps required for problem solving.
2. What do you understand by Algorithm? Explain with the help of an example
3. Name the two ways to write the algorithm.
4. Write an algorithm using flowchart to
   a. check if the number N is a positive or a negative number.
   b. check if the number N is a multiple of 5 or not.
   c. Find the largest of the two numbers A and B.
5. Draw the symbols used in flowchart to:
   a. To decision making
   b. To accept input or display output
   c. To perform arithmetic operations
   d. To start/end a program

5 Python

Introduction to Python

Python is a general-purpose high-level programming language which was conceived in the year 1980 and implemented in the year 1989 by Dutch programmer Guido Van Rossum at CWI in the Netherlands as a successor to the ABC programming language. Today, Python is one of the most widely used programming languages with features like code readability with simple to understand syntax and also to express the concepts/ programs in fewer lines of codes. It's an interpreted language which means you type the command and get the result instantly.

It supports multiple programming paradigms like object-oriented as well as structured programming. Python is an open-source language which means that anyone can contribute to it and anyone can freely download it and use it. Today, Python is used in every part of our lives starting from web searches to gaming, scientific and mathematical computing, and even in AI projects. Websites like Instagram, YouTube use Python. Today, Python is used in AI, Machine learning, Data Mining, Data Science, Graphic Design Applications, Product development, Testing, Automation Scripting and many such fields.

Being an open-source language, Python can be downloaded free of cost from the website https://www.python.org/downloads/ . The latest version of Python is 3.9.4 which was released on 4th April 2021 but we can work on version 3.6 and above.

Features of Python are as follows:

- It is a simple and a versatile language. It can be run on various systems.
- Beginners just learning to program appreciate Python's simplicity and interactivity. It is an easy to learn language.
- Python can be learned quickly, and for many experienced programmers, the initial investment of effort into learning enough about Python to use it practically is remarkably small.
- Python is a free and open-source language. It is an example of FLOSS (Free/Libré and Open Source Software). In simple terms, you can freely distribute copies of this software, read it's source code, make changes to it, use pieces of it in new free programs.
- Python is a High Level Language.
- Python can be easily ported to many platforms which allows python programs to work on any platform without making any major changes. You can use Python on Linux, Windows, FreeBSD, Macintosh, Solaris etc.
- It is an interpreted language. This means that unlike other programming languages like, C, C++, where the source code has to be converted to binary code by the compiler before execution,

Python converts the source code into an intermediate form called bytecodes and then translates this into the native language of your computer and then runs it. And thus you see the execution of the commands line by line as no intermediate file is created in Python.

- Python supports Object Oriented programming, which means the program is built around objects which include data and functionality. It also supports Procedure Oriented programming, where the program is built around procedures or functions.
- Python has extensive libraries, which can be used to develop a lot of applications.

Installing Python

1. Python is an open source language and hence it can be downloaded free from the website www.python.org. To install python go to https://www.python.org/downloads/
2. Choose the operating system
3. You can choose any version from 3.6 and above. The current version is 3.9.4.

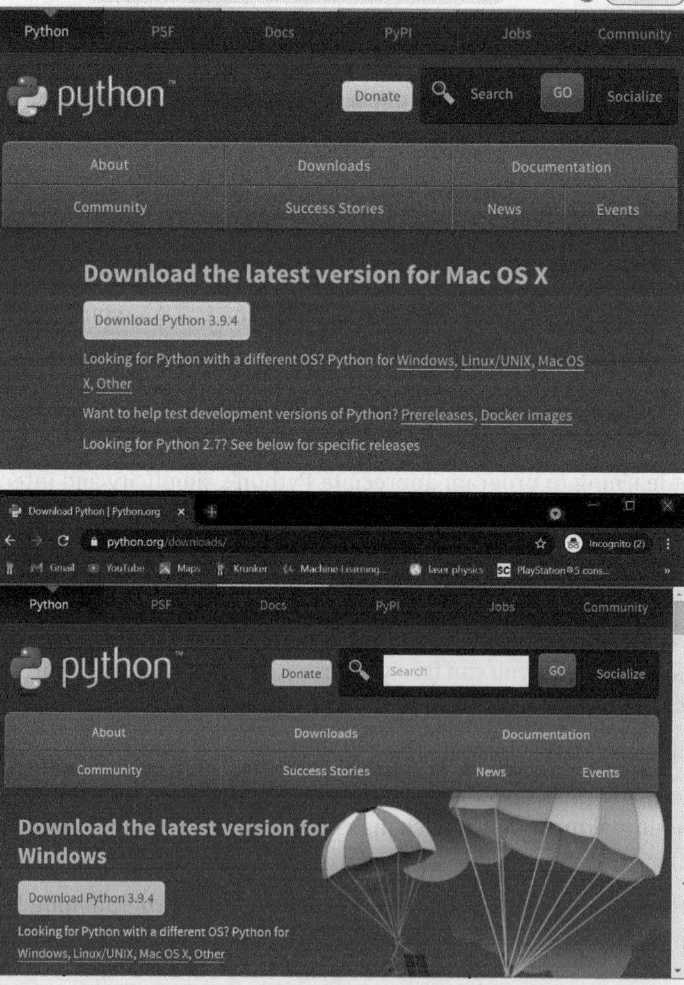

Release version	Release date		Click for more
Python 3.7.2	Dec. 24, 2018	Download	Release Notes
Python 3.6.8	Dec. 24, 2018	Download	Release Notes
Python 3.7.1	Oct. 20, 2018	Download	Release Notes
Python 3.6.7	Oct. 20, 2018	Download	Release Notes
Python 3.5.6	Aug. 2, 2018	Download	Release Notes

4. You must choose the executable installer from the various files shown. This is advisable for the offline version.

Files

Version	Operating System	Description
Gzipped source tarball	Source release	
XZ compressed source tarball	Source release	
macOS 64-bit/32-bit installer	Mac OS X	for Mac OS X 10.6 and later
macOS 64-bit installer	Mac OS X	for OS X 10.9 and later
Windows help file	Windows	
Windows x86-64 embeddable zip file	Windows	for AMD64/EM64T/x64
Windows x86-64 executable installer	Windows	for AMD64/EM64T/x64
Windows x86-64 web-based installer	Windows	for AMD64/EM64T/x64
Windows x86 embeddable zip file	Windows	
Windows x86 executable installer	Windows	
Windows x86 web-based installer	Windows	

5. When you start installing, make sure that you know the path where the python is getting installed as it will be required later when we work with multiple modules. It is therefore advisable to create a folder say python367 in C drive and install python within that folder. So click on Customize installation→ Next→ Change the install location to C:\python367

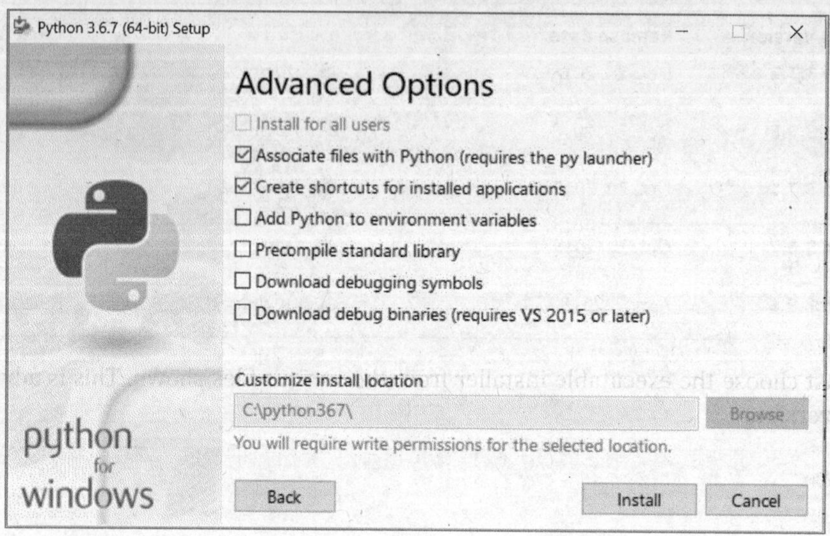
Python 3.6.7 (64-bit) Setup
Advanced Options
Install for all users
Associate files with Python (requires the py launcher)
Create shortcuts for installed applications
Add Python to environment variables
Precompile standard library
Download debugging symbols
Download debug binaries (requires VS 2015 or later)
Customize install location
C:\python367\
Browse
You will require write permissions for the selected location.
Back
Install
Cancel
python for windows

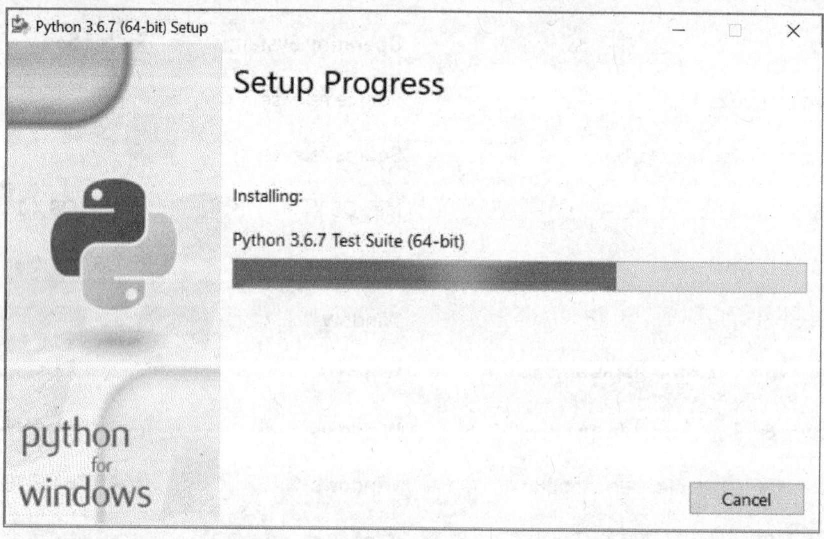
Python 3.6.7 (64-bit) Setup
Setup Progress
Installing:
Python 3.6.7 Test Suite (64-bit)
Cancel
python for windows

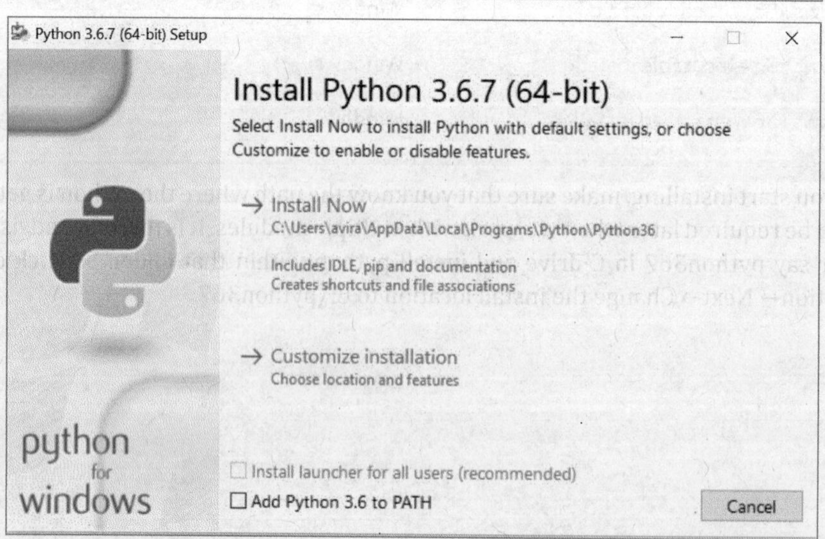
Python 3.6.7 (64-bit) Setup
Install Python 3.6.7 (64-bit)
Select Install Now to install Python with default settings, or choose
Customize to enable or disable features.
→ Install Now
C:\Users\avira\AppData\Local\Programs\Python\Python36
Includes IDLE, pip and documentation
Creates shortcuts and file associations
→ Customize installation
Choose location and features
Install launcher for all users (recommended)
Add Python 3.6 to PATH
Cancel
python for windows

6. Once Python is installed, go to run → IDLE and the python interpreter window will appear.

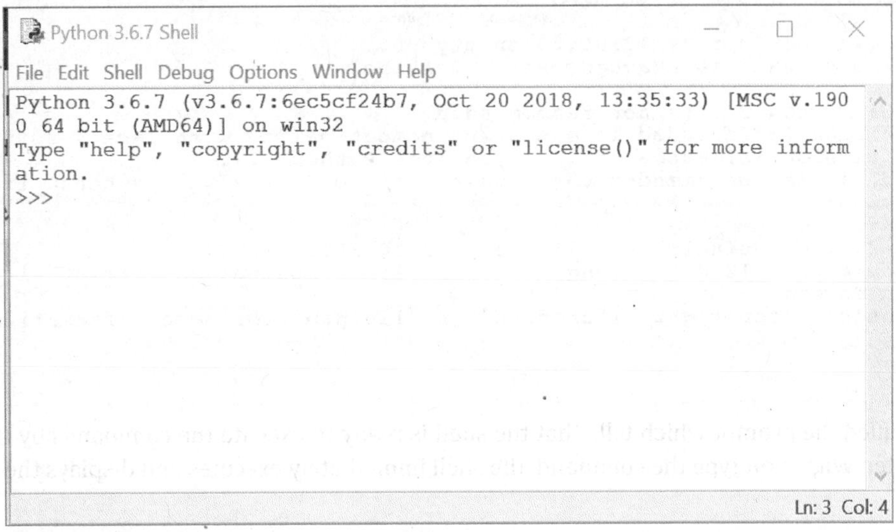

```
Python 3.6.7 Shell
File Edit Shell Debug Options Window Help
Python 3.6.7 (v3.6.7:6ec5cf24b7, Oct 20 2018, 13:35:33) [MSC v.190
0 64 bit (AMD64)] on win32
Type "help", "copyright", "credits" or "license()" for more inform
ation.
>>>
Ln: 3 Col: 4
```

Execution modes

There are two modes to execute a python commands/programs:

1. Interactive Mode
2. Script Mode

Interactive mode

This mode is also called as RELP (Read Eval Print Loop) where the single line commands written by the user are executed. The commands are executed by Python shell. This mode comes with the python installation.

To access python shell:

Open Terminal (or command prompt) of your Operating System (Mac / Windows) → Type Python

The following screen will appear in windows:

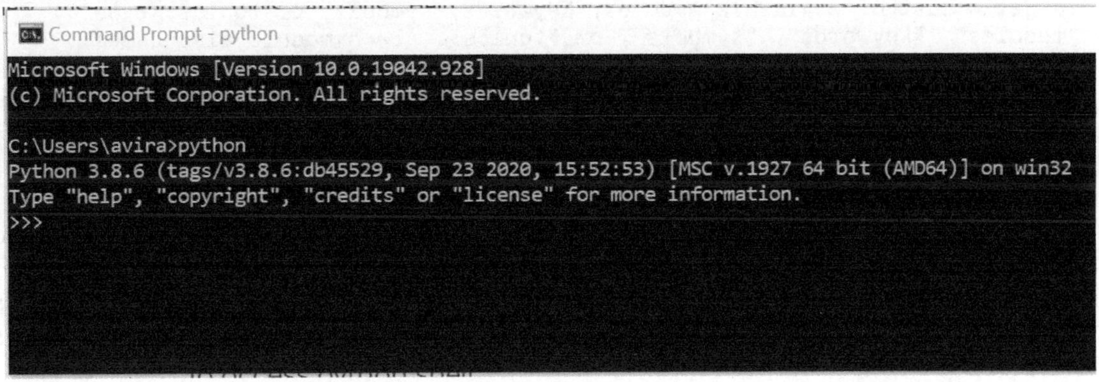

```
Command Prompt - python
Microsoft Windows [Version 10.0.19042.928]
(c) Microsoft Corporation. All rights reserved.

C:\Users\avira>python
Python 3.8.6 (tags/v3.8.6:db45529, Sep 23 2020, 15:52:53) [MSC v.1927 64 bit (AMD64)] on win32
Type "help", "copyright", "credits" or "license" for more information.
>>>
```

The following screen will appear in mac:

```
sarikakaushal — Python — 75×16
Last login: Sat Apr 24 12:00:00 on ttys000
sarikakaushal@Sarikas-MacBook-Air ~ % python

WARNING: Python 2.7 is not recommended.
This version is included in macOS for compatibility with legacy software.
Future versions of macOS will not include Python 2.7.
Instead, it is recommended that you transition to using 'python3' from with
in Terminal.

Python 2.7.16 (default, Dec 21 2020, 23:00:36)
[GCC Apple LLVM 12.0.0 (clang-1200.0.30.4) [+internal-os, ptrauth-isa=sign+
stri on darwin
Type "help", "copyright", "credits" or "license" for more information.
>>> 
```

>>> is called the prompt which tells that the shell is ready to execute the commands by the Python interpreter. When you type the command, the shell immediately executes and displays the result.

Try it!

Type >>>help( ) .

You will be able to get the help related to python command and other python related topics, which we will do in the following chapters.

```
Python 3.7.7 (v3.7.7:d7c567b08f, Mar 10 2020, 02:56:16)
[Clang 6.0 (clang-600.0.57)] on darwin
Type "help", "copyright", "credits" or "license()" for more information.
>>> help()

Welcome to Python 3.7's help utility!

If this is your first time using Python, you should definitely check out
the tutorial on the Internet at https://docs.python.org/3.7/tutorial/.

Enter the name of any module, keyword, or topic to get help on writing
Python programs and using Python modules.  To quit this help utility and
return to the interpreter, just type "quit".

To get a list of available modules, keywords, symbols, or topics, type
"modules", "keywords", "symbols", or "topics".  Each module also comes
with a one-line summary of what it does; to list the modules whose name
or summary contain a given string such as "spam", type "modules spam".

help> |
```

Interactive mode is convenient to use especially when your script is small and you would like to check the result quickly. It helps the beginners to check the python commands result / execution. But for long programs the shell is not recommended. Also you cannot make changes in the commands written in shell. You have to rewrite them to see the changed result. So the second mode called is 'Script Mode' is used.

Script Mode

This mode is used when you need to write a complete python program and save the file written in a text editor like sublime with the file extension .py

There are two ways to work on the script mode:

a. Since the file gets stored in the default folder where python is installed, just write the file name with the complete path at the command prompt. For example to execute a python file 'try.py', we write the following at the command prompt

```
Microsoft Windows [Version 10.0.19042.928]
(c) Microsoft Corporation. All rights reserved.

C:\Users\avira>c:\python367\try.py
My first program
completed successfully

C:\Users\avira>
```

b. IDLE (Integrated Development and Learning Environment) comes with the Python installation in Windows and Mac and it provides a text editor with features like syntax highlighting and auto indentation. It allows you to execute single line python statements or complete Python program. Go to run and type IDLE to open the editor window.

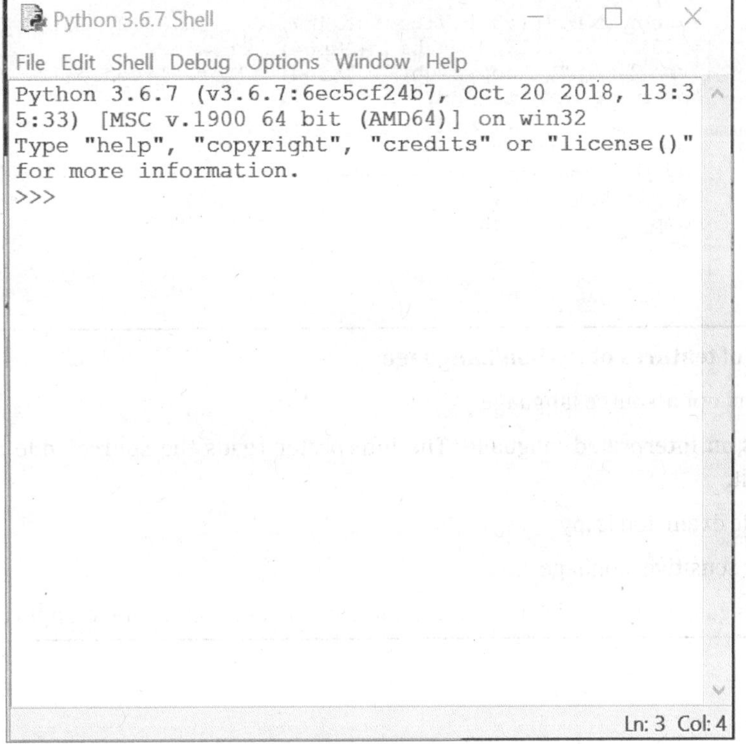

To open a new file select File→ New File, write the 'very first Python program' and Save with the name 'try.py'.

Program

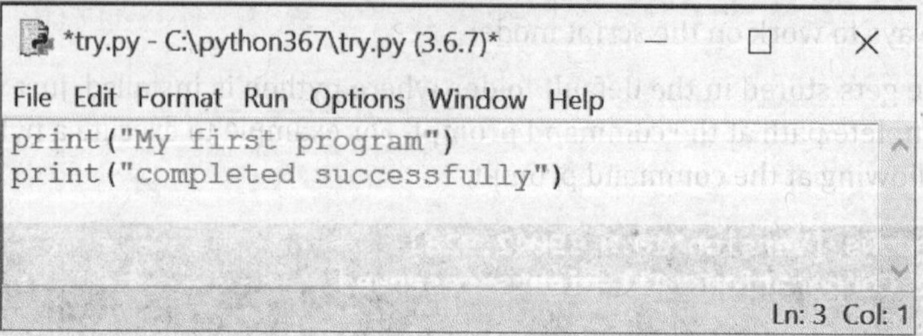

To execute the program select Run→ Run Module. You can also use the function key F5 to execute your program.

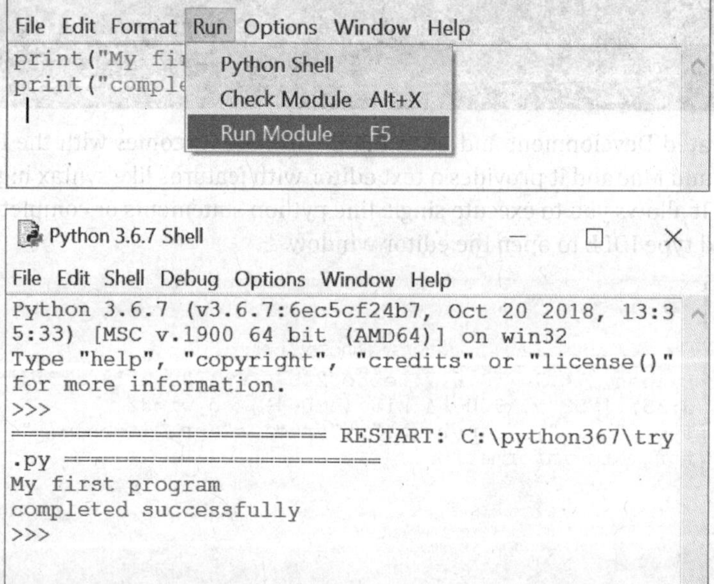

Quick recap of features of Python Language

1. Its free and open-source language
2. Python is an interpreted language. The interpreter reads the source code line by line, and executes it.
3. Python file extension is .py
4. It's a case sensitive language
5. Python language come which GUI based libraries to make GUI enabled applications

Python character set

Every programming language recognizes and allows a certain set of characters to be used in a program. These are called character sets. Following are the character sets allowed by Python programming language:

Letters A-Z / a-z

Numbers/Digits 0-9

Special characters + - * / % // ( ) [ ] { } \ # , ; :: ' ' " " @ _ < > = & ** != ==

Python can also recognize all ASCII and UNICODE characters too.

Tokens

The smallest unit in a programming language used in building a program is called Token. This includes keyword, identifier, literal, operator, punctuator.

1. **Keywords**

   Every programming language has some predefined words which have some meaning in the programming language. These predefined words are called as keywords. To see the list of keywords type the following in interactive mode:

```
>>>help("keywords")

OR type

>>> help( )        and then

help>keywords
```

```
>>> help("keywords")

Here is a list of the Python keywords.  Enter any keyword to get more help.

False               class               from                or
None                continue            global              pass
True                def                 if                  raise
and                 del                 import              return
as                  elif                in                  try
assert              else                is                  while
async               except              lambda              with
await               finally             nonlocal            yield
break               for                 not
```

   There are 35 keywords as per version 3.6.7. One more keyword is added in the latest version 3.9 and above

2. **Literal**

   The data which we use in a program is called a literal. Data can be numeric, alphanumeric, complex no or any other value required for a program.

   Following are the different types of literals:

a. **String literal :** It's any alphanumeric value represented in quotes. Examples are, "`Num123`", "`Have a Great Day`", "`Rahul`" etc.

b. **Numeric literal :** They are further categorized as:

   i. Integer literal- They are values without decimal. Examples are `12, 78 , 1234` etc.

   ii. Float literal. They are values with decimal. Examples `12.0, 99.90, 3.1414` etc.

   iii. Complex literal: This has two parts real and imaginary. It is represented as a+bj. Examples are `12+5j, 12.3+45.3j, 89j` etc.

   iv. Binary literal : Python can store the binary number by prefixing it with '0b'. Examples of binary literal are `0b1001, 0b1110` etc.

   v. Octal literal: Octal numbers also can be directly represented in python by directly prefixing the no with 0c. For example `0c234, 0c567` etc.

   vi. Hexadecimal literal: Hexadecimal numbers are represented in python by directly prefixing the no with 0x. For example `0xA34, 0x5B7` etc.

c. **Boolean literal:** This has only two values, True and False.

3. **Identifier**

They identify the memory location. They are the names given to a variable/object which store the value. So we identify the memory location by giving them a name and thus is called a variable.

Rules for naming an identifier

- It can have alphabets A-Z, a-z and numbers 0-9.
- It cannot be a keyword
- It cannot have a space
- It cannot start with a number
- The only special character allowed is _ (underscore)
- Variable name can start with _ (underscore)

Few examples of a valid identifiers are : `Num, Num123, Num_123, _Num123, Data_xyz, Else, IF`

Few examples of invalid identifiers are : `else, 23Num, Data XYZ, Data-XYZ, Num$123`

In Python, the variables are declared by simply assigning a value or literal. The type of the variable is implicitly assigned as per the value it points to. So variables must be assigned values before they are used.

For example:

```
>>>X=12  #X is variable of the type integer
>>>PI=3.14  #PI is variable of the type float
>>>Name="Kavin" #X is variable of the type string
>>>B=0b1101 #B is variable of the type Binary
```

4. **Operators**

There are various types of operations we can perform on a variable. Operators provide different results as per their use. Following are the different type of operators:

1. **Arithmetic :** They perform arithmetic operations. Following are the arithmetic operators:

operator	Purpose	Example	Output
+ (Addition)	Used to add numeric values	>>>12+34 >>>3+6.77	36 9.77
- (Subtraction)	Used to subtract the given numeric values	>>> 34-67 >>> 22.123-6.78	-33 15.343

* (Multiplication)	Used to multiply the numeric values	>>> 9*7
		>>> 45*2.2
		>>> 1.2*1.2
			63
			99.00000000000001
			1.44

Note: Floating-point numbers are stored as binary fractions, as the computer only understands binary (0 and 1) but most of the fractions cannot be accurately stored in our computer due to the hardware limitation. Due to this reason, you might see the floating point calculations with long fraction part. This is generally with odd fraction nos, like 1.1, 4.33, 7.89 etc			
/ (Division)	Used to divide numerator by denominator and gives precise answer	>>>5/2 >>>4/2 >>>6.7/3	2.5 2.0 2.2333333333333334
Note: In python the final result is always a number with decimal point (float value) irrespective of whether the numerator and denominator both are integers.			

// (Floor Division)	Returns the nearest possible integer less than or equal to the result	>>>4//2
		>>> 4.0//2
		>>> 3//2
		>>>-3//2
			2
			2.0
			1
			-2

Note: The final result will be float if either or both the numbers are float.			
% (Remainder)	Gives the remainder when numerator is divided by denominator	>>>3%2 >>>-3%2 >>>3%-2 >>>-3%-2 >>>10.5%5	1 1 -1 -1 0.5

Note: Remainder can be found for the floating point data also. Remainder works using the given formula:

N%D = N-(N//D * D)

Explanation of the above Examples:

3%2 → 3 - (3//2 * 2) → 3-(1 *2) → 3-2=1

-3%2 → -3 - (-3//2 *2) → -3 - (-2 * 2) → -3+ 4 → 1

3%-2 → 3 - (3//-2 *-2) → 3 - (-2 * -2) → 3- 4 → -1

-3%-2 → -3 - (-3//-2 *-2) → -3 - (1 * -2) → -3+ 2 → -1

10.5%5 → 10.5 - (10.5//5 * 5) → 10.5 - (2.0 *5) → 10.5-10.0 → 0.5

** (Exponentiation)	Results in power of a number (a^b)	>>>3**2 (3^2) >>>2**3**2 (2 ** 3^2) → 2^9	9 512

Note: All operators work from left to right except the exponentiation operator, which is executed from right to left, if occurs in an expression consecutively.

Examples:

15//2//3 → 7//3 → 2

15/2/3 → 7.5/3 → 2.5

15 ** 2** 3 → 15 ** 8 → 15^8 → 2562890625

2. Relational

These operators do the comparison when used with the operands/variables and give the result in True and False. Following are the relational operators:

Operator	Purpose	Example a=10 b=20	Output
>	Returns True if the first operand is greater than the second operand else returns False.	>>>a>b >>>15>a >>>10>a	False True False
>=	Returns True if the first operand is greater than or equal to the second operand else returns False.	>>>a>=6 >>>a>=15 >>>10>=a	True False True
<	Returns True if the first operand is smaller than the second operand else returns False.	>>>a<14 >>>a<b >>>a<10	True True False
<=	Returns True if the first operand is greater than or equal to the second operand else returns False.	>>>a<=14 >>>a<=b >>>a<=10	True True True
!=	Returns True if the two operands are not equal to each other else returns False	>>>a!=10 >>>a!=b	False True
==	Returns True if the two operands are equal else returns False	>>>a==b	False

3. Logical

The operators which generate results by combining multiple conditions are called logical operators. The final result generated is in terms of True or False. Following are the examples of logical operators:-

Operator	Purpose	Example a=10 b=0	Output
and	It combines multiple conditions where the final result will be true all the conditions in an expression are true.	`>>>a>5 and b>=0` `>>>a!=10 and b<1`	True False
or	It combines multiple conditions and generates the final result if either one or all the conditions are true.	`>>>a>5 or b>=0` `>>>a!=10 or b<1`	True True

not	Returns True if the operand is False and Returns False if the operand is True.	`>>>not a`
		`>>>not b`
		`>>>not -10`
		`>>>not 10`
		`>>>not 0`
			False
			True
			False
			False
			True

Note the following:

1. A variable with a non zero value is True and with zero value is False. Hence if a=10, then **not a** is False. Similarly, if b=0 (Which is False), its inverse, i.e. **not b** is True
2. When these Logical operators are used in a single expression without any bracket, then the priority is in the hierarchy not→ and→ or.

   Example:

```
>>> a=5
>>> b=10
>>> c=-23
>>> print(a>4 or b==10 and c>-25)
True

Steps of execution:
b==10 and c>=-25 → T and T → T
a>4 or T → T or T → True

>>> print(a>14 or b==10 and c>-25)
True

Steps of execution:
b==10 and c>=-25 → T and T → T
a>14 or T → F or T → True

>>> print(a>14 or b==10 and c>-20)
False
```

```
Steps of execution:
b==10 and c>=-20 → T and F → F
a>14 or F → F or F → False

>>> print(a>14 or b==10 and not c>-25)
False

Steps of execution:
not c>=-25 → not T → F
b==10 and F → T and F → F
a>14 or F → F or F→ False

>>> print(a>14 or b==10 and not c>-20)
True

Steps of execution:
not c>=-20 → not F → T
b==10 and T → T and T → T
a>14 or T → F or T→ True
```

4. Assignment Operator

This operator assigns the value to the operand.

Operator	Purpose	Example a=10 b=3	Output
=	It assigns the value to the operand.	>>>a=10 >>>print(a)	10

5. Augmented Assignment:

These operators also work with two operands and modifies the first operand by taking values from both the operands. Following are the augmented operators:

Operator	Purpose	Example a=10 b=3	Output
+=	It adds the values of the two operands a and b and restore the result a+b in the first operand a	>>>a+=b print(a)	13
-=	It subtracts the values of the two operands a and b and restore the result a-b in the first operand a	>>>a-=b print(a)	7
*=	It multiplies the values of the two operands a and b and restore the result a*b in the first operand a	>>>a*=b print(a)	30

Operator	Purpose	Example a=10 b=3	Output
/=	It divides the values of the two operands a and b and restore the result a/b in the first operand a	>>>a/=b print(a)	3.3333333333333335
//=	It does the floor division of the values of the two operands a and b and restore the result a//b in the first operand a	>>>a//=b print(a)	3
**=	It finds the power the values of the two operands as a^b and restore the result a^b in the first operand a	>>>a**=b print(a)	1000
%=	It finds the remainder of the values of the two operands a and b and restore the result a%b in the first operand a	>>>a%=b print(a)	1

6. **Membership Operator:**

The following membership operators are used to find substring / value in a given string/object. The result is returned as True if the value is found else False.

Operator	Purpose	Example	Output
in	Returns True if the value/substring is **found** in a given string/value else returns False	>>>a="AEIOU" >>>print("OK" in a) >>>print("O" in a)	False True
not in	Returns True if the value/substring is **not found** in a given string/value else returns False	>>>a="SCHOOL" >>>print("CH" not in a) >>>print("LO" not in a)	False True

7. **Identity Operator:**

This operator returns True if the operands point to the same value else returns False

Operator	Purpose	Example	Output
is	Returns True if the operands/objects point to the same value	>>>a="AEIOU" >>>print("OK" in a) >>>print("O" in a)	False True
not is	Returns True if the value/substring is not found in a given string/value else returns False	>>>a="SCHOOL" >>>print("CH" not in a) >>>print("LO" not in a)	False True

8. **Bitwise operators**

These operators are used for bitwise calculations on integers where the data is converted into binary language and then the operations are performed bit by bit. Following are the different Bitwise operators:

Operator	Name	Example
&	Bitwise AND	x&y
|	Bitwise OR	x|y
~	Bitwise NOT	~x
^	Bitwise XOR	x^y
>>	Bitwise right shift	x>>1
<<	Bitwise left shift	x<<2

Punctuator

They are the ASCII characters which separate the data.

"*, /, &, (,), { , }, \, |,;,:" are the few delimiters used in python.

Variables and Objects

Everything stored in memory is considered as an object in python language. Each object has a unique ID (identity) which remains there for the lifetime of the object till the time it is used in a program. When we store the data in a variable the implicit declaration of the type occurs depending upon the data stored and the variable points to the address which stores the data. The address of the object/data can be accessed using the `ID()` function. Have a look at the example given below:

For example:

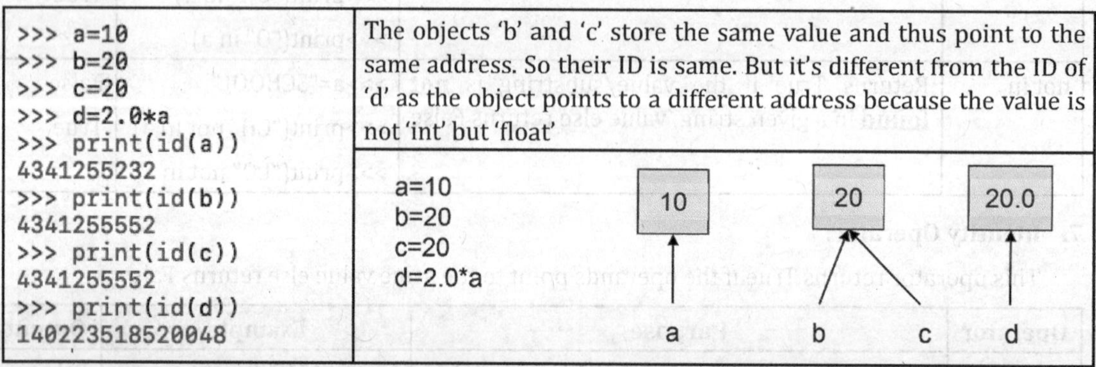

```
>>> a=10
>>> b=20
>>> c=20
>>> d=2.0*a
>>> print(id(a))
4341255232
>>> print(id(b))
4341255552
>>> print(id(c))
4341255552
>>> print(id(d))
140223518520048
```

The objects 'b' and 'c' store the same value and thus point to the same address. So their ID is same. But it's different from the ID of 'd' as the object points to a different address because the value is not 'int' but 'float'

Different ways of assigning values to variables

Way-1

```
#finding Simple interest
P=1000
R=5
T=6
SI=P*R*T/100
print("Simple Interest",SI)
```

Way-2

```
#finding Simple interest
P,R,T=1000,5,6
SI=P*R*T/100
print("Simple Interest",SI)
```

Way=3

```
#finding Simple interest
P=1000;R=5;T=6
SI=P*R*T/100
print("Simple Interest",SI)
```

Way-4

```
#finding Simple interest
(P,R,T)=(1000,5,6)
SI=P*R*T/100
print("Simple Interest",SI)
```

Interesting thing to know:

When we perform operation on variables in a single statement, then it is important to remember that the operations are performed on the original values and not the modified values as shown below:

```
a,b=10,20

c=40

a,b=c,a

#This means that the variable 'b' will take old value of 'a' which is #10 and not 40
print("a=",a,"b=",b,"c=",c)
```

Output

```
a= 40 b= 10 c= 40
```

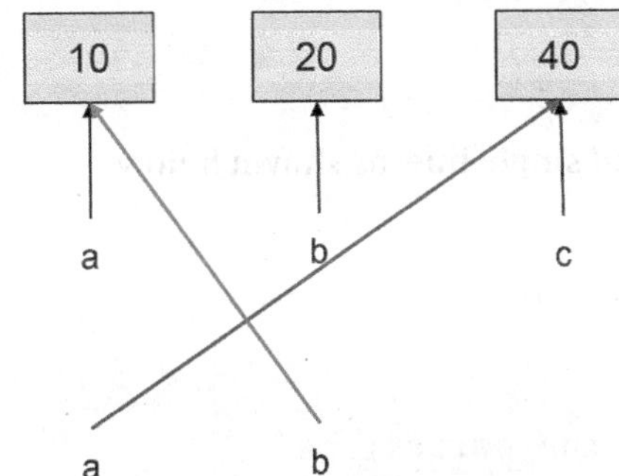

The above diagram indicates that the objects/variables point to the address which stores the value. When the calculations happen, the variable points to the address of the new value. Hence the result.

Concept of l-value and r-value

In a programming language, when we use the assignment operator to assign the data to a variable, the value on the left side of the assignment operator is called l-value, while the value on the right side of the assignment operator is called the r-value.

The l-value is an assignable object which can be modified as it has an identifiable memory location. R-value is the one which is fetched and stored in the l-value. Look at the examples given below:

Example: 1

```
>>>Num-43
```

Here the l-value is Num which fetches the r-value 43 and stores.

Example: 2

```
>>> Data1=10
>>> Data2=Data1
>>> print(Data2)
10
>>> Data1=30
>>> print(Data2)
10
>>> print(Data1)
30
```

In the first command the l-value is Data1 which stores a constant r-value 10.

But in the second command, the l-value Data2, fetches the value stored in Data1 (which is an r-value) and changes in Data1 later doesn't affect the Data2.

Comments in Python

It is always a good practice to keep on providing the details of the task performed by your program at various intervals. This not only helps you to recall the program but also to modify or update your program whenever needed without going through the whole code. Since the details are not to be part of the executable program but for programmer's reference, they are provided as comment. Thus, comment is a text which is a part of our program but doesn't get executed. There are two ways to write a comment in python:

1. Single line Comment : It is provided using #. The text after '#' is taken as a comment and is not executed. But it works for a single line, hence the name.

Example

```
>>> per=(89+78+97)/3 #finding the percentage
>>> print(per)
88.0
>>>
```

Single line comment won't work beyond single line as shown below

```
>>> per=(89+78+97)/3 #finding the percentage
>>> of the three numbers
SyntaxError: invalid syntax
```

Correct Way

```
>>> per=(89+78+97)/3 #finding the percentage
>>> #of the three numbers
```

2. Multiline comment: When you need to provide comment which exceed single line, then instead of using # before every comment line, you can enclose the comment either in :

   a. """ Comment…. """ → Three starting and ending double quotes

   b. ''' Comment…. ''' → Three starting and ending single quotes

Example:

```
"""
Name       : ABC
RollNo     : 10
Program No: 1
"""

print("My First Program")
print("Great Work")
```

```
'''
Name       : ABC
RollNo     : 10
Program No: 1
'''

print("My First Program")
print("Great Work")
```

Summary

1. Python is a general purpose high level programming language which was implemented in the year 1989 by Dutch programmer Guido Van Rossum. It can be downloaded from the website www.python.org.
2. Two modes to execute a python program are interactive and script.

3. The smallest unit in a programming language used in building a program is called Token. This includes keyword, identifier, literal, operator, punctuator.
4. Keywords are predefined words which have some meaning in the programming language.
5. The data which we use in a program is called a literal. Data can be numeric, alphanumeric, complex no or any other value required for a program.
6. Identifier is the name given to a variable/object which stores the value.
7. Different types of operators which can be used in python program are Arithmetic, Relational, Logical, Assignment, Membership, Identity and Bitwise.
8. Arithmetic operators perform arithmetic operations. Examples are `+,-,*,/,//,%,**`
9. Relational operators do the comparison when used with the operands/variables and give the result in True and False. Examples are `>,>=,<,<=,!=,==`
10. The operators which generate results by combining multiple conditions are called logical operators. Examples are `and, or, not`.
11. Assignment operator assigns the value to the operand. Example =
12. Augmented assignment is the combination, in a single statement, of a binary operation and an assignment statement. Examples are `+=,-=,*=,/=,//=,**=,%=`
13. Examples of membership operators are `in` and `not in`. It is used to find substring / value in a given string/object.
14. Identity operator returns True if the operands point to the same value else returns False. Examples are `is` and `not is`.
15. Bitwise operators are used for bitwise calculations on integers where the data is converted into binary language and then the operations are performed bit by bit.
16. When we use the assignment operator to assign the data to a variable, the value on the left side of the assignment operator is called l-value, while the value on the right side of the assignment operator is called the r-value.
17. Comment is a text which is ignored by the compiler during the execution of the program. Two types of comments are single line comment (#) and multiline comment (“””)

? EXERCISE

Multiple Choice Questions

1. Which of the following is a valid identifier:

   a. True b. 12ABC c. _False d. one&two

2. Which of the following is a relational operator:

   a. > b. ** c. in d. is

3. Choose the correct logical operator/s:

   a. + b. /= c. and d. in

4. Identify the membership operator from the following:

a. in b. not in c. both a and b d. None of the above

5. Choose the correct arithmetic operator/s

a. is b. += c. % d. in

6. What will be the correct output of the statement ?

>>>7//2.0

a. 3 b. 3.0 c. 3.5 d. .35

7. Choose correct output of the given statement :

>>> 4+2**2*10

a. 18 b. 80 c. 44 d. None of the above

8. Give the output of the following code:

>>>X,Y,Z=7,3,4

>>>X-Y**2+Z

a. 3 b. 2 c. 2.0 d. 3.0

9. Give the output of the following code:

>>> a,b = 7,3.5

>>> (a-b)//2**2

a. 7.0 b. 7 c. 0 d. 0.0

10. Give the output of the following code:

>>>a,b,c=1,2,3

>>> a//b**c+a-c*a

a. -2 b. -2.0 c. 2.0 d. None of the above

11. If a=1, b=2 and c=3 then which statement will give the output as : 2.0 from the following:

a. >>>a%b%c+1 b. >>>a%b%c+1.0

c. >>>a%b%c d. >>>a%b%c-1

12. Which statement will give the output as : True from the following :

a. >>>not -5 b. >>>not 5 c. >>>not 0 d. >>>not(5-1)

13. Give the output of the following code:

>>>2**3**2

a. 512 b. 64 c. 128 d. 27

14. Give the output of the following code:

>>>(2**3)**2

a. 512 b. 64 c. 128 d. 27

15. Choose the correct keyword from the given options:

a. Global b. Data c. continue d. never

16. True and False are which type of literals:

a. Arithmetic b. String c. Numeric d. Boolean

17. The two identity operators are:

a. in,not in b. is, not is c. and, or d. True, False

18. Identify the incorrect way of declaring variables:

a. a=10;b=20;c=30
b. a=10,b=20,c=30
c. a,b,c=10,20,30
d. None of the above

19. The symbol for giving a single line comment in Python is:

a. % b. $ c. & d. #

20. >> operator is also called as:

a. Bitwise left shift
b. Bitwise right shift
c. Bitwise AND
d. Bitwise OR

Subjective Questions

1. What are Tokens?
2. Name at least 2 tokens.
3. Differentiate between the following:
   a. Arithmetic and relational operators
   b. / and // operator
   c. Keyword and identifier
   d. and or logical operators
   e. Membership and identity operators
4. Write single line Python statements for the following
   a. Declare two variables 'X' and 'Y' with same value 0
   b. Given a=89;b=98, display the remainder when a is divided by b
   c. Print the identity of the above python object 'a'
   d. Check whether 'a' is greater than 'b' or not and display the result.
   e. Display the average of the three variables N, M and W
   f. Declare a string literal with the value 'Calculate'
   g. Declare an integer literal with the vale 99
5. Write rules to name a variable in python.
6. What are comments? How are single line and multi-line comments inserted in a program?
7. What is the extension of a python file?

6 Data Types

Data Types

When we store data in a variable, the implicit type is assigned to the variable and the value stored decides the data type of the object. Python provides the following types of data to be stored in python objects:

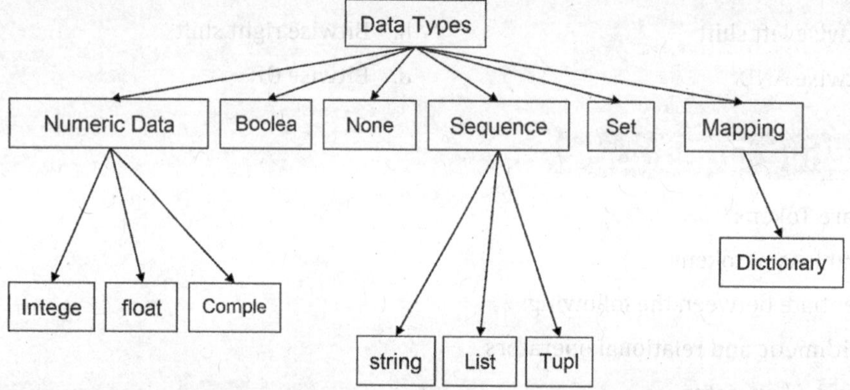

1. Numeric Data Type : It stores number data. It can further be categorized as
   a. integer- which store integer values, i.e values without decimal.
   b. float - which allows values with decimal.
   c. complex - which allows to store complex value having real and imaginary part

All the above numeric data types are immutable, which means as soon as the value is changed/ modified, the ID of the object changes.

Examples

Data type/ Class	Example	Description

integer	>>> X=12
	>>> print(type(X))
	<class 'int'>
	>>> Y=-12
	>>> print(type(Y))
	<class 'int'>
		All integer values (positive or negative) come under class integer, like 12, 45, -90, 78 etc.

float	>>> Z=12.90
	>>> print(type(Z))
	<class 'float'>
		All decimal value data comes under float class 12.0,-9.89,56.8 etc

complex	>>> W=12j
	>>> print(type(W))
	<class 'complex'>
	>>> R=12+6.5j
	>>> print(type(R))
	<class 'complex'>
		Examples of complex data are in the format a+bj (where a and b are real and imaginary part respectively)

Example showing that the numeric data types are immutable. As soon as the values are modified, the ID of the objects change.

```
>>> X,Y,Z=12,12.5,12+3j
>>> print(id(X),id(Y),id(Z))
4431469696 140643410285616 140643398298512
>>> X+=10
>>> Y+=X
>>> Z+=10
>>> print(X,Y,Z)
22 34.5 (22+3j)
>>> print(id(X),id(Y),id(Z))
4431470016 140643400637168 140643398298576
```

***Note:** The type() function tells you the data type of the value and shows the class to which it belongs as shown in the above examples.*

2. Boolean: It stores only two values 'True' and 'False'.

Data type/ Class	Example	Description

Bool	`>>> Status=True`
	`>>> print(type(Status))`
	`<class 'bool'>`
	`>>> ReStatus=False`
	`>>> print(type(ReStatus))`
	`<class 'bool'>`
		Note that the two boolean values `True` and `False` have the first letter capital.

3. None : 'None' is similar to Null value in other programming languages. It is not similar to 0 or False. It is an instance of None class.

Data type/ Class	Example	Description

None	`>>> Chk=None`
	`>>> print(type(Chk))`
	`<class 'NoneType'>`
		Note that None is a keyword and belongs to class NoneType

	`>>> Data=None`
	`>>> print(id(Chk))`
	`4384022616`
	`>>> print(id(Data))`
	`4384022616`
		None value is not equal to any value. A variable assigned None in Python points to an instance of 'NoneType' class and since there is only one instance of the NoneType class, therefore all the variables with value None point to the same object.

	`>>> Data==Chk`
	`True`
	`>>> print(not Data)`
	`True`
		Note that None is taken as False. Hence not None is True.

4. **Sequence:** Python language allows the storage of multiple values under a single object in an ordered manner. This means the order in which the data is stored, in the same order it can be accessed too. Few types of sequence data types are string, list and tuple.

a. **String :** It is a collection of alphanumeric characters stored in quotes.

Example:

```
>>> Name="Python Language"
>>> print(Name)
Python Language
>>> print(type(Name))
<class 'str'>
```

The characters in the string are stored in consecutive memory locations, where each character is called an element and each element can be accessed using the subscript number, as shown in the diagram. The subscript is enclosed in a square bracket. The subscript is also called as **key or index**

P	y	t	h	o	n		L	a	n	g	u	a	g	e
0	1	2	3	4	5	6	7	8	9	10	11	12	13	14

```
>>> Name="Python Language"
>>> print(Name[0],Name[3])
P h
```

Once the value is stored, the sequence of the characters remains in an ordered manner. It is an immutable data type, where the changes are **not allowed.**

```
>>> Name[0]="p"
Traceback (most recent call last):
  File "<pyshell#2>", line 1, in <module>
    Name[0]="p"
TypeError: 'str' object does not support item assignment
```

b. **List :** It is a heterogeneous collection of data. Heterogeneous means any data of any type can be an element of a list. The data is stored within a square bracket. It can store duplicate values also. It is also called as a mutable data type, which means changes in the object in terms of addition, updating Some of the examples of list are given below:

```
>>> List1=[10,12,56,90]
>>> List2=["one","two","three","four"]
>>> List3=[56,"Anu","F",89.5,True]
>>> print(type(List1),type(List2),type(List3))
<class 'list'> <class 'list'> <class 'list'>
>>> List4=[12,56,12,34,56]
>>> print(id(List1),id(List2),id(List2),id(List4))
140312698554160 140312698624432 140312698624432 140312698623872
```

List1

10	12	56	90
0	1	2	3

List2

"one"	"two"	"three"	"four"
0	1	2	3

List3

56	"Anu"	"F"	89.5	True
0	1	2	3	3

The element of a list can be extracted using the subscript/key/index (similar to strings). Lists are mutable, which means the changes can be made in a list. The following code will help you understand it:

```
>>> List3=[56,"Anu","F",89.5,True]
>>> print(List3[0],List3[4])
56 True
>>> print(id(List3))
140643397179264
>>> List3[0]=10
>>> print(List3)
[10, 'Anu', 'F', 89.5, True]
>>> print(id(List3))
140643397179264
```

→ The first element changed to 10.

→ Since it is a mutable object, its ID is not changed even after changing the element.

Note : To create a blank List , we write `L=[]`, where `L` is the name of a List.

c. **Tuple :** The third type of sequence data type is Tuple. It is also a heterogeneous collection of data where the elements are stored in a round bracket.

```
>>> Tup1=(1,3,5,2)
>>> Tup2=("Ravi","Ankit","Rajiv","Neha")
>>> Tup3=(1,"XI","Aniket",16)
>>> print(id(Tup1))
140643401394128
>>> print(Tup1)
(1, 3, 5, 2)
```

Tup1

1	3	5	2
0	1	2	3

You can access any element of a tuple by using the subscript/key/index

```
>>> print(Tup1[2])#will print third element
5
```

Tuple is an immutable data type where the changes are not allowed. That is, a new tuple can be created but an existing tuple cannot be modified.

Note:

- To create a blank tuple , we write T=(), where T is the name of a tuple.
- But it is important to know that a tuple with one element is created in the following manner:

  T=(10,) and not T=(10). This is because T=(10) will create an object of type integer

```
>>> T=(10)
>>> print(type(T))
<class 'int'>
>>> T=(10,)
>>> print(type(T))
<class 'tuple'>
```

5. **Set:** It is an unordered collection of data, where no duplicate value is allowed. The elements in a set are enclosed in a curly bracket. The data in a set is not sequenced, which means the order in which the data is stored is not the same when extracted.

```
>>> SET={1,45,23,78}
>>> print(SET)
{1, 45, 78, 23}

>>> SET={3,2,2,1,7}
>>> print(SET)
{1, 2, 3, 7}
```

Set is also a mutable data type but it is interesting to note that only those values can be added to a set which are immutable like integer, float, boolean, complex, string and tuple. Also, the new element can be added or the existing elements can be removed, but the elements cannot be modified. Also, since the sets are unordered, so they are not subscriptable, which means you cannot extract the elements location-wise.

```
>>> s
{(4, 5), 1, 'aa', 1.1}
>>> s[0]
Traceback (most recent call last):
  File "<pyshell#34>", line 1, in <module>
    s[0]
TypeError: 'set' object is not subscriptable
>>> s[0]+=1
Traceback (most recent call last):
  File "<pyshell#35>", line 1, in <module>
    s[0]+=1
TypeError: 'set' object is not subscriptable
```

6. **Mapping:** It is a data type where a key is mapped with an object. This means that the key is not default like in the case of list, tuple, string but is provided while declaring a mapping data type. Example of mapping data type is dictionary.

A dictionary maps keys to values. Keys are immutable objects, while values can be of any data type. Dictionaries are mutable objects. The values in dictionary are enclosed within curly bracket as key:value pair in the following manner:

```
>>> D={1:"one",2:"two",3:"three"} # 3 elements
```

In the above example, a dictionary object D is created with three elements with keys `1,2,3` and their respective values as "one", "two" and "three" respectively.

"one"	"two"	"three"
0	1	2

Few more examples:

```
>>> Mks={"Ruhana":[89,78,90],"Hitesh":[90,67,86],"Bharat":[67,56,67]}
```

"Ruhana"	"Hitesh"	"Bharat"
[89,78,90]	[90,67,86]	[67,56,67]

```
>>> Data={89:"pen",45:"Pencil",6.7:True}
```

"pen"	"Pencil"	True
89	45	6.7

To extract the values, we need to provide the key in the following manner:

```
>>> print(Mks["Ruhana"])
[89, 78, 90]
>>> print(Mks["Bharat"])
[67, 56, 67]
```

Note : Keys in a dictionary are immutable objects, while values can be of any data type. This means the key can be either integer, float, tuple, complex, string **but not list or dictionary.** Key cannot be duplicate also.

```
>>> Num={(1,3):(23,56),12:"string"} #accepted

>>> Num={[1,3]:(23,56),12:"string"} #not allowed

Traceback (most recent call last):
  File "<pyshell#57>", line 1, in <module>
    Num={[1,3]:(23,56),12:"string"} #not allowed
TypeError: unhashable type: 'list'
```

Interesting to know:

If you try to create a dictionary object with the same key, then instead of showing error, the last value of the same key is accepted as shown in the example below:

```
>>> Num={10:"s1",12:"s2",10:89,34:78,12:"created"} #Key cannot have duplicate values
>>> print(Num)
{10: 89, 12: 'created', 34: 78}
```

Mutable and Immutable data types

The data types are broadly categorized into type types, mutable and immutable. A mutable object is an object whose value can change once created. An Immutable object is an object whose value can't change once created. Mutable objects store a collection of data. Example: List, set and dictionary. Examples of immutable objects are int, float, bool, str, tuple.

We can use the `id()` function to check the mutability of an object. `id()` returns the identity of an object as an integer. This integer usually corresponds to the object's location in memory. After any modification in an object, if the ID of that object remains same, then it indicates that the object is mutable.

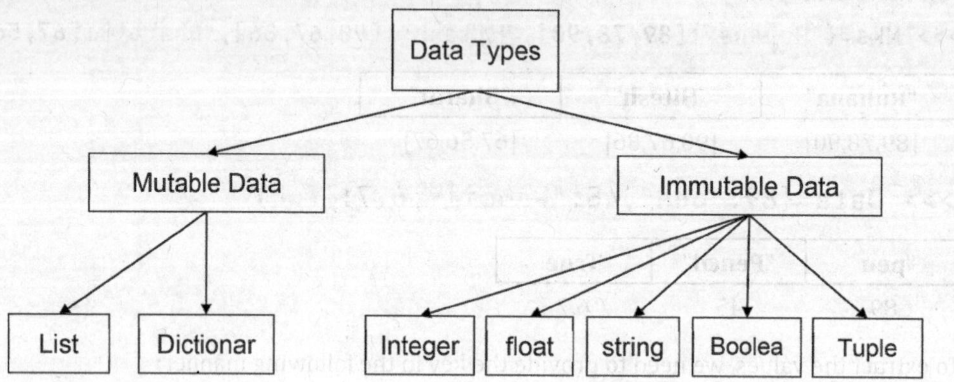

Let us see few examples to understand mutable and immutable objects

Example-1

```
>>> X=10
>>> Y=X
>>> print(id(X),id(Y))
4431469632 4431469632
>>> id(X)==id(Y)
True
```

We will make some changes in the above object X and see the result

```
>>> X+=10
>>> print(X,Y)
20 10
>>> print(id(X),id(Y))
4431469952 4431469632
>>> id(X)==id(Y)
False
```

→ The ID changes after making change in X

Example-2

```
>>> L=[45,12,8,3,45]
>>> print(id(L))
140643411106624
```

Making changes in 1st element

```
>>> L[0]+=10
>>> print(L)
[55, 12, 8, 3, 45]
>>> print(id(L))
140643411106624
```

→ ID remains same, which shows its mutability.

Expressions

An expression is a combination of values which include variables, literals, operators which evaluate to a single result. Following are the few examples of expression:

```
>>>10-5+15              #Evaluate to 20
>>>X**2**4//2           #X is a variable with some value
>>>X+Y-7                #X and Y are variables
>>>12+7j + 34           #Evaluate to (46+7j)
>>>"One" + "Two"        #Evaluate to 'OneTwo'
>>>(7-2)*13//5**2       #Evaluate to 2
```

Operator Precedence

While solving an expression, some operators are given priority over others when the brackets are not there. We need to remember the precedence to solve an expression. Follow the given rules of operator precedence:

()	Brackets, list display, dictionary display, set display
**	Exponentiation
+x, -x, ~x	Positive, negative, bitwise NOT
*, /, //, %	Multiplication, Division, Floor Division, Remainder (All same, evaluated which comes from left to right)
+, -	Addition, Subtraction ((All same, evaluated which comes from left to right)
<<, >>	Bitwise Shifts
&	Bitwise And
^	Bitwise XOR
|	Bitwise OR
in, not in, is, is not, <, <=, >, >=, !=, ==	Comparison Operator including membership and identity tests
not	Boolean NOT
and	Boolean AND
or	Boolean OR
if else	Conditional Statement
lambda	Lambda Expression

Note:

1. **Operators in the same box have the same precedence.**
2. **Operators in the same box group and evaluated from left to right (except for exponentiation, which groups and evaluates from right to left)**
3. **Comparisons, membership tests, and identity tests, all have the same precedence whichever comes from left-to-right**

Examples: Evaluate the following expression

a. **12%3**2+6*7**

Steps:

(12%**3**2**+6*7) → 12%9+6*7

(12%9+6*7) → 3+6*7

(**3+**6*7) → 3+42

45

b. 4*2**2**3 #1024

Steps:

(4*2****2**3**) → 4*2**8

(4***2**8**) → 4*256

1024

c. 56//12/3 #1.3333333333333333

Steps:

(**56//12**/3) → 4/3

1.3333333333333333

d. 2 + 3 * 4

Steps:

(2 + **3 * 4**) → 2+12

14

e. (2 + 3) * 4

Steps

(**2 + 3**) * 4 → 5*4

20

f. 56>45 and not 7!=8 or 4<2

Steps:

(56>45 and **not 7!=8** or 4<2) → 56>45 and **False** or 4<2

(**56>45** and False or 4<2) → **True** and False or 4<2

(**True and False** or 4<2) → **False** or 4<2

(False or **4<2**) → False or **False**

False

g. "S" in "SUBJECTS" and 7<7 or 10 in [78,34,10] #True

Steps:

"S" in "SUBJECTS" and 7<7 or 10 in [78,34,10]

True and 7<7 or 10 in [78,34,10]

True and True or 10 in [78,34,10]

True or **10 in [78,34,10]**

True or **True**

True

input() function

When we work on a program, data is required which we provide using variables. We can assign the values to variables to provide the data. But to make our program more flexible and interactive, we also need to take the data from the user during the execution of the program. The function which is used to accept the data into a python object while the program is running is the `input()` function. By default, the data accepted using this function is in the form of a string.

Using Interactive Mode | Using Script Mode | Output

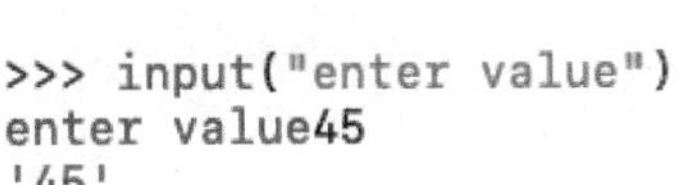

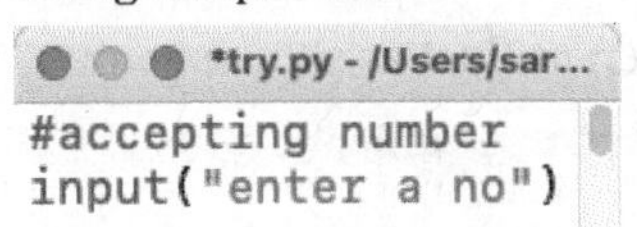

In the above example, it is clear that function accepts the value at the runtime, but the value accepted is not stored anywhere to be used later in the program. So we use an object to accept the value, in the following manner:

Syntax :

```
<Object Name>=input("Message which is optional")
```

Example:

```
>>> Num=input("Enter a number")
Enter a number56
>>> type(Num)
<class 'str'>
```

Note: The value accepted using the `input ()` function is by default a string.

To accept the values in other data types, we use the following functions:

1. int() : For accepting the integer value at the run time, we can use this function in the following manner:

```
>>> Num=int(input("Enter a number"))
Enter a number12
>>> type(Num)
<class 'int'>
```

Note: Error will occur if we try to enter a value if we try to put a float value or an alphabet

```
>>> Num=int(input("Enter a number"))
Enter a number34.5
Traceback (most recent call last):
  File "<pyshell#7>", line 1, in <module>
    Num=int(input("Enter a number"))
ValueError: invalid literal for int() with base 10: '34.5'
```

```
>>> Num=int(input("Enter a number"))
Enter a numberA
Traceback (most recent call last):
  File "<pyshell#8>", line 1, in <module>
    Num=int(input("Enter a number"))
ValueError: invalid literal for int() with base 10: 'A'
```

2. float() : For accepting the floating point value at the run time, we can use this function in the following manner:

```
>>> Num=float(input("Enter a number"))
Enter a number56.3
>>> type(Num)
<class 'float'>
```

Integer value entered is also taken as float as shown below:

```
>>> Num=float(input("Enter a number"))
Enter a number12
>>> type(Num)
<class 'float'>
>>> print(Num)
12.0
```

Note : Error will occur if we try to enter a value if we try to put an alphabet value.

```
>>> Num=float(input("Enter a number"))
Enter a numberA
Traceback (most recent call last):
  File "<pyshell#12>", line 1, in <module>
    Num=float(input("Enter a number"))
ValueError: could not convert string to float: 'A'
```

We will do some more functions later.

print() function

To display the output of the program, print() function is used.

```
Name=input("Enter you Name:")
print(Name)
```

Output:

```
Enter you Name:Python
Python
```

To display multiple values using the same print () function, we separate it with comma ','

```
Name=input("Enter you Name:")
print("Hello",Name)
```

There are two important parameters of the print() function, which are explained below:

a. sep   b. end

The sep parameter is called as a separator. It is used to separate multiple values when used with a single print(). By default the multiple values are separated by a single column space. The sep parameter only takes a string value. The given examples will make the function sep more clear:

```
>>> print("one","two","three")
one two three
```

The three values "one","two","three" are separated by a single space.

```
>>> A,B=12,14
>>> print("Numbers are : ",A,B,"and the sum is :",A+B)
Numbers are :  12 14 and the sum is : 26
```

By default the values are separated by a single column space. But to separate the values with another string, we specify it explicitly with the parameter as shown below:

```
>>> print("one","two","three",sep='#')
one#two#three
>>> print("one","two","three",sep=' and ')
one and two and three
>>> print("one","two","three", sep='123')
one123two123three
>>> print("Great Work",sep='@')
Great Work
```

→ In this last print statement, sep value '@' is not displayed as the separator value is displayed between the multiple values used with a single print function, which is not happening in this case.

Few more examples:

```
>>> A,B=23,67
>>> print("sum ",A+B,"Product",A*B,"Difference",A-B,sep=" # ")
sum  # 90 # Product # 1541 # Difference # -44

>>> print("one","two","three","fishes",sep=' LITTLE ')
one LITTLE two LITTLE three LITTLE fishes
```

The end parameter is used to specify how the print function should terminate. By default every `print()` terminates with a line break also written as `'\n'`.

Example1: Without using end parameter.

```
A,B=56,12
print(A,B,sep='+')
print(A+B)
```

Output

```
56+12
68
```

Example2: With using end parameter.

```
A,B=56,12
print(A,B,sep='+',end="=")
print(A+B,end=" is the sum")
```

Output

```
56+12=68 is the sum
...
```

Example3:

```
print("one","two","three",sep=" BIG ",end=" Monkeys ")
print("four","five","six",sep=" LITTLE ", end=" Donkeys ")
print("Clap","Clap",sep=" CLAP ")
print("We got them in a", "Trap", sep=" TRAP ")
```

Output

```
one BIG two BIG three Monkeys four LITTLE five LITTLE six Donkeys Clap CLAP Clap
We got them in a TRAP Trap
>>>
```

Example4: Here '\n' used with a string will give a line break.

```
print("one","two","three",sep=" BIG ",end=" Monkeys\n")
print("four","five","six",sep=" LITTLE ", end=" Donkeys\n")
print("Clap","Clap",sep=" CLAP ")
print("We got them in a", "Trap", sep=" TRAP ")
```

Output

```
one BIG two BIG three Monkeys
four LITTLE five LITTLE six Donkeys
Clap CLAP Clap
We got them in a TRAP Trap
...
```

Type conversion

When we write a statement or an expression, it is evaluated as per certain programming norms/ rules. The final result gets converted either automatically using certain commands/functions. The expression in python is evaluated using :

a. Explicit conversion

b. implicit conversion

Consider the example given below:

```
A=input("Enter a number")
print("The sum is : ",A+A)
print("The product is : ",A*5)
```

And the output:

```
Enter a number12
The sum is :  1212
The product is :  1212121212
```

Since the requirement of the program was to accept a number and to find the sum, we didn't get the correct result as the data is accepted as a string by default. So 'concatenation' happened using addition, which means the same string 'A' is added one after the other. Similarly, 'repetition' happened using multiplication, so the string was repeated 5 times and hence the above result. To get the desired output, we need to explicitly convert the data. This is called **Explicit Conversion.** Following functions are used to explicitly convert data into specific data type:

Function	Purpose	Example	Output
int()	This function converts a string or float number into an integer. Note that the string must be a numbers from 0-9	a,c="12",3.9 b=int(a) print(2*b) print(int(c)) x="89.7" print(int(x))	24 3 #Error
float()	This function converts a string or integer number into float. Note that the string must be a numbers from 0-9	a,c="78.5",99 print(float(a)+5) print(float(c))	83.5 99.0
chr()	It takes integer as a parameter and converts it to character, where the integer value is the ascii code of the character returned. Note that the ascii code for 'A' is 65, '0' is 48, 'a' is 97	a,b=65,48 print(chr(a)) print(chr(b))	A 0
ord()	It converts and displays the ascii code of the character which is passed as parameter.	a,b='A','g' print(ord(a)) print(ord(b))	65 103
str()	It converts anything passed as a parameter to string.	print(str(34)) print(str(34.7)) print(str(2+8j)) L=[3,4,5] print(str(L))	34 34.7 (2+8j) [3, 4, 5] (Note: all the above are string values)
list()	It is used to convert an iterable to a list	S="data" L=list(S) print(L) T=(12,45,78) print(list(T)) D={"301":"Eng", "083":"CS"} print(list(D))	['d', 'a', 't', 'a'] [12, 45, 78] ['301','083']

Function	Purpose	Example	Output
tuple()	It is used to convert an iterable to a tuple	S="data" T=list(S) print(T) L=[12,45,78] print(list(T)) D={"301":"Eng", "083":"CS"} print(tuple(D))	('d', 'a', 't', 'a') (12,45,78) ('301','083')
dict()	It is used to convert a list or tuple of pair of values into a dictionary.	a=((1,2),(2,3)) >>>dict(a) b=[(1,2),(2,3)] >>>dict(b) c=[[1,2],[2,3]] >>>dict(c)	{1: 2, 2: 3} {1: 2, 2: 3} {1: 2, 2: 3}
complex()	It converts the two parameters passed as real and imaginary values to complex no. Note that the first arguments can be a string(with number value) or a number. But it cannot take the second argument as a string.	a=12 >>> complex(a) b=6 >>>complex(a,b) a="68" >>>complex(a,a) a="68" >>>complex(a)	(12+0j) (12+6j) #Error (68+0j)
hex()	It converts an integer value to hexadecimal string	a=hex(23) print(a) print(type(a))	'0x17' <class 'str'>
oct()	It converts an integer value to Octal string	a=oct(99) print(a)	'0o143'
bin()	It converts an integer value to binary string	a=89 print(bin(a))	'0b1011001'

Implicit Conversion is done by the interpreter when data of different types are involved in calculation. We will see the following examples to understand it:

```
A=12
B=90.3
C=A+B
print(C, type(C))    →    102.3 <class 'float'>
```

When any arithmetic operation occurs between integer value and float value, the result is converted into float, as shown in the above example:

```
A=4
B="String"
C=A*B
print(C, type(C))    →    StringStringStringString <class 'str'>
```

The only arithmetic operator which can be used with a string data is asterisk (*), which is used to repeat the given string some specific number of times.

Errors

When we write a program, there is a possibility when either the program doesn't run successfully or runs but doesn't generate correct output. This means that there is/are errors in the program. To make the program run successfully, one needs to identify the type of errors. There are three types of errors which can occur in a program:

- Syntax errors
- Logical errors
- Runtime errors

Syntax Error

The error which occurs due to wrong syntax of the code is called as Syntax error

Some of the examples of syntax errors are:

- inappropriate use of operators

```
>>> a=12
>>> a=*89
SyntaxError: can't use starred expression here
```

#Wrong use of augmented assignment operator in the above example.

- wrong indentation

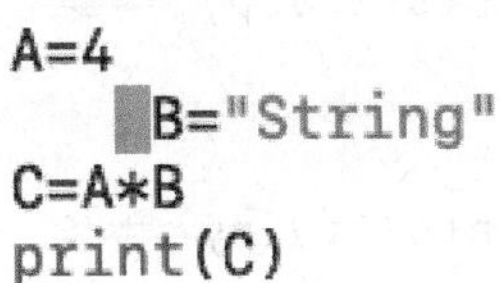

→

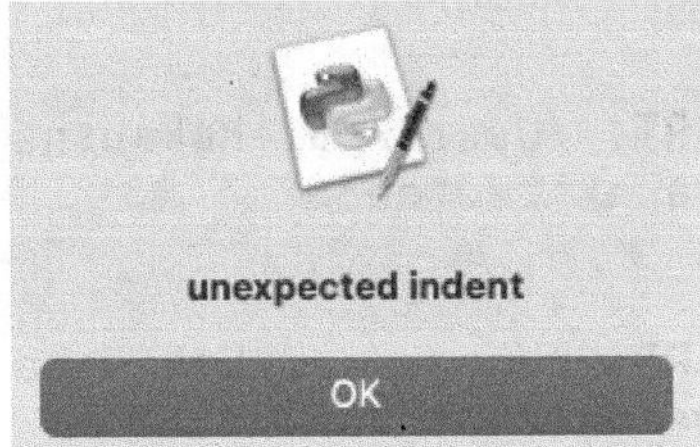

- Missing brackets, quotes

```
>>> print"hello"
SyntaxError: invalid syntax
```

#brackets missing with print()

Logical Error

The error which occurs by giving the wrong output/result is called a Logical Error. Since the program executes but generates an incorrect result and due to this, these errors are difficult to find. Logical errors are also called as Semantic errors. A good example to illustrate it is to find the average of three numbers 13,15,45.

```
>>> print("Average is : ",13+15+45/3)
Average is :  43.0
```

Incorrect average is calculated due to missing bracket. The program executes but gives the wrong result. The correct code would be:

```
>>> print("Average is : ",(13+15+45)/3)
Average is :  24.333333333333332
```

Runtime error

The error which occurs due to inappropriate values taken at the runtime of the program is called runtime error. The interpreter will stop the execution if it comes across a runtime error. Few examples are given below:

Example 1: Division by zero

```
A=int(input("Enter Numerator"))
B=int(input("Enter Denominator"))
print("Division :",A/B)

Enter Numerator12
Enter Denominator0
Traceback (most recent call last):
  File "/Users/sarikakaushal/Documents/try.py", line 3, in <module>
    print("Division :",A/B)
ZeroDivisionError: division by zero
```

Example 2: Extractive the element from an iterable which doesn't exist.

```
L=[5,6,7,8]
A=int(input("Enter the element to be extracted"))
print(L[A])

================ RESTART: /Users/sarikakaushal/Documents/try.py ====
Enter the element to be extracted3
8
>>>
================ RESTART: /Users/sarikakaushal/Documents/try.py ====
Enter the element to be extracted6
Traceback (most recent call last):
  File "/Users/sarikakaushal/Documents/try.py", line 3, in <module>
    print(L[A])
IndexError: list index out of range
```

Summary

1. Numeric Data Type stores number data.
2. Boolean data type stores only two values 'True' and 'False'.
3. Python language allows the storage of multiple values under a single object in an ordered manner called a sequence. Examples are strings, lists, tuples.
4. String is a collection of alphanumeric characters stored in quotes.
5. List is a heterogeneous collection of data which can store data of any type. The data is stored within a square bracket. Eg `L=["XI",32,"CS"]`
6. Tuple is also a heterogeneous collection of data where the elements are stored in a round bracket.
7. Set is an unordered collection of data, where no duplicate value is allowed. The elements in a set are enclosed in a curly bracket.
8. A dictionary object is a mapping data type where the data is inserted in the form of items. Each item is a key value pair. The values in the dictionary are enclosed within the curly bracket.
9. A mutable object is an object whose value can change once created. An Immutable object is an object whose value can't change once created. Mutable objects store a collection of data. Example: List, set and dictionary.
10. Immutable objects are the one which doesn't allow the data to change once stored. Examples are String, Tuples.
11. The following operator precedence is followed to solve an expression brackets→**(Exponentiation) → Bitwise Operators → *,/,//,% → +,- → Bitwise operators → comparison operators → Logical operators → if else
12. The function which is used to accept the data into a python object while the program is running is the `input()` function. By default, the data accepted using this function is in the form of a string.
13. `int()` is used to convert the data into integer.
14. `float()` is used to convert the data into floating point value.
15. `print()` is used to display the output of the program.
16. `sep` parameter of the `print()` is used to separate multiple values when used with a single `print()`. The default value of the sep function is a single column space. The sep function takes string value
17. `end` parameter is used to specify how the print function should terminate. By default every `print()` terminates with a line break also written as `'\n'`. The end parameter takes string value.
18. `chr()` takes integer as a parameter and converts it to character, where the integer value is the ascii code of the character returned.
19. `str()` converts anything passed as a parameter to string.
20. There are three types of errors which can occur in a program, namely, Syntax errors, Logical errors and Runtime errors.
21. The error which occurs due to wrong syntax of the code is called as Syntax error.
22. The error which occurs by giving the wrong output/result is called a Logical Error.
23. The error which occurs due to inappropriate values taken at the runtime of the program is called runtime error.

? EXERCISE

Multiple Choice Questions

1. Choose the correct type of error in the codes given below:

a. `>>>print 10+20`

1. Syntax 2. Logical 3. Runtime 4. No Error

b.
```
>>>a,b=12,13
>>>print("Sum is",a-b)
```
1. Syntax 2. Logical 3. Runtime 4. No Error

c.
```
>>>X,Y=12,0
>>>print(X//Y)
```
1. Syntax 2. Logical 3. Runtime 4. No Error

d
```
>>>X=12
>>>print(sep="*", "The correct value is",X)
```
1. Syntax 2. Logical 3. Runtime 4. No Error

e `>>> print(ord("X"))`

1. Syntax 2. Logical 3. Runtime 4. No Error

f
```
>>> Num=23
>>> Num*=10
>>> print("Number is :",num)
```
1. Syntax 2. Logical 3. Runtime 4. No Error

(The above program will generate runtime NameError)

g
```
>>>S=input("Enter a no")
>>> print(34+S)
```
1. Syntax 2. Logical 3. Runtime 4. No Error

(The above program will generate runtime TypeError)

2. The following object is declared in a python program. Which type of Object is this?

`>>>L=[23,77,12,90,66]`

1. Set 2. Dictionary 3. List 4. Tuple

3. To declare a tuple with a single value, which of the following command is used:

1. `T=(23)` 2. `T(23)` 3. `T=(23,)` 4. `T=23`

4. The example of a mapping data type is...

1. List 2. Dictionary 3. Tuple 4. String

5. An example of Immutable data type is:

   1. String 2. List 3. Dictionary 4. Set

6. An example of Mutable data type is:

   1. String 2. List 3. Tuple 4. All the above

7. The output of the following command will be:

```
X,Y=23,45
print("The remainder of:",X,"and",Y,"is",X%Y,sep="**")
```

   1. The remainder of: 23 and 45 is**23
   2. The remainder of:**23**and 45 is 23**
   3. The remainder of:**23**and**45**is**23
   4. The remainder of:**23 and 45**is**23

8. Write the output of the following python expression:

```
print((4>5) and (2!=1) or (4<9))
```

9. `>>>A=B=10`

   `>>>print(str(A)+str(B))`

   1. 20 2. 10 3. 1001 4. 1010

10. `T="Good Day"`

    `print(T[2],T[6],sep="89")`

    1. 89a 2. 089 3. o89a 4. 890a

11. Boolean Data Type is

    1. Mutable data type
    2. Immutable data type
    3. Can be mutable and immutable data type
    4. Neither mutable nor immutable data type

12. The operator which calculates the power of two numbers is:

    1. // 2. % 3. && 4. **

13. `33>55 and not 5!=9 or 3<4`

    1. True 2. False 3. 33 4. 0

14. The function which accepts the value at the runtime is:

    a. `int()` b. `input()` c. `float()` d. `print()`

15. The two parameters of the print() are:

    a. `break and input` b. `end and input`

    c. `end and sep` d. `int and sep`

16. `print(float(34//12))` will generate the output :

    a. 2 b. 2.0 c. 2.8 d. 2.83333

17. Give the output of the commands given below

```
CLASS='["one","two","three"]'
print(type(CLASS))
```

a. <class 'list'> b. <class 'str'>

c. <class 'tuple'> d. <class 'set'>

18. Which type of operator is !=

a. Augmented assignment b. Relational

c. Logical d. Assignment

19. Give the output for the following commands:

```
U=10;V=25
U+=20
V-=5
W=2*(2*V+U)
print(U,V,W,sep='###')
```

a. 20###30###140 b. 30###30###140

c. 30######140 d. 30###20###140

20. `print(int(3>7)+int(15.5+6),not(5<3+1)+190/10,sep=" OR ")`

a. 21 OR 22 b. 21 OR False c. True OR False d. 21 OR True

Subjective Questions

1. What is the difference between the following?
   a. Mutable and Immutable data types
   b. "55" and 55
   c. Logical and Syntax Errors
   d. Implicit and Explicit conversion
   e. int() and float()
2. Write Python single liner codes for the following statements:
   a. Assign the values "Tank" and 1500 to the python objects Name and Price
   b. Calculate the 10% of the above price using formula and store the result in another object called Discount.
   c. Find the TotalPrice by subtracting discount from Price and display the Name and TotalPrice on the same line.

3. Write a program to accept three sides of a triangle and check if the triangle is an isosceles triangle or not.
4. Rewrite the following code after removing the errors from it. Underline each of the corrections done by you.

```
input("Enter number:")=Num
X=23,Y=78
X+Y+Num=Sum
print("SUM is:",sep="**",Sum)
```

5. Write at least two features of Python Programming language

7 Flow of Control

Flow of control: An introduction

Suppose you want to eat an icecream (orange bar) from the vendor outside your house. What steps will you follow to achieve it? You will go outside your house and then go to the ice cream vendor. You will ask for an ice cream. You will ask specifically for an orange bar. If the vendor has an orange bar, he will give you and you will come back home and eat it. If the vendor doesn't have an orange bar, then you won't take any other ice cream and come back home without it. To achieve a goal, one needs to follow some simple steps.

Similarly, in programming also we need to follow steps to achieve a task. For doing so, we need to break the task into simple and small steps and execute them in a specific order. The order in which an operation in a programming language is executed is called flow of control.

In python, the following are the flow of control statements:

1. Sequential
2. Conditional statements
3. Loop Control statements/iterative flow

Sequential flow of control happens when the statements are executed one after the other in a given sequence. For example:

```
N1=10
N2=int(input("Enter a number"))
Avg=(N1+N2)/2
print("Average of two numbers is :",Avg)
print("Program Over")
```

Execution:

```
Enter aa number33
Average of two numbers is : 21.5
Program Over
```

In programming, when we execute a task based on the condition criteria, then this is called a ***conditional flow of statement.*** For example, we can check whether the average of the two numbers calculated in the above example is an even number or an odd number. If the average is even, then the result 'EVEN' should be printed, otherwise, the result 'ODD' should be printed. This follow of control needs an if else statement, which will be discussed in the later section.

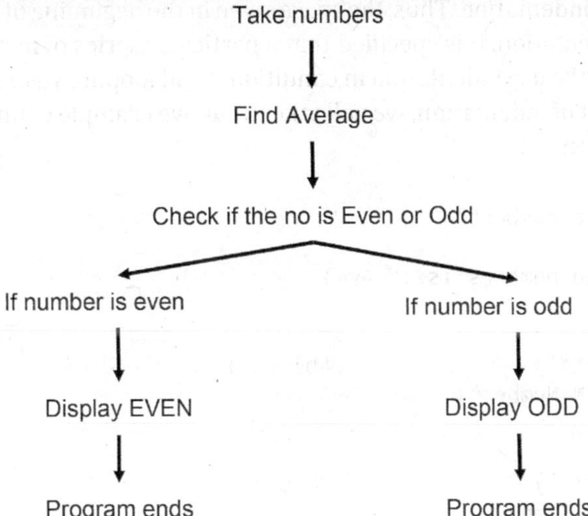

When a given task or series of instructions are required to be repeated a certain number of times then this flow of control is known as ***iterative flow***. We use for and while loop for loop flow of control. In continuation to the above example, if we want to repeat the message "EVEN" or "ODD" say 15 times, then we use a loop.

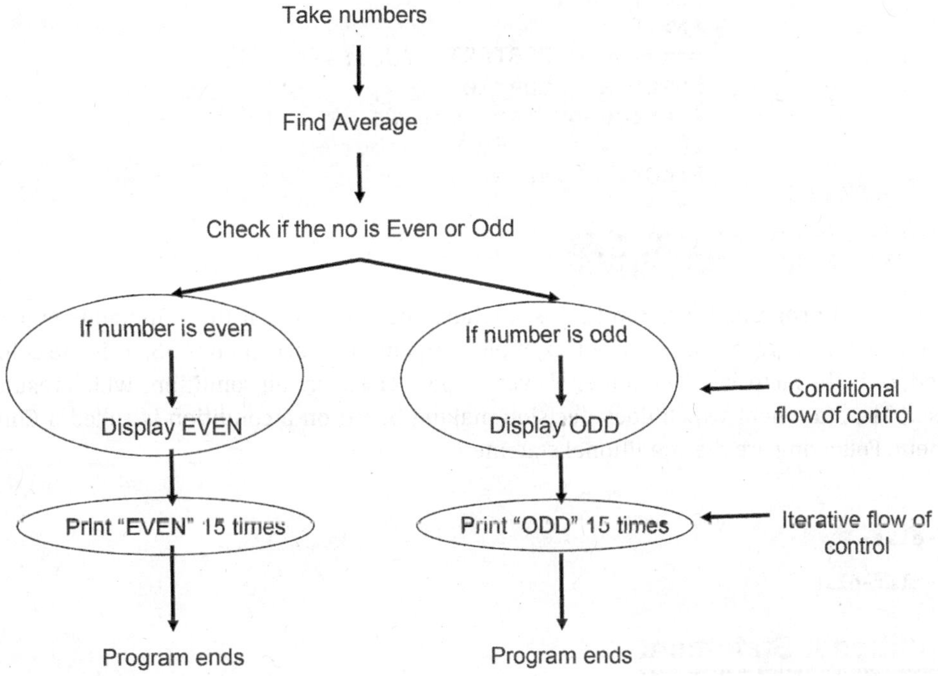

Use of indentation

A block of code is the series of instructions which should be executed in a sequential order one after the other. In programming languages like C, C++, a block is written within curly brackets. In python, a block is specified using indentation. Thus, the space given in the beginning of the block of code is called ***indentation***. Using indentation, it is specified that a particular series of instructions/commands is a part of a specific block. We use indentation in conditional and looping statements, with functions etc. To illustrate the concept of indentation, we will take the above example of finding the number as even or odd using if else statement:

```
N1=10
N2=int(input("Enter a number"))
Avg=(N1+N2)/2
print("Average of two numbers is :",Avg)

if Avg%2==0:
    print(Avg,end='***')                    #block 1
    print("is an EVEN Number")

else:
    print(Avg,end='***')                    #block 2
    print("is an ODD Number")

print("Program Over")
```

```
Enter a number28
Average of two numbers is : 19.0
19.0***is an ODD Number
Program Over
>>>
========= RESTART: /Users/sarikak
Enter a number10
Average of two numbers is : 10.0
10.0***is an EVEN Number
Program Over
```

Conditional Statements

While writing a program, there can be cases where the execution of the commands is based on a decision made on a given condition. For example, if the number accepted is >5, or is the color of the ball 'Red', or is the factorial of a number N even or odd. These are all conditions which result in True or False. The statement which does decision making based on a condition is called a Conditional Statement. Following are the conditional statements:

- **if**
- **if-else**
- **if-elif-else**

if conditional Statement

Syntax:

```
if <condition specified is True> :
    Commands to be executed
```

#Program 1: To accept a number and print the message "BIG" is the number accepted is greater than 10

Code	Output
Num=int(input("Enter a number")) if Num>10: print("BIG")	Enter a number31 BIG >>> ========== RESTART Enter a number9 >>>

Note: If the number accepted is not greater than 10, then no result will be printed as we didn't give statements to handle the case when the condition is False.

```
Enter a number9
>>>
```

#Program 2: Accept first name of a student. If the name accepted is "John" then print the last name as "Mathew"

Code	Output
Name=input("Enter first name")) if Name=="John": print(Name, "Mathew")	Enter first nameJohn John Mathew

if else conditional Statement

We have seen in the above examples that the 'if construct' will handle the True case and would not display anything if the case is False. else does that. So else contains statements which should be executed if the condition specified with if goes False. We will modify the above programs and see the difference in the output.

Syntax:

```
if <condition specified is True> :
   Commands to be executed
else :
    Commands to be executed if the condition is False
```

#Program 1: To accept a number and print the message "BIG" is the number accepted is greater than 10 else print "SMALL"

Code	Output

Num=int(input("Enter a number"))
if Num>10:
    print("BIG")
else:
    print("SMALL")
	Enter a number19
	BIG
	Enter a number9
	SMALL

Flowchart Explanation:

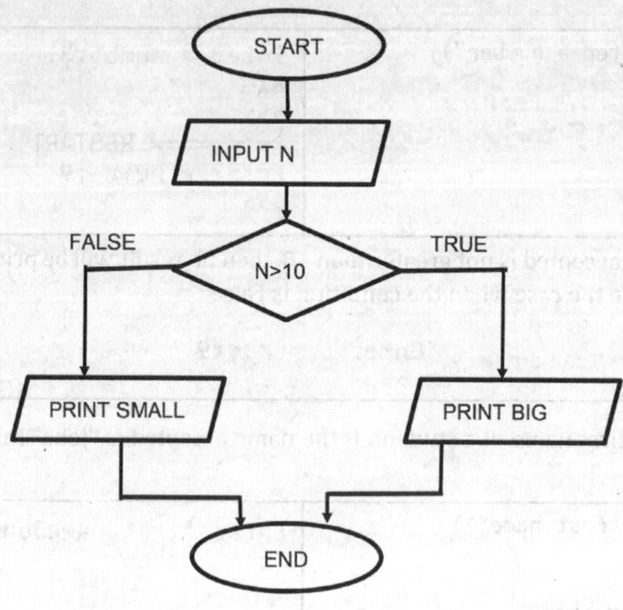

#Program 2: Accept first name of a student. If the name accepted is "John" then print the last name as "Mathew" else print the message "Unknown Name"

Program	Output

`Name=input("Enter first name")`
`if Name=="John":`
`    print(Name, "Mathew")`
`else:`
`    print("Unknown Name")`
	Enter first nameJohn
	John Mathew
	
	Enter first nameKevin
	Unknown Name

#Program 3: Accept a number and find its Absolute value

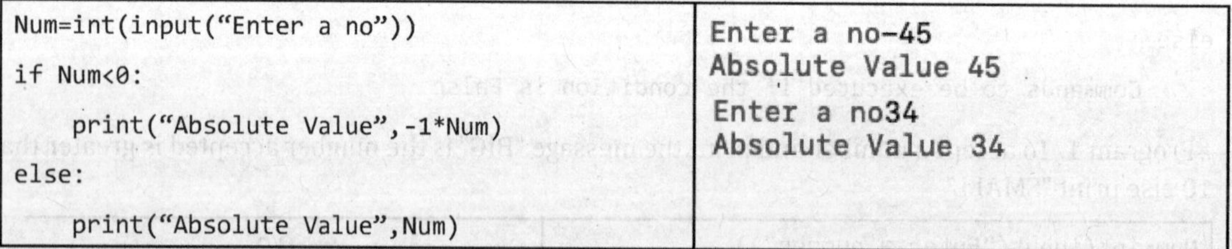

Program	Output

`Num=int(input("Enter a no"))`
`if Num<0:`
`    print("Absolute Value",-1*Num)`
`else:`
`    print("Absolute Value",Num)`
	Enter a no-45
	Absolute Value 45
	Enter a no34
	Absolute Value 34

#Program 4: Accept a number Num and check whether it is an even number or an odd number

Program	Output

`Num=int(input("Enter a no"))`
`if Num%2==0:`
`    print(Num,"is an Even No")`
`else:`
`    print(Num,"is an Odd No")`
	Enter a no22
	22 is an Even No
	
	Enter a no45
	45 is an Odd No

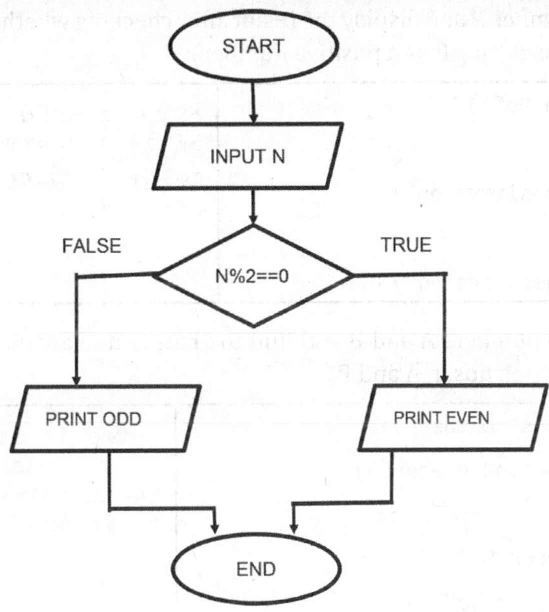

#Program 5: Accept a number N and Check whether it is a factor of M or not, where M is also accepted by the user. (Note that N will be factor of M if M is divisible by N)

Code	Output

`N=int(input("Enter first Number"))`
`M=int(input("Enter Second Number"))`
`if M%N==0:`
`    print(N, "is a factor of", M)`
`else:`
`    print(N,"is not a factor of", M)`
	Enter first Number15
	Enter Second Number32
	15 is not a factor of 32
	Enter first Number2
	Enter Second Number22
	2 is a factor of 22

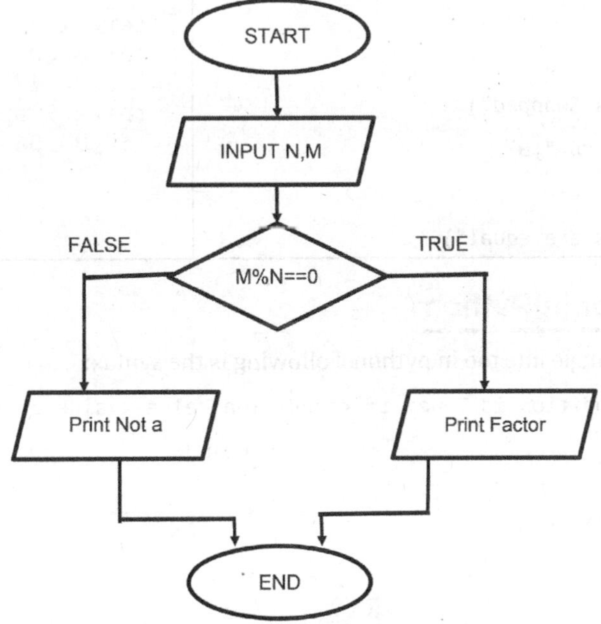

#Program 6: Accept a number N and display the result after checking whether the number is a positive number or negative (considering 0 as a positive number)

Code	Output

N=int(input("Enter a No"))
if N>=0:
    print(N, "is a positive no")
else:
    print(N, "is a negative no")
	Enter a No56
	56 is a positive no
	Enter a No-66
	-66 is a negative no

#Program 7: Accept two numbers A and B and find the Larger and Smaller Number (assuming that the user is not entering same nos in A and B)

Code	Output

A=int(input("Enter first Number"))
B=int(input("Enter Second Number"))
if A>B:
    print(A, "is Larger No")
    print(B, "is Smaller No")
else:
    print(B, "is Larger No")
    print(A, "is Smaller No")
	Enter first Number54
	Enter Second Number45
	54 is Larger No
	45 is Smaller No

#Program 8: Accept two numbers A and B. Display them. If the two numbers are not equal, then swap (interchange) the values of A and B and redisplay the result.

Code	Output

A=int(input("Enter first Number"))
B=int(input("Enter Second Number"))
print("A=",A, "B=",B)
if A!=B:
    A,B=B,A
    print("Numbers Swapped")
    print("A=",A, "B=",B)
else:
    print("Numbers are equal")
	Enter first Number12
	Enter Second Number12
	A= 12 B= 12
	Numbers are equal
	Enter first Number56
	Enter Second Number67
	A= 56 B= 67
	Numbers Swapped
	A= 67 B= 56

Ternary operator in Python

We can use if else in single line too in python. Following is the syntax:

```
<var>=<value if condition is True> if <condition> else <value if condition False>
```

Example 1:

```
N=int(input("Enter a number"))
a="YES" if N%3==0 else "NO"
print(a)
```

Result:

```
Enter a number12
YES
```

Other alternative:

```
N=int(input("Enter a number"))
print("YES") if N%3==0 else print("NO")
```

Example 2:

```
N,M=2,3
R=5 + (N if N>M else M)
print(R)
```

Since the condition N> M is False, so 3 is added 5 and 8 is stored in R. Hence the output 8

Another way of using Single liner decision making statement

Syntax:

```
Val=[Value/“Msg if condition is False”, Value/“Msg if condition is True”][Condition”]
```

OR

```
print([Value/“Msg if condition is False”, Value/“Msg if condition is True”][Condition”])
```

Example 1: To display message True, if the number Num is a multiple of 5 else display False

```
Num=int(input("Enter a number"))
print(["False","True"][Num%5==0])
```

Output:

```
Enter a number12
False
```

Example 2: To increase the value of N by 10% if N<50 else increase by 5%

```
N=int(input("Enter a number"))
N=N+[N*5/100,N*10/100][N>=50]
print(N)
```

Output:

```
Enter a number45
47.25
```

if elif else conditional Statement

Simple if else will work if we have exactly one condition which results in True or false. But if there are multiple conditions to be evaluated, then we expand the if statement to if elif..else. Here the conditions are specified everytime if occurs. Referring to the above #program 7, we explicitly mentioned that the user enters unequal values for A and B. But if the user enters the same number for A and B, both, then we need to modify the above program.

Syntax:

```
if <condition 1 specified is True> :
    Commands to be executed
```

```
elif  <condition 2 specified is True> :
     Commands to be executed
elif  <condition 3 specified is True> :
     Commands to be executed
.
.
.
.
else :
     Commands to be executed none of the above condition is True
```

#Program 1: Accept two numbers A and B and find the Larger and Smaller Number.

Program	Output

`A=int(input("Enter first Number"))`
`B=int(input("Enter Second Number"))`
`if A>B:`
`    print(A, "is Larger No")`
`    print(B, "is Smaller No")`
`elif B>A:`
`    print(B, "is Larger No")`
`    print(A, "is Smaller No")`
`else:`
`    print(A,"and", B, "are same")`
	Enter first Number34
	Enter Second Number43
	43 is Larger No
	34 is Smaller No
	
	Enter first Number4
	Enter Second Number4
	4 and 4 are same

#Program 2: Accept three numbers A, B and C and find the Largest of the three Numbers.

Program	Output

`A=int(input("Enter first Number"))`
`B=int(input("Enter Second Number"))`
`C=int(input("Enter Second Number"))`
`if A==B==C:`
`    print("All numbers are same")`
`elif A>=B and A>=C:`
`    print(A, "is Largest No")`
`elif B>=A and B>=C:`
`    print(B, "is Largest No")`
`else:`
`    print(C, "is Largest No")`
	Enter first Number4
	Enter Second Number4
	Enter Second Number4
	All numbers are same
	
	Enter first Number56
	Enter Second Number56
	Enter Second Number4
	56 is Largest No

#Program 3: Accept three numbers and arrange then in ascending order. Display the final result.

```
A=int(input("Enter first Number"))
B=int(input("Enter Second Number"))
C=int(input("Enter Second Number"))
if A>B:
    A,B=B,A
if C<B:
    if C<A:
        A,B,C=C,A,B
    else:
        A,B,C=A,C,B

print("Numbers in ascending order :",A,B,C)
```

```
Enter first Number56
Enter Second Number34
Enter Second Number7
Numbers is ascending order : 7 34 56
```

#Program 4: Accept marks of a child in 5 subjects. Calculate the percentage and display the grade based on the following criteria:

Grade A+ : 91-100

Grade A : 81-90

Grade B+ : 71-80

Grade B : 61-70

Grade C+ : 51-60

Grade C : <51

Method 1

```
A=float(input("Enter Mks in Sub1"))
B=float(input("Enter Mks in Sub2"))
C=float(input("Enter Mks in Sub3"))
D=float(input("Enter Mks in Sub4"))
E=float(input("Enter Mks in Sub5"))
per=(A+B+C+D+E)/5
print("Your Percentage is:",per,"and you got",end=' ')
if per>50:
    if per>60:
        if per>70:
            if per>80:
                if per>90:
                    print("Grade A+")
```

```
                else:
                    print("Grade A")
            else:
                print("Grade B+")
        else:
            print("Grade B")
    else:
        print("Grade C+")
else:
    print("Grade C")
```

```
Enter Mks in Sub167
Enter Mks in Sub289
Enter Mks in Sub378
Enter Mks in Sub468
Enter Mks in Sub585
Your Percentage is: 77.4 and you gotGrade B+
```

Method-2

```
A=float(input("Enter Mks in Sub1"))
B=float(input("Enter Mks in Sub2"))
C=float(input("Enter Mks in Sub3"))
D=float(input("Enter Mks in Sub4"))
E=float(input("Enter Mks in Sub5"))
per=(A+B+C+D+E)/5
print("Your Percentage is:",per,"and you got",end=' ')
if 100>=per>90: #per>90 and per<=100
    print("Grade A+")
elif 90>=per>80: #per>80 and per<=90
    print("Grade A")
elif 80>=per>70: #per>70 and per<=80
    print("Grade B+")
elif 70>=per>60: #per>60 and per<=70
    print("Grade B")
elif 60>=per>50: #per>50 and per<=60
    print("Grade C+")
else:
    print("Grade C")
```

```
Enter Mks in Sub180
Enter Mks in Sub280
Enter Mks in Sub380
Enter Mks in Sub480
Enter Mks in Sub580
Your Percentage is: 80.0 and you got Grade B+
```

#Program 5: Accept the year and check if it's a leap year or not.

```
Year=int(input("Enter Year"))
if Year%400==0:
    print("Leap Year")
elif Year%4==0:
    if Year%100!=0:
        print("Leap Year")
    else:
        print("Not a Leap Year")
else:
    print("Not a leap Year")
```

```
Enter Year2000
Leap Year
>>>
=================
Enter Year1900
Not a Leap Year
```

Note: A leap year is the one which is either divisible by 400 or if divisible by 4 and not divisible by 100.

Summary

1. ***Sequential flow of control*** happens when the statements are executed one after the other in a given sequence.
2. The space given in the beginning of the block of code is called ***indentation***.
3. The statement which does decision making based on a condition is called a Conditional Statement. if, if-else, if-elif-else are conditional statements.
4. We can also use if-else in single line. For example to display "Positive"/"Negative" message depending upon whether a number is less than 0 or not, we can write single liner if else in the following manner:

   ```
   print("Positive") if Num>=0 else print("Negative")
   ```

5. There are two ways to write single liner if else decision making statements:

   a. First Method:

   ```
   <var>=<value if condition is True> if <condition> else <value if condition False>
   ```

   b. Second Method:

   ```
   Val=[Value/“Msg if condition is True”, Value/“Msg if condition is False”][Condition”]]
   ```

? EXERCISE

Multiple Choice Questions

1. ```
   a = 100
   b = 20
   print(“a”) if a > b else print(“b”)
   ```

   a. `100` b. `20` c. `a` d. `b`

2. Print “Good Work” if a is not equal to b

   ```
   a = 20
   b = 10
   ________a ________b_________
    print(“Hello World”)
   ```

   a. `if,!=,:` b. `if,<>,:` c. `if,<!,:` d. `if,<,:`

3. ```
   number = 0
   if number > 0:
      print(“positive”)
   else:
      print(“negative”)
   ```

   a. `positive` b. `negative` c. `0` d. `None of the above`

4. Can we write if-else in a single line in python?

   a. Yes b. No

   c. Only possible with loops d. None of the above

5. Which one of the following is a valid Python if statement?

   a. `if a>=100 :` b. `if (a >= 100)`

   c. `if (a => 100)` d. `if a = 100`

6. Give the output of the given below program?

```
if 1 + 3 == 7:
    print("Yes")
else:
    print("Invalid")
```

a. Yes b. Invalid c. No Output. d. Error

7. Give the output

```
a=25
if a < 15:
    print("Hi", end="**")
if a <= 30:
    print("Hello",end="&&")
else:
 print("Know Program")
```

a. `Hello&&` b. `Hi&&` c. `Know Program` d. `Hi**Known Program`

8.
```
a, b, c = 2,4,6
if a > 0:
  if b >= 4:
    print("Inside")
  elif c > 5:
    print("Super Inside")
else:
  print("None")
```

a. Inside b. Super Inside c. None d. Error

9.
```
X,Y=0,0
if X+Y:
    print("False")
else:
    print("True")
```

a. False b. True c. No output d. Error

10. What is the output of the given below program?

```
a = b = false
if (a and b):
    print("Yes")
```

```
else:
    print("No")
```

a. Yes b. No

c. Compiled Successfully, No Output. d. Error

11. Which of the following is not a decision-making statement?

a. if-elif statement b. for statement

c. if -else statement d. if statement

12. Give the output

```
if True:
    print(2021)
else:
    print(2022)
```

a. 2022 b. 2021 c. Error d. 202122

13. If you have multiple conditions, then which clause can be used to specify them?

a. else if b. elseif c. elif d. None of the above

14. The .... statement is used for decision making in Python.

a. if else if b. if elif else c. For ; d. for

15. In Python, ... defines a block of statements.

a. block b. loop c. indentation d. {}

16. The two membership operators are .... and ....

a. in, not in b. true , false c. =,== d. None

17. A graphical representation of an algorithm to solve a problem is called ....

a. flow of data b. barchart c. flow chart d. None

18. What is the logical expression for the following?

Either A is greater than B or A is less than C

a. A>B or A<C b. A>B and A<C c. A>Band C d. A>B or C

19. Give the statement for the following case

Either name is SK or age between 45 and 55

a. name==SK and age >=45 and age<=55 b. name==SK and age >=45 or age<=55

c. name==SK or age >=45 and age<=55 d. None

20. Which statement will check if a is equal to b or not?

a. `if a = b:` b. `if a == b:` c. `if a === c:` d. `if a == b`

8 Iteration

Repetition of a series of instructions in programming is called iteration. We use loops to perform iteration. In Python, iteration is performed by for and while loop.

for loop

There are different ways to use the for loop. One way is using the range function.

Syntax:

```
for <variable> in range(start, end, step):
      statements
```

Example:

```
for i in range(1,5):
    print("Learning Loops")
```

Output:

```
Learning Loops
Learning Loops
Learning Loops
Learning Loops
```

The variable `(i)` in the above for loop takes the value from the range( ) function. range() function has three parameters.

start	It provides the starting value of the range. It is an optional value. If start is not provided, then its default value is taken as 0.	In the above example, the starting value of i is taken as 1.
end	It provides the ending value of the range. It is not an optional value. It's compulsory to provide an end value. The loop will execute till end-1. This means that if end value is 5, then the last value taken by the range function will be 5-1=4.	In the above example, the end value is taken as 5-1=4
step	It provides the step value. It is also an optional value and is taken as 1 if not provided.	In the above example, the step value is not provided, so it is taken as 1.

Explanation of the above example:

1. The loop begins with i=1. The condition is True as i<5. So the control goes inside the loop.
2. "Learning Loops" is printed and then the control goes back to the loop.

3. Because of the step value, the value of i changes to 2 (i=1 + step value). Since i<5 (2<5), the control again goes inside the loop. Again 'Learning Loops' is printed for the second time. The control goes back to the beginning of the loop and changes the value of i to 3 (2+1)
4. Since 3<5, Learning Loops is printed 3rd time. Again the value of i changed to 4 and 4<5 so the condition is True and Learning Loops is printed 4th time. The value of i changes to 5 now.
5. Since 5<5 condition is False, so the loop terminates and hence the above result.

Few examples of range function with for loop

`for i in range(5):` `    print("i=",i)`	start=0 (default) end=5-1=4 step=1 (default) Hence numbers printed from 0 to 4	i= 0 i= 1 i= 2 i= 3 i= 4
`for i in range(2,6):` `    print("i=",i)`	start=2 end=6-1=5 step=1 (default) Hence numbers printed from 2 to 5	i= 2 i= 3 i= 4 i= 5
`for i in range(2,6,2):` `    print("i=",i)`	start=2 end=6-1=5 step=2 Hence numbers printed 2, 4(2+2)	i= 2 i= 4
`for i in range(2,6,-1):` `    print("i=",i)`	start=2 end=6-1=5 step=-1 Since the loop is expected to be in reverse order due to -1 step, the condition became false in the very first statement and hence no result.	>>> |
`for i in range(6,2,-1):` `    print("i=",i)`	start=6 end=2+1=3 (as the loop is going in reverse order, i>2 or 1>=3) step=-1 Hence numbers printed from 2 to 5	i= 6 i= 5 i= 4 i= 3

Very Important
`for i in range(1,10,2):`
`    print("i=",i)`
`print(i)`
	In this example, note that the value of i printed outside the loop is 9 and not 11. This is because the range function behaves as if it's a list and returns the successive items of the desired sequence. And the last element in the list in this example is 9. Hence 9 printed outside the loop.	i= 1
		i= 3
		i= 5
		i= 7
		i= 9
		9

Note: the range function can only have integer values. Any other type value will give an error.

for loop with iterables

Unlike other programming languages, it is important to know that for loop in Python can iterate over the iterable objects of python like a list or a string or a tuple or dictionary as shown in the examples below:

Syntax:

```
for <variable> in <iterable Object>:
    statement/statements
```

Example1:

```
L=[56,23,89,90]
for i in L:
    print("Value is ",i)
```

Output

```
Value is  56
Value is  23
Value is  89
Value is  90
```

Example2:

```
Name="PYTHON"
for i in Name:
    print("Value is ",i)
```

Output

```
Value is  P
Value is  Y
Value is  T
Value is  H
Value is  O
Value is  N
```

Example3:

```
Data=(9,"XI Class","Komal",89.5)
for i in Data:
    print("Value is ",i)
```

Output

```
Value is  9
Value is  XI Class
Value is  Komal
Value is  89.5
```

The above programs can be done using the range function also, using the len function. The len function returns the length of an iterable, which means the count of the total number of elements in the iterable. In the example below, the start value will be 0 by default and step value will be 1 by default.

Example 1:

```
L=[56,23,89,90]
for i in range(len(L)):
    print("Value is ",L[i])
```

```
Value is  56
Value is  23
Value is  89
Value is  90
```

Example 2:

```
Name="PYTHON"
for i in range(len(Name)):
    print("Value of",i,"is",Name[i])
```

```
Value of 0 is P
Value of 1 is Y
Value of 2 is T
Value of 3 is H
Value of 4 is O
Value of 5 is N
```

Example 3:

```
Data=(9,"XI Class","Komal",89.5)
for i in range(len(Data)):
    print("Value of Data[",i,"] is",Data[i])
```

Output

```
Value of Data[ 0 ] is 9
Value of Data[ 1 ] is XI Class
Value of Data[ 2 ] is Komal
Value of Data[ 3 ] is 89.5
```

while loop

While loop is the other way to perform iteration. This loop is used to execute the statements till the given condition is True. Here is the syntax of the while loop:

Syntax:

```
while <condition is True>:
    ...statements.....
```

Example:

Code	Output	Explanation

#To print Python 5 time
C=1
while C<=5:
    print("Python")
    C+=1
print("Done")
	Python
	Python
	Python
	Python
	Python
	Done
		Here a variable C is initialized with the value 1. Till the value is less than or equal to 5, the control will move inside the loop and the statements are executed. That is why the string "Python" is printed 5 times

#Print first 5 numbers
C=1
while C<=5:
    print(C)
    C+=1
	1
	2
	3
	4
	5
		This program is similar to the above example except the value of C being printed in this case.

#Print first 5 even numbers
C=1
while C<=5:
    print(2*C)
    C+=1
	2
	4
	6
	8
	10
		Alternate method to do this program is:
		C=2
		while C<=10:
		    print(C)
		    C+=2

#Print first 5 odd numbers
C=1
while C<=5:
    print(2*C-1)
    C+=1
	1
	3
	5
	7
	9
		Alternate method to do this program is:
		C=1
		while C<=10:
		    print(C)
		    C+=2

Note: Unlike range function in for loop, in while loop object of any data type can be used to provide the condition.

```
C=1.2                   1.2
while C<=5:             2.2
      print(C)  →       3.2
      C+=1              4.2
```

Also, we need to be careful with the conditions provided. The while loop can go infinite, if the False condition is not reached as shown in the example below:

```
C=1
while C<=5:
      print(C)
      C-=1
```

→ Here the loop will go infinite as the value of C will always be smaller than 5.

break and continue statements in loops

break statement is used to terminate the loop. The statements after the loop continue to get executed. Let us see few examples to understand the break statement:

Example 1

```
for i in range(1,6):
      a=int(input("Enter a number"))
      if a==0:
            print("Loop terminated")
            break
      else:
            print("No entered",a)
print("Loop executed",i,"times")
```

The above program accepts 5 numbers using for loop. But the loop will terminate as soon as the number accepted is 0.

```
Enter a number3
No entered 3
Enter a number1
No entered 1
Enter a number56
No entered 56
Enter a number88
No entered 88
Enter a number5
No entered 5
Loop executed 5 times
```

In this case, all the numbers accepted are non-zero. Thus the loop runs 5 times.

```
Enter a number34
No entered 34
Enter a number56
No entered 56
Enter a number0
Loop terminated
Loop executed 3 times
```

In this second execution, the third number accepted is zero. Thus the loop terminates after executing the loop 3 times.

Example 2:

```
S=0
while True:
    a=int(input("Enter a number"))
    if a%7==0:
        break
    S+=a
print("Sum is :",S)
```

This program will find the sum of all the numbers accepted in the loop. But as soon as the number accepted is multiple of 7, the loop terminated.

```
Enter a number4
Enter a number67
Enter a number63
Sum is : 71
```

continue statement is used to continue with the loop by skipping the rest of the statements in the loop, if it is encountered. For example, to print only the odd numbers between 1 and 10, program below, skips the statements in the loop if the counter C is an even number and that's why the print statement is also ignored.

```
C=0
while C<=10:
    C+=1
    if C%2==0:
        continue
    print("Number is :",C)
```

Can you guess the output if the above program is modified as shown below:

```
C=1
while C<=10:
    if C%2==0:
        continue
    print("Number is :",C)
    C+=1
```

→ ?

else clause with loops

It is interesting to know that in python we can use the else statement not only with if else construct but with loops also. *A loop's else clause runs when no break occurs.* else at the end of the loop will only be executed if the loop is not terminated and the loop completes all its iterations. If the loop terminates due to the encounter of the **break** statement, then the else written after the loop is not executed. The following example shows the use of else with for and while loops, both.

<table>
<tr><td><pre>#print the sum of all numbers in a list L
L=[67,45,89,33,10]
s=0
for i in L:
    s+=i
else:
    print("Sum is : ",s)</pre></td><td>Sum of all the elements of a list L is calculated. Since the loop completes its iterations so else will be executed and hence the result :

<code>Sum is : 244</code></td></tr>
<tr><td><pre>#print the sum of elements in a list L
#till an even number is encountered
L=[67,45,66,89,33,10]
s=0
for i in L:
    if i%2==0:
        print("Sum",s)
        break
    s+=i
else:
    print("Sum is : ",s)</pre></td><td>Sum of only the first two elements of list L is calculated as the third element is even and hence the result.

<code>Sum 112</code></td></tr>
<tr><td><pre>#program to check if the number is prime
N=int(input("Enter a number"))
for i in range(2,N//2+1):
    if N%i==0:
        print(N,"is not a prime number")
        break
else:
    print(N,"is a Prime Number")</pre></td><td>Program checks whether the number N is a prime number or not. A prime number is the one which is not divisible by any number from 2 to half of the number. If divisible, then the loop is terminated. If the loop stops without completing the iterations, then else will not be executed.</td></tr>
<tr><td><pre>#print sum of first five numbers
C=1
S=0
while C<=5:
    S+=C
    C+=1
else:
    print("Sum is :",S)</pre></td><td><code>Sum is : 15</code></td></tr>
</table>

Flowchart representation of loops using examples:

Program to print sum of 1st five numbers

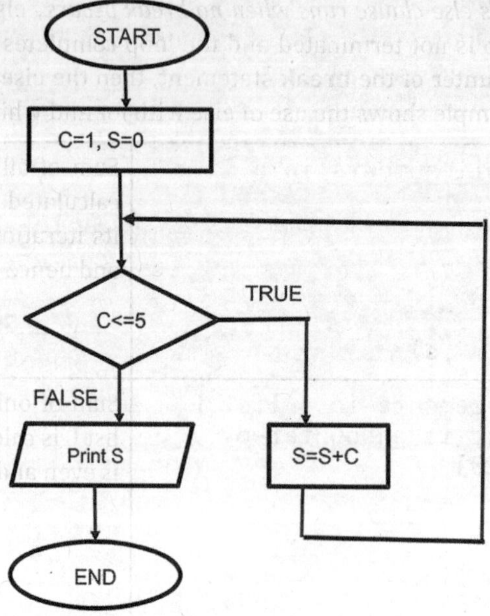

Program to display the first 10 multiples of 3

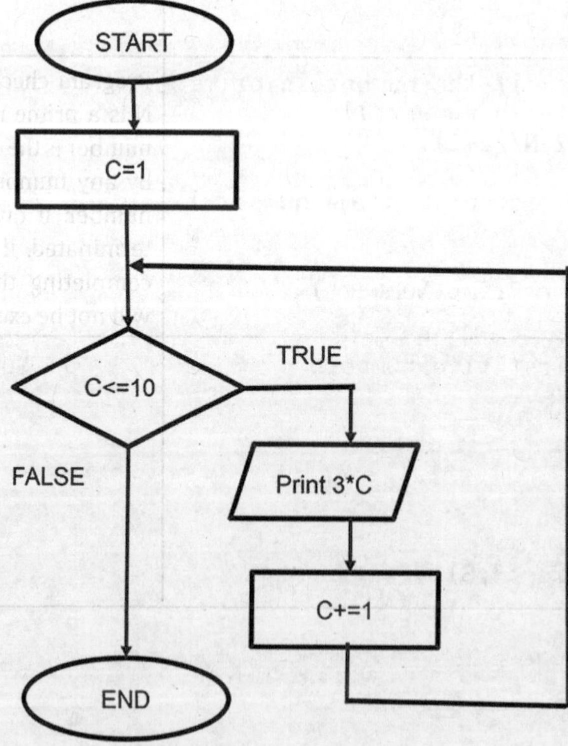

Nested Loop

When one loop is used within another, then we say the loop is nested. In a nested loop, we can use for within another for loop or while within another while loop or for within while loop or vice versa.

In a nested loop, it is to be remembered that for every value of the outer loop, the inner loop gets executed completely. For example:

Example 1

```
for i in range(1,5):
    for j in range(1,3):
        print(i,j,i+j)
    print(i)
```

In the above example, the execution goes in the following manner:

i	j	print(i,j,i+j)	Output	
1	1	1 1 2	1 1 2	1 1 2 1 2 3 1 2 1 3 2 2 4 2 3 1 4 3 2 5 3 4 1 5 4 2 6 4
	2	1 2 3	1 2 3	
			1	
print(i)	1			
2	1	2 1 3	2 1 3	
	2	2 2 4	2 2 4	
			2	
print(i)	2			
3	1	3 1 4	3 1 4	
	2	3 2 5	3 2 5	
			3	
print(i)	3			
4	1	4 1 5	4 1 5	
	2	4 2 6	4 2 6	
			6	
print(i)	4			

Example 2: Program to generate the following pattern till N rows, where N is accepted by the user:

```
1
12
123
1234 till N rows
```

```
N=int(input("Enter a number"))
for i in range(1,N+1):
    for j in range(1,i+1):
        print(j,end=' ')
    print()
```

In the above example, the execution goes in the following manner for N=5:

i	j	print(j,end=' ')	Output
1 print()	1	1	Enter a number5 1 1 2 1 2 3 1 2 3 4 1 2 3 4 5
2	1 2	1 2	
3	1 2 3	1 2 3	
4	1 2 3 4	1 2 3 4	
5	1 2 3 4 5	1 2 3 4 5	

Example 3: Find the output of the program below:

Code	Output

<pre>for A in range(3):
    c=A
    while c>0:
        print(c,A,c+A,sep='#')
        c-=1
    print("Loop -",A+1)</pre>	

Solved examples of questions suggested in the syllabus

1.	**#Find the factorial of a number N.** N=int(input("Enter a number")) fact=1 for i in range(1,N+1): fact*=i print("Factorial of",N, "is",fact)	Enter a number5 Factorial of 5 is 120

<table>
<tr><td>2.</td><td><pre>#Find the sum of first N odd numbers
N=int(input(“Enter a number”))
S=0
for i in range(1,N+1):
    if i==N:
        print(2*i-1,end=’ ‘)
    else:
        print(2*i-1,end=’+’)
    S+=2*i-1
print(“=”,S)</pre></td><td><pre>Enter a number5
1+3+5+7+9 = 25</pre></td></tr>
<tr><td>3.</td><td><pre>#Find the sum of given series
#x - x2 + x3 - x4 + ...xn
N=int(input(“Enter number of terms”))
X=float(input(“Enter value of X”))
S,pro=0,X
for i in range(1,N+1):
    if i%2!=0:
        S+=pro
        print(pro,end=’-’)
    else:
        S-=pro
        print(pro,end=’+’)
    pro*=X
print(“=”,S)</pre></td><td><pre>Enter number of terms4
Enter value of X2
2.0-4.0+8.0-16.0+= -10.0</pre></td></tr>
<tr><td>4</td><td><pre>#Find the sum of given series
#x/1! + x2/2!+ x3/3!+ x4/4!- ....
xn/n!
N=int(input(“Enter number of terms”))
X=float(input(“Enter value of X”))
S,pro,fact=0,1,1
for i in range(1,N+1):
    pro*=X
    fact*=i
    S+=pro/fact
    if i==N:
        print(pro,”/”,fact,sep=’’,end=’ ‘)
    else:
        print(pro,”/”,fact,sep=’’,end=’+’)
print(“=”,S)</pre></td><td><pre>Enter number of terms4
Enter value of X3
3.0/1+9.0/2+27.0/6+81.0/24 = 15.375</pre></td></tr>
</table>

5	**#Determine whether a number is a perfect number or not**
	(A perfect number is a positive integer that is equal to the sum of its positive divisors, excluding the number itself)
	N=int(input("Enter a number"))
	S=0
	for i in range(1,N):
	    if N%i==0:
	        S+=i
	if N==S:
	    print(N,"is a perfect number")
	else:
	    print(N,"is not a perfect number")
		**Enter a number56
		56 is not a perfect number
		Enter a number28
		28 is a perfect number
		Enter a number6
		6 is a perfect number**

6	**#Check whether number N is a perfect number or not. Repeat the task till the number N is not entered as 0**
	while True:
	    N=int(input("Enter a number"))
	    if N==0:
	        break
	    S=0
	    for i in range(1,N):
	        if N%i==0:
	            S+=i
	    if N==S:
	        print(N,"is a perfect number")
	    else:
	        print(N,"is not a perfect number")
		**Enter a number3
		3 is not a perfect number
		Enter a number5
		5 is not a perfect number
		Enter a number6
		6 is a perfect number
		Enter a number9
		9 is not a perfect number
		Enter a number1
		1 is not a perfect number
		Enter a number0**

7	**#Determine whether a number is an armstrong number** (An armstrong number is the number that is equal to the sum of cube of all its digits (for a three-digit number)) N=int(input("Enter a number")) N1,SUM=N,0 while N1>0:	**Enter a number370 370 is an armstrong number Enter a number23 23 is not an armstrong number**

<table>
<tr><td></td><td><pre>   SUM+=(N1%10)**3
    N1//=10
if N==SUM:
    print(N,"is an armstrong number")
else:
    print(N,"is not an armstrong number")</pre></td><td></td></tr>
<tr><td>8</td><td>#Determine whether a number is a palindrome.
(A palindrome number is the one which remains unchanged when its digits are reversed.)<pre>N=int(input("Enter a number"))
N1,rev=N,0
while N1>0:
    rev=rev*10+N1%10
    N1//=10
if N==rev:
    print(N,"is a palindrome")
else:
    print(N,"is not a palindrome")</pre></td><td><pre>Enter a number123
123 is not a palindrome

Enter a number12321
12321 is a palindrome

Enter a number370
370 is an armstrong number</pre></td></tr>
<tr><td>9</td><td>#Display the terms of a Fibonacci series.<pre>N=int(input("Enter a number"))
a,b=0,1
for i in range(1,N+1):
    print(a,end=',')
    a,b=b,a+b</pre></td><td><pre>Enter a number6
0,1,1,2,3,5,</pre></td></tr>
<tr><td>10</td><td>#Compute the greatest common divisor and least common multiple of two integers<pre>N=int(input("Enter a number N"))
M=int(input("Enter a number M"))
small=N if N<M else M
for i in range(small,0,-1):
    if N%i==0 and M%i==0:
        HCF=i
        break
LCM=int(N*M/HCF)
print("LCM=",LCM,"and HCF=",HCF)</pre></td><td><pre>Enter a number N12
Enter a number M6
LCM= 12 and HCF= 6

Enter a number N5
Enter a number M4
LCM= 20 and HCF= 1

Enter a number N6
Enter a number M4
LCM= 12 and HCF= 2</pre></td></tr>
</table>

Summary

1. Repetition of a series of instructions in programming is called iteration.
2. In Python, iteration is performed by for and while loop.
3. The statement used to terminate the loop is *break*. The statements after the loop continue to get executed.
4. continue statement is used to continue with the loop by skipping the rest of the statements in the loop, if it is encountered.
5. A loop's else clause runs when no break occurs.
6. When one loop is used within another, then we say the loop is nested.

Practice Questions

1. Write a program to calculate the sum of first N natural numbers, where N is accepted by the user.
2. Write a program to keep on accepting the numbers till the user wants and at the end it should display the count of positive numbers, negative numbers and zeros entered.
3. Write a program to print out all Armstrong numbers between 1 and 999.
4. Write a program to print the result of the following series till N terms
   a. `1 - 1/2 + 1/3 - 1/4 + 1/5 -... 1/N!`
   b. `2+4+6+8+10+.......`
   c. `1!+2!+3!+4!+.............N!`
   d. `2!+4!+6!+8!+................`
   e. `1!+3!+5!+7!+9!+..................`
   f. `X+X3+X5+X7+...................`
   g. `X2+X4+X6+X8+.....................`
   h. `1+(1+2)+(1+2+3)+(1+2+3+4)+...............`
   i. `2+(2+4)+(2+4+6)+.............`
   j. `1+(1+3)+(1+3+5)+..................`
   k. `X+X3/3!+X5/5!+X7/7!+............`
5. Write a program to print the following patterns till N rows

1	1	1	*
1 2	2 2	2 1 2	***
1 2 3	3 3 3	3 2 1 2 3	*****
1 2 3 4	4 4 4 4	4 3 2 1 2 3 4	*******
1 2 3 4 5	5 5 5 5 5	5 4 3 2 1 2 3 4 5	*********

5	5	1	2
45	54	23	24
345	543	456	246
2345	5432	78910	2468
12345	54321	1112131415	246810

6. Store 10 elements in a list L. iterate it, and display numbers divisible by five. Stop the loop iteration if the element is greater than 150.
7. Accept a number N and count the total number of digits in it.
8. Write a program to display all prime numbers within a range from 1 to N, where N is accepted by the user.
9. Find the sum of the series 2 +22 + 222 + 2222 + .. N terms
10. Choose the correct options.

? EXERCISE

Multiple Choice Questions

1.
```
x = 33 / 4 * (5+  2) * 4 + 2
print(x)
```
a. 233.0 b. 37.0 c. 233 d. 235

2.
```
for x in range(0.5, 3.5, 0.5):
  print(x)
```
a. 0.5*1.0*1.5*2.0*2.5*3.0*
b. 0.5 1.0 1.5 2.0 2.5 3.0*
c. 0.5*1.0*1.5*2.0*2.5*3.0*3.5*
d. Error

3.
```
One = 5 ** 2
Two = 5 ** 3
print(One,end='&')
print(Two,end='@')
```
a. 32&27@ b. 25&125@ c. 125@25& d. 32&125@

4.
```
for i in range(5, 19, 3):
  print( i, end=', ')
```
a. 5, 8, 11, 14, 17,
b. 8, 11, 14, 17,
c. 17,14,11,8,5,
d. 5,6,7,8........18

5. Which operator has higher precedence in the following list
a. % Modulus b. & BitWise AND c. **, Exponent d. > Comparison

6.
```
x=0.5
while x<3.5:
    print(x,end='*')
    x+=0.5
```
a. 0.5*1.0*1.5*2.0*2.5*3.0*   b. 0.5 1.0 1.5 2.0 2.5 3.0*

c. 0.5*1.0*1.5*2.0*2.5*3.0*3.5*   d. Error

7
```
for num in range(-2,-5,-1):
    print(num, end="8")
```
a. -8-8-48   b. -2-3-48   c. 28 38 48   d. -28-38-48

8
```
for num in range(11, 14):
    for i in range(3, num):
        if num%i == 1:
            print(num)
            break
```
a. 11
12
13   b. 11
12   c. 13
12
11   d. None

9 Which of the following is/are valid operator in Python:

a. */   b. is   c. ^   d. like

10 Which of the following is/are Keywords in Python ?

a. break   b. Check   c. range   d. for

11
```
x = 0
a = 0
b = -5
if a > 0:
    if b < 0:
        x = x + 5
    elif a > 5:
        x = x + 4
    else:
        x = x + 3
else:
    x = x + 2
print(x)
```
a. 1   b. 2   c. 3   d. 4

12
```
var = 10
for i in range(10):
    for j in range(2, 10, 1):
        if var % 2 == 0:
            continue
            var += 1
    var+=1
else:
    var+=1
print(var)
```

a. 34 b. 56 c. 21 d. 97

13
```
x = 0
a = 5
b = 5
if a > 0:
    if b < 0:
        x = x + 5
    elif a > 5:
        x = x + 4
    else:
        x = x + 3
else:
    x = x + 2
print(x)
```

a. 1 b. 2 c. 3 d. 4

14
```
x = 6
y = 2
print(x ** y,end-'+')
print(x // y)
```

a. 6+36 b. 36+3 c. 3+36 d. 36 3 +

15 What is the output of print(5%10)

a. 0 b. 2 c. 5 d. Error

16 What is the output of print(2**3**2)

a. 512 b. 64 c. 256 d. 128

17 **Give Output**

```
for i in range(2.0):
    print(i)
```

a. 1 b. 1 2 c. Error d. None of the above

18

```
i=1
while True:
    if i%3==0:
        break
    print(i,end=' ')
    i+=1
```

a. 1 b. 1 2 c. Error d. None of the above

19

```
i=1
for i in range(0,10,3):
    print(i+2,end='*')
    i+=2
```

a. 2*5*8*11* b. 0*2*5*8* c. 3*8*11*13* d. 2*8*8*11*

20

```
while True:
    i=10
    print(i+5,end='8')
    if i%5==0:
        break
    else:
        i=i+2
```

a. 58 b. 15 c. 158 d. 185

9 Strings

Introduction to Strings

Strings are the series of characters stored in a sequence within single, double quotes or triple quotes. For example, the name of a person/product, address etc.

```
>>>a='Python Language' #String declaration within single quotes
>>>a
'Python Language'
```

OR

```
>>>a="Python Language" #String declaration within double quotes
>>>a
'Python Language'
```

OR

```
>>>a="""Python Language""" #String declaration within triple double quotes
>>>a
'Python Language'
```

OR

```
>>>a='''Python Language''' #String declaration within triple single quotes
>>>a
'Python Language'
```

Some of the key features we need to know about strings are:

1. Any data enclosed either in single or double quotes is a string in Python.
2. String is an iterable object which stores characters in a sequence
3. String is an immutable object, which means we cannot change a specific character in a string.
4. To know the total number of characters in a string, we use a function called len(string). For example:

   ```
   >>>a="Good Day"
   >>>print(len(a))
   8 #Total letters in String are 8, from index 0 to 7
   ```

5. We can use escape sequence (\) to include line break (\n) or tab (\t) or to show quotes with a string as shown in the examples:

```
>>>a="Python\nLanguage" #using \n as Newline
>>>print(a)
Python
Language

>>>a="Python\tLanguage" #using \t as tab
>>>print(a)
Python  Language
>>> a='\'Python\' Language' #using \ to include quotes with a string
>>> print(a)
'Python' Language

>>>a="Python: It's a very interesting Language"
>>>print(a)
Python: It's a very interesting Language
#To include single quotes within a string, enclose the string in double quotes.

>>>a='Python: It's a very interesting Language' #Error

>>>a='"Python" Language'
>>>print(a)
"Python" Language
#To include double quotes within a string, enclose the string in single quotes.
```

String indexing

Since a string is an iterable object, each character has an index number using which the character of a string can be extracted.

a='Python Language'

0	1	2	3	4	5	6	7	8	9	10	11	12	13	14
P	y	t	h	o	n		L	a	n	g	u	a	g	e
-15	-14	-13	-12	-11	-10	-9	-8	-7	-6	-5	-4	-3	-2	-1

Each character in the string has a positive index as well as negative index number, using which the character can be extracted. The index number is provided in a square brackets as shown below:

```
>>>print(a)        #Python Language
>>>print(a[5])     #n
>>>print(a[-5])    #g
```

String operations

Following operations are possible in this iterable object:

a. **Concatenation :** Concatenation means combining 2 or more strings. Concatenation is possible using '+' (plus) sign. Following example illustrate concatenation in strings:

Example 1

```
>>> a="Twinkle"
>>> b="Little Star"
>>> a+b
'TwinkleLittle Star'
```

Note:

1. Concatenation is possible **only** between strings.
2. Also, two or more string literals (i.e. the ones enclosed between quotes) next to each other are automatically concatenated as shown below:

Example 2

```
>>> "Twinkle" +12
#Error
    TypeError: can only concatenate str (not "int") to str
```

Example 3

```
>>> "Twinkle" "Little Star"
'TwinkleLittle Star'
```

Example 4

```
>>> X="PY" "thon"
>>> X
'PYthon'
```

Example 5

```
Enter first name :Aviral          A=input("Enter first name :")
Enter second name :Kaushal        B=input("Enter second name :")
Hello  Aviral Kaushal          →  print("Hello ", A+' '+B)
```

Example 6

```
str1='hello'
str2='Class XI'
str3=str4="Students"
print(str1,str3,sep=' to ',end=' and ')
print(str1,end=' '+str2)
  hello to Students and hello Class XI
```

b. Repetition: We can repeat a strings using asterisk (*) in the following manner:

Example 1

```
A="•" #this character is printed using Option+8 (in Mac)
print(A*10) #The character is repeated 10 times
print("WOW") →  ••••••••••
print(A*10)     WOW
                ••••••••••
```

Note that repetition in string is possible when the string is multiplied **only** with an integer

Example 2

```
A="Twinkle "
B="Little Star"
print(A*2+B)
```

```
Twinkle Twinkle Little Star
```

Example 3

```
str1='Tippy '
str2='Which Color you want'
print(str1*5+" Tap",end="\n"+str2)
```

Output

```
Tippy Tippy Tippy Tippy Tippy  Tap
Which Color you want
```

c. Membership: There are two membership operators 'in' and 'not in'. They are used to find a substring in a given string (when used with string)

in : The 'in' operator results True if the given value/string is found in the given variable.

Example 1

```
A="Every moment is a fresh beginning"
B="fresh"
C="e"
D="every"
print(B in A) #True as 'fresh' is present in string A
print(C in A) #True as 'e' is present in string A
print(D in A) #False as Python is case sensitive
```

Explanation: In the above example, the substring to be searched can either be a single character or a substring, irrespective to the whether the substring appears once or more times in the string. 'Fresh' substring is present in string A and hence gives True result. Similarly, 'e' is present and hence True. But 'every' is not similar to 'Every' as Python is case sensitive and hence it generates False result.

Output

```
True
True
False
```

not in: Evaluates to true if the given value/string is not found in the given variable.

Example 2

```
A="Every moment is a fresh beginning"
B="fresh"
C="e"
D="every"
print(B not in A) #False
print(C not in A) #False
print(D not in A) #True
```

```
False
False
True
```

Example 3

```
#program to check whether a string has vowel 'A' or not
A=input("Enter a string")
if 'A' in A:
  print("Vowel A Found")
else:
  print("Vowel A not found")
```

Output

```
Enter a stringgurgaon
Vowel A not found
```

#Since 'A' is not same as 'a'

```
Enter a stringGurgAon
Vowel A Found
```

d. **Slicing:** It is a feature which allows you to extract a part of the string using the index numbers. To understand slicing we will refer to the following string

a='Python Language'

0	1	2	3	4	5	6	7	8	9	10	11	12	13	14
P	y	t	h	o	n		L	a	n	g	u	a	g	e
-15	-14	-13	-12	-11	-10	-9	-8	-7	-6	-5	-4	-3	-2	-1

There are 3 parameters which can be provided in slicing.

String[start:end:step]

start → specifies the beginning index number. If not provided, then it's 0.

end → specifies the ending index. If it's not provided, then it takes the length of the strings (which is the count of the total number of characters in the string). The last character printed is always end-1

step → It is also optional. If not provided then it's taken as 1. It specifies that by how many steps the index should be jumped to display the next character. If the step provided is positive then the direction of display of the element is from left to right. If the step is negative, then the direction of display of the element is from right to left. Also, if step is negative, then start becomes len(string)-1 by default while end goes till the first character on left.

Examples with reference to above string 'a', with explanation:

```
>>> print(a)
Python Language #String printed

>>> print(a[:]) #Start is default 0 and end is default < len(a)
Python Language

>>> print(a[::])#Start is default 0 and end is default < len(a)
Python Language

>>> print(a[1:4]) #start is 1 and end is <4, step=1 (default)
yth
```

0	1	2	3	4	5	6	7	8	9	10	11	12	13	14
P	y	t	h	o	n		L	a	n	g	u	a	g	e
-15	-14	-13	-12	-11	-10	-9	-8	-7	-6	-5	-4	-3	-2	-1

```
>>> print(a[6:]) #Start is 6, end is < len(a)
Language
```

0	1	2	3	4	5	6	7	8	9	10	11	12	13	14
P	y	t	h	o	n		L	a	n	g	u	a	g	e
-15	-14	-13	-12	-11	-10	-9	-8	-7	-6	-5	-4	-3	-2	-1

```
>>>print(a[::2]) #Start and end default, but step is 2
Pto agae
```

0	1	2	3	4	5	6	7	8	9	10	11	12	13	14
P	y	t	h	o	n		L	a	n	g	u	a	g	e
-15	-14	-13	-12	-11	-10	-9	-8	-7	-6	-5	-4	-3	-2	-1

```
>>>print(a[::-1])
egaugnaL nohtyP
```

0	1	2	3	4	5	6	7	8	9	10	11	12	13	14
P	y	t	h	o	n		L	a	n	g	u	a	g	e
-15	-14	-13	-12	-11	-10	-9	-8	-7	-6	-5	-4	-3	-2	-1

```
#As step is negative, the direction of printing characters is from right to left,
hence reverse string printed
>>> print(a[::-3])
euant
```

0	1	2	3	4	5	6	7	8	9	10	11	12	13	14
P	y	t	h	o	n		L	a	n	g	u	a	g	e
-15	-14	-13	-12	-11	-10	-9	-8	-7	-6	-5	-4	-3	-2	-1

#The step is negative, so direction is right to left. Also, every third character is printed from right to left as step=-3

```
>>> print(a[1:8:3])
yoL
```

0	1	2	3	4	5	6	7	8	9	10	11	12	13	14
P	y	t	h	o	n		L	a	n	g	u	a	g	e
-15	-14	-13	-12	-11	-10	-9	-8	-7	-6	-5	-4	-3	-2	-1

#Start =1, while end<8. step=3 will print every third character starting from index 1.

```
>>> print(a[1:8:-1])
```

#This won't print anything as direction of printing of characters should be right to left, but the values of start and end indicate left to right direction

```
>>> print(a[-1:-5:-1])
egau
```

0	1	2	3	4	5	6	7	8	9	10	11	12	13	14
P	y	t	h	o	n		L	a	n	g	u	a	g	e
-15	-14	-13	-12	-11	-10	-9	-8	-7	-6	-5	-4	-3	-2	-1

#Here negative indexing is specified, so according to the index number as shown in the picture we see characters from -1 till -4 from right to left direction

```
>>> print(a[3:-5])
hon Lan
```

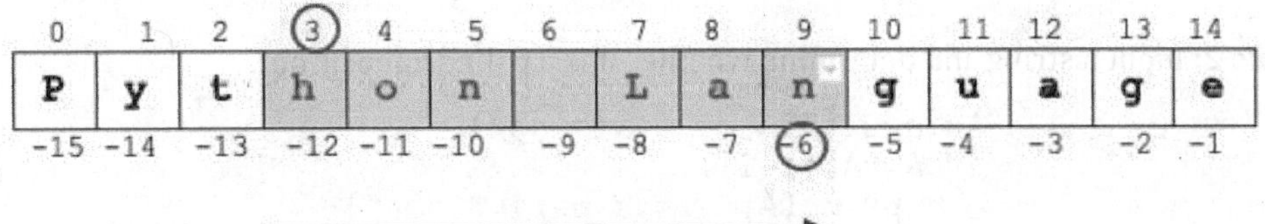

#In this example, there is a combination of positive and negative indexing. Start is 3, end one less than -5 position and since the step is 1 by default and the direction of index is also from left to right, the characters as per the index are printed.

```
>>> print(a[-4:-12:-1])
ugnaL no
```

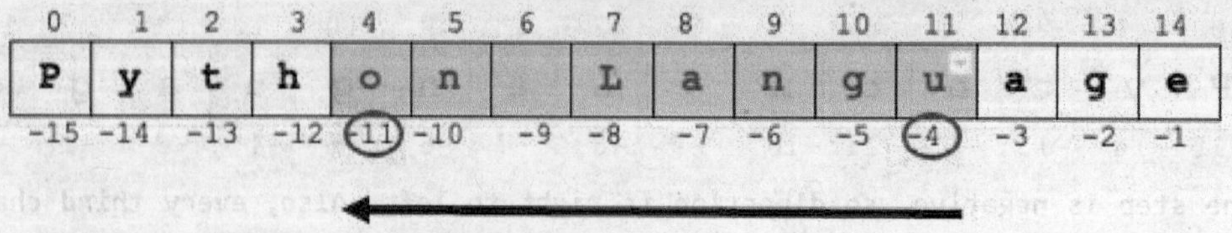

Traversing a string using loops

Since a string is an iterable object, we can reach each and every element of the string one after the other in a sequence using loops.

Two ways to traverse a string

<table>
<tr>
<td>

#Here character is taken from the string A and given to i, which is printed

```
A=input("Enter a string")
for i in A:
        print(i,end="//")

    Enter a stringTASK
    T//A//S//K//
```

</td>
<td>

#Here the index is extracted using the range function and to display the character, the index is specified in square brackets with string variable.

```
A=input("Enter a string")
for i in range(len(A)):
        print(A[i],end="//")

        Enter a stringTASK
        T//A//S//K//
```

</td>
</tr>
</table>

Example1: To count the number of vowels in a string accepted by the user

```
A=input("Enter a string")
count=0
vowels="aeiouAEIOU"
for i in A:
    if i in vowels:
        count+=1
else:
    print("Total Vowels are :",count)

   Enter a stringThis is a pAradISE
   Total Vowels are : 7
```

Example 2: Input a string and determine whether it is a palindrome or not.

```
A=input("Enter a string")
if A==A[::-1]:
    print(A, "is a palindrome")
else:
    print(A, "is not a palindrome")

        Enter a stringhannah
        hannah is a palindrome

      Enter a stringDABAR
      DABAR is not a palindrome
```

Built-in functions used with strings

Following are the functions which can be used for string manipulation as well as to check or extract a desired output from the string.

	Function	Description	Syntax
1	len()	This function finds the length of the string, which means it returns the total number of characters in a string.	len(string)
	Example:	A=input("Enter a string") print(len(A)) **Enter a stringGood Job** **8**	
2	capitalize()	This function returns a new string after converting the first letter of the string to uppercase and the rest of the letters to lowercase. The original string remains unchanged.	string. capitalize()
	Example:	>>>a="Python. Interesting Language" >>>print(a.capitalize()) **Python. interesting language** >>>print(a) **Python. Interesting Language** >>> print("wow. Nice".capitalize()) **Wow. nice**	
3	title()	This function displays the string after converting the first letter of every word in uppercase. The original string remains unchanged	string.title()
	Example:	>>>A="Change the world by being yourself." >>>print(A.title()) **Change The World By Being Yourself.** **>>>print(A)** Change the world by being yourself.	
4	lower()	It displays the string after converting all the letters of the string in lowercase. The original string remains unchanged	string.lower()

	Example:	>>>A="Whatever you do, do it well. By Walt Disney" >>>print(A.lower()) **whatever you do, do it well. by walt disney** >>>print(A) **Whatever you do, do it well. By Walt Disney**	
5	upper()	It displays the string after converting all the letters of the string in uppercase. The original string remains unchanged	string.upper()
	Example:	>>>A="Whatever you do, do it well. By Walt Disney" >>>print(A.lower()) **whatever you do, do it well. by walt disney** >>>print(A) **Whatever you do, do it well. By Walt Disney**	
6	count()	▪ This function counts and displays the total number of occurence of a substring in a string. ▪ For searching in a specific part of the string, the start and the end index number of the string for search can be provided. ▪ If start and end parameter is not provided then the whole string is searched	string.count(Substr, start,end) #The searching is from start index till end-1 index
	Example:	>>>A="If you tell the truth you do not have to remember anything" >>>print(A.count("you")) **2 #'you' appears 2 times in the string A** >>>print(A.count("you",0,5)) **0 #'you' doesn't occur between index 0 and 4.** >>>print(A.count("you",0,6)) **1 #'you' occurs once between index 0 and 5.** >>>print(A.count("e")) **6 #'e' appears 6 times in the entire string A.** #If you tell the truth you do not have to remember anything	

7	find()	▪ find( ) function returns the smallest beginning index of the substring if it is found in the string. ▪ Returns -1 if the substring is not found. ▪ The start and the end index number of the string for search can be provided. ▪ If not provided then the whole string is searched.	string.find(Substr, start,end) #The searching is from start index till end-1 index

	Example:	>>> S="One little two little three little cups"
		>>> S.find("little")
		4
		#One little two little three little cups
		>>> S.find("little",5)
		15
		#One little two little three little cups
		>>> S.find("little",16)
		28
		#One little two **little three little cups**
		>>> S.find("little",16,len(S))
		28
		#One little two **little three little cups**
		>>> S.find("little",16,22)
		-1
		#One little two **little** three little cups	

8	index()	▪ index( ) function returns the smallest beginning index of the substring if it is found in the string. ▪ Generates 'ValueError' exception if the substring is not found. ▪ The start and the end index number of the string for search can be provided. ▪ If not provided then the whole string is searched.	string. index(Substr, start,end) #The searching is from start index till end-1 index

	Example:	>>> S="One little two little three little cups"
		>>> S.index("little")
		4
		#One little two little three little cups
		>>> S.index("little",5)
		15	

		#One little two little three little cups
		>>> S.index("little",16)
		28
		#One little two little three little cups
		>>> S.index("little",16,len(S))
		28
		#One little two little three little cups
		>>> S.index("little",16,22)
		#ValueError: substring not found	

	ONLY DIFFERENCE BETWEEN find( ) and index( ) If substring is not found find( ) returns -1 but index( ) raises ValueError exception		
9	endswith()	This function returns True if the string ends with the given substring, else it returns False. You can also provide tuple of substrings. You can provide the start and end position of the main strings in which searching is done. If not provided, then default the whole string is With optional start, test beginning at that position. With optional end, stop comparing at that position.	str.endswith(sub-string, start, end) #The searching is from start index till end-1 index

		>>>A="One little two little three little cups"
		>>> A.endswith(' ')
		False #as the string doesn't end with space
		
		>>> A.endswith((' ','le','ps'))
		True #as the string doesn't end with space or 'le' but ends with 'ps'
		
		>>> A.endswith(' ',1,4)
		True #as the ending string is space from index no 1 to 3 'ne '
		
		>>> A.endswith(' ',1,3)
		False #as the ending string is not space from index no 1 to 2 'ne'	

10	startswith()	This function returns True if the string starts with the given substring, else it returns False. You can also provide tuple of substrings. You can provide the start and end position of the main strings in which searching is done. If not provided, then default the whole string is With optional start, test beginning at that position. With optional end, stop comparing at that position.	str.startswith(-substring, start, end) #The searching is from start index till end-1 index

	Examples:	>>>A="One little two little three little cups"
		>>> A.startswith(' ')
		False #as the string doesn't start with space
		
		>>> A.startswith((' ','One','one'))
		True #as the string doesn't start with space or 'one' but ends with 'One'
		
		>>> A.startswith('n',1,5)
		True #as the starting string is 'n' from index no 1 to 3 'ne l'
		
		>>> A.startswith('e',10,15)
		False #as the starting string is 'e' from index no 10 to 14
		' two'	

11	isalnum()	Returns **True** if all the characters in the string are either alphabets (A-Z,a-z) or digits (0-9) or their combination else it returns **False**	string.isalnum( )
	Example:	>>>a="Hello Everyone" >>>print(a.isalnum()) False #as space(special char) is there and is not allowed >>>b="Hello Every123" >>>print(b.isalnum()) False #as space(special char) is there and is not allowed >>>c="Hello" >>>print(c.isalnum()) True #as characters are part of alphanumeric and are allowed >>>d="123" >>>print(d.isalnum()) True #as numbers are part of alphanumeric and are allowed >>>f="Hello123" >>>print(f.isalnum()) True #as numbers and characters are alphanumeric >>>g="45%" print(g.isalnum()) False #as %(special char) is there and is not allowed	

12	isalpha()	It returns **True** if the characters in a string are alphabets only (A-Z, a-z) else it returns **False** . If the string has special characters or digits then isalpha( ) will return **False**	string.isalpha( )
	Examples:	>>>a="What a Great Work!" >>>print(a.isalpha()) False #due to spaces and ! (exclamation mark) >>>b="GREAT WORK" >>>print(b.isalpha()) False #due to spaces >>>c="GREAT" >>>print(c.isalpha()) True >>>d="123" >>>print(d.isalpha()) False #due to numbers which are not alphabets >>>e="GREAT123" >>>print(e.isalpha()) False #due to numbers >>>f="GREAT***" >>>print(f.isalpha()) False #due to special characters >>>g="***%***" >>>print(g.isalpha()) False #due to special characters >>>h="GREATwork" >>>print(h.isalpha()) True #as the string has only alphabets	
13	isdigit()	This function returns **True** if the characters in a string are digits only (0-9) else it returns **False** . So if the string has special characters or alphabets then isdigit( ) will return **False**	string.isdigit()

	Examples:	>>>a="What a Great Work!" >>>print(a.isdigit()) False #due to presence of characters >>>b="GREATWORK" >>>print(b.isdigit()) False #due to presence of characters >>>c="GREAT123" >>>print(c.isdigit()) False #due to presence of characters >>>d="123" >>>print(d.isdigit()) True >>>e="**123" >>>print(e.isdigit()) False #due to presence of special characters ** >>>f="123 456" >>>print(f.isdigit()) False #due to special character space	
14	islower()	It returns **True** if **ALL** the characters in the string are in lowercase (a-z) else it returns **False**	**string.islower( )**
	Example	>>>a="What a wonderful Day!" >>>print(a.islower()) False #due to the presence of uppercase letters also. >>>b="what a wonderful day" >>>print(b.islower()) True #as all letters are in lowercase >>>c="day" >>>print(c.islower()) True #as all letters are in lowercase >>>d="123" >>>print(d.islower())	

		False #as only digits are there >>>e="wonderful 1-2-3 days" >>>print(e.islower()) True #as all letters present are in lowercase >>>f="***wonderful days***" >>>print(f.islower()) True #as lowercase letters are there >>>g="**$$**" >>>print(g.islower()) False #as only special characters present	
15	isupper()	It returns **True** if **ALL**the characters in the string are in uppercase (A-Z) else it returns **False**	string.isupper( )
	Example:	>>>a="What a wonderful Day!" >>>print(a.isupper()) False #due to the presence of lowercase letters also. >>>b="WHAT A WONDERFUL DAY!" >>>print(b.isupper()) True #as all letters are in uppercase >>>c="WONDERFUL" >>>print(c.isupper()) True #as all letters are in uppercase >>>d="123" >>>print(d.isupper()) False #as only digits are there >>>e="HAVE 1-2-3 AWESOME DAYS" >>>print(e.isupper()) True #as all letters present are in uppercase >>>f="***WONDERFUL DAYS***" >>>print(f.isupper()) True #as uppercase letters are there	

		>>>g="**$$**" >>>print(g.isupper()) False #as only special characters present	
16	isspace()	Returns **True** if **ALL** the characters in a string are whitespace characters else it returns **False**	string.isspace( )
	Example	>>>a="" >>>print(a.isspace()) False #as no whitespace characters >>>b=" " >>>print(b.isspace()) True #as whitespace characters are present >>>c="Good Luck" >>>print(c.isspace()) False #as alphabets are present >>>d="123 SPACE" >>>print(d.isspace()) False #as digits and characters are there	
17	lstrip()	lstrip( ) function returns a copy of the string after removing the specified character/ characters from the left side of the string, if they exist. If the parameter is not provided, then leading whitespaces are removed	string. lstrip('str')

		>>> A=" train on track "
		>>> A.lstrip()
		'train on track '#spaces in beginning removed but not at the end
		
		>>> A="ttrain on track"
		>>> A.lstrip('t')
		'rain on track' #'t' removed from the left of string
		
		>>> A="train on track"
		>>> A.lstrip('tt')
		'rain on track' #'t' removed from the left of string
		
		>>> A='*.ttrain of track'	

		>>> A.lstrip('*.')
		'ttrain of track' #if either '*' or '.' appears, its removed from left of string
		
		>>> A='*.*ttrain of track'
		>>> A.lstrip('*.')
		'ttrain of track' #if either '*' or '.' appears, its removed from left of string
		
		>>> A='*.*ttrain of track'
		>>> A.lstrip('*')
		'.*ttrain of track' #'*'removed from the left side of the String. Since the second '*' comes after '.', it is not removed	

18	rstrip()	rstrip( ) function returns a copy of the string after removing the specified character/characters from the right side of the string, if they exist. If the parameter is not provided, then trailing whitespaces are removed	string. rstrip('str')

	Examples	>>> A=" train on track "
		>>> A.rstrip()
		' train on track'#spaces at the end removed but not in the beginning
		
		>>> A="ttrain on track"
		>>> A.rstrip('k')
		'rain on track' #'k' removed from the right of string
		
		>>> A="train on track"
		>>> A.lstrip('t')
		'train on track' #'t' is not present on the right side of the string so nothing removed.
		
		>>> A='**.ttrain of track.**'
		>>> A.lstrip('*.')
		'**.ttrain of track' #if either '*' or '.' appears on the right side of the string, it is removed	

		>>> A='*.*ttrain of track*.**'
		>>> A.lstrip('*')
		'*.*ttrain of track*.' #'*' removed from right side of the string	

19	strip()	strip( ) function returns a copy of the string after removing the specified character /characters from the beginning as well as from the end of the string, if they exist. If the parameter is not provided, then leading and trailing whitespaces are removed	string.strip('str')

	Example:	>>> A=" train on track "
		>>> A.strip()
		'train on track' #spaces at the beginning as well as the end removed
		
		>>> A="ttrain on track"
		>>> A.strip('tk')
		'rain on trac' #if either 't' or 'k' appears either on the left or right side of the string then it is removed.
		
		>>> A="train on track"
		>>> A.strip('t')
		'rain on track' #'t' present either on left or right side of the string removed.
		
		>>> A='**.ttrain of track.**'
		>>> A.strip('*.')
		'ttrain of track' #if either '*' or '.' appears on either side of the string, it is removed
		
		>>> A='*.*ttrain of track*.**'
		>>> A.strip('*')
		'.*ttrain of track*.' #'*' removed from either side of the string	

20	replace()	replace( ) function returns a copy of the string after replacing 'old' string with 'new' string. It also allows us to specify the number of replacements to be done. If not specified, then all the 'old' strings are replaced with 'new'	string.replace('old','new',count='no of replacements from left side')

<table>
<tr><td></td><td>Examples</td><td colspan="2">>>>A="One little two little three little cups"
>>>print(A.replace('little','big'))
One big two big three big cups #all replacements done

>>>print(A.replace('little','big',1))
One big two little three little cups #only 1 replacement done

>>>print(A.replace('little','BIG',2))
One BIG two BIG three little cups #2 replacements done

>>>print(A.replace('LITTLE','big',1))
One little two little three little cups #No replacement done</td></tr>
<tr><td>21</td><td>join()</td><td>This function takes an iterable as an argument in the form of a string. It concatenates the string with the elements of the iterable.
Note that if the iterable contains a non-string value then the exception is raised.</td><td>string.join(iter-able)</td></tr>
<tr><td></td><td>Examples:</td><td colspan="2">>>>A.join()
TypeError #One argument compulsory

>>> A="HI"
>>> A.join("RED")
'RHIEHID' #String A concatenated with iterable string RED → R+HI+E+HI+D → RHIEHID

>>> A=" HI "
>>> A.join("RED")
'R HI E HI D' #String A (this time with spaces) concatenated with iterable string RED → R+ HI +E+ HI +D → R HI E HI D

>>>A=" Present "
>>> print(A.join(("Nisha","Vibha","Kusum")))
'Nisha Present Vibha Present Kusum'
#Here the iterable has 3 elements and hence the result is Nisha+ Present +Vibha+ Present +Kusum

>>>B=" Present\n"
>>>print(B.join(("Nisha","Vibha","Kusum")))
Nisha Present
Vibha Present
Kusum
#Because of '\n' in string B, the like break appears after 'Present' and hence the above result</td></tr>
</table>

22	partition()	This function searches for a specified string and returns a **tuple** of three elements. The first element is the string before the specified string. The second element is the specified string and the third element is the string after the specified string.	string.partition('str')

	Examples	>>> A="We should work together"
		>>> A.partition("We")
		('', 'We', ' should work together') #'We' found so it's the second element. No string before 'We', so the first element is blank string. Everything after 'We' till the end is the third element of the tuple.
		
		>>> A.partition("WE")
		('We should work together', '', '') #'WE' is not found as Python is case sensitive, so second and third elements are blank strings and the rest of the string is first element
		
		>>> A.partition("work")
		('We should ', 'work', ' together') #'work' is present in the string, so all characters before it will be the first element, and all characters after 'work' will be the third element and 'work' is the second element.
		
		>>> A.partition("together")
		('We should work ', 'together', '')#All characters before 'together' is first element, 'together' is second element and since nothing is left so blank string is the third element.	

23	split()	This function is one of the most important and frequently used functions of string. Using this function, the string is divided into a **list** of strings based on the given separator. If the separator is not provided then the string is divided on the occurrence of a space. Note: the character used in split doesn't appear in the list.	str.split('separator', 'max no of splits') Max no of splits specifies the maximum no of times split will occur
	Examples	>>>A="this is split function" >>>print(A.split()) ['this','is','split','function'] #The words are split into a list of strings on the basis of space. >>>print(A.split(' ',2)) ['this','is','split function']	

		#2 specifies that a maximum of 2 splits of spaces will occur. This means this is split function"
		split-1 split-2
		`>>>print(A.split('is'))`
		`['th', ' ' , 'split function']`
		`#'is' occurs twice in the string, so`
		this is split function
		split-1 split-2
		`>>>print(A.split('i',3))`
		`['th','s ', 's spl', t function']`
		
		`#To display the words in a string #in different lines`
		
		`A=input("Enter a string")`
		`for i in A.split():`
		`  print(i)`

Example1: To Count and display the number of vowels, consonants, uppercase, lowercase characters in string.

```
Name=input("Enter a string")
vow=con=upper=lower=total=dig=spchar=0
for i in Name:
    if i.isalpha()==True:
        if i in "AEIOUaeiou":
            vow+=1
        else:
            con+=1
        if i.isupper()==True:
            upper+=1
        else:
            lower+=1
    elif i.isdigit()==True:
        dig+=1
    else:
        spchar+=1
print("Total Characters :",len(Name))
```

```
print("Total Consonants :",con)
print("Total Vowels :",vow)
print("Total Uppercase letters :",upper)
print("Total lowercase letters :",lower)
print("Total Digits :",dig)
print("Total Special Characters :",spchar)
```

```
Enter a stringAnyone can Learn Programming. It's like counting 123
Total Characters : 52
Total Consonants : 25
Total Vowels : 15
Total Uppercase letters : 4
Total lowercase letters : 36
Total Digits : 3
Total Special Characters : 9
```

Example2: To Count and display the number of words in a string. Also convert all letters in uppercase and display the string

```
Name=input("Enter a string")
words=Name.split()
print("Total Words :",len(words))
print("String in uppercase",Name.upper(),sep="\n")
```

```
Enter a stringThats an awesome Program
Total Words : 4
String in uppercase
THATS AN AWESOME PROGRAM
```

Summary

1. Strings are the series of characters stored in a sequence within single, double quotes or triple quotes.
2. Concatenation means combining 2 or more strings. Concatenation is possible using '+' (plus) sign. Concatenation is possible only between strings.
3. We can repeat a strings by multiplying string with an integer, using asterisk (*).
4. There are two membership operators 'in' and 'not in'. They are used to find a substring in a given string (when used with string)
5. Slicing is a feature which allows you to extract a part of the string using the index numbers.
6. The process of extracting every character from a string using a loop is called traversing.
7. `len()` function finds the length of the string.
8. `capitalize()` function returns a string after converting the first letter of the string to uppercase and rest of the letters to lowercase.

9. `title()` function returns a string after converting the first letter of every word in uppercase.
10. `lower()` function displays the string after converting all the letters of the string in lowercase.
11. `upper()` function displays the string after converting all the letters of the string in uppercase.
12. `count()` function counts and displays the total number of occurence of a substring in a string.
13. `find()` function returns the smallest beginning index of the substring if it is found in the string.
14. `index()` function returns the smallest beginning index of the substring if it is found in the string.
15. `endswith()` function returns True if the string ends with the given substring, else it returns False.
16. `startswith()` function returns True if the string starts with the given substring, else it returns False.
17. `isalnum()` function returns True if all the characters in the string are either alphabets (A-Z,a-z) or digits (0-9) or their combination else it returns False.
18. `isalpha()` returns True if the characters in a string are alphabets only (A-Z, a-z) else it returns False.
19. `isdigit()` function returns True if the characters in a string are digits only (0-9) else it returns False.
20. `islower()` returns True if all the characters in the string are in lowercase (a-z) else it returns False.
21. `isupper()` returns True if all the characters in the string are in uppercase (A-Z) else it returns False.
22. `isspace()` returns True if all the characters in a string are whitespace characters else it returns False
23. `lstrip()` function returns a copy of the string after removing the specified character/ characters from the left side of the string, if they exist.
24. `rstrip()` function returns a copy of the string after removing the specified character/characters from the right side of the string, if they exist.
25. `strip()` function returns a copy of the string after removing the specified character /characters from the beginning as well as from the end of the string, if they exist.
26. `replace()` function returns a copy of the string after replacing 'old' string with 'new' string. It also allows us to specify the number of replacements to be done.
27. `join()` function concatenates the string with the elements of the iterable.
28. `partition()` function searches for a specified string and returns a tuple of three elements.
29. `split()` function is used to divide the string into a list of strings based on the given separator.

Programs to practice

1. Accept a string and print the number of characters in each word. Example If the string is "Welcome to the world of programming", then the result should be

```
Welcome : 7
to : 2
```

```
the : 3
world : 5
of : 2
programming : 11
```

2. Accept two strings A and B and form a new string, which is the combination of first, middle and the last characters of strings A and B. For example, `A="Great" B="Work"`

   `NewString="GWertk"`

3. Accept description of product in the form of a sentence. Display the occurrence of a word "the" in the sentence. The case sensitivity should be ignored.

   For example: if

   `A="Toothpaste comes in a variety of colors and flavors, intended to encourage use of the product. The three most common flavorants are peppermint, spearmint, and wintergreen."`

   `Count: 2`

4. Accept a string, which is the combination of lowercase and uppercase letters. Form a new string with lowercase letters in the beginning and uppercase letters in the end.

   For example: `A="ThisGReatwORk", the Newstring: hiseatwkTGROR`

5. Accept a string from the user and replace all white spaces with an asterisk.
6. Accept a string and display its reverse using a loop.
7. Accept a string and display the work with the maximum length. For example If the string is "Welcome to the world of programming", then the result should be 'programming'
8. Accept a string and print all the words in reverse. For example is the string `A="Python Programming Language"`. Then the result should be :

   ```
   nohtyP
   gnimmargorP
   egaugnaL
   ```

9. Accept a string and Replace all instances of a substring 'in' with 'IN' in a string
10. Accept a string and remove all the special characters and digits, if any, except space from the string. For example, if string is **`A="If you %%cannot be &123a poet, then be a poem"`**, then the final string should be **`A="If you cannot be a poet then be a poem"`**.
11. Write a program to accept a string and remove the word 'the' from it and print the modified string.
12. Write a program to accept two string and check if the two strings are Anagrams or not. Two words are said to be Anagrams if the letters of one word can be rearranged to form the other word. For example, madam and adamm are anagrams of each other.

? EXERCISE

Multiple Choice Questions

1. `str = "POSITIVE"`

   `print (str[1:3])`

   a. `SO` b. `PO` c. `OS` d. `IT`

2. Which operator is used to concatenate two strings?

   a. + b. * c. ^ d. .

3. What will the following commands do?

   `S = "California Video Library"`

   `print(s[::-1])`

   a. Print the String S as it is. b. Prints the last character of the string S

   c. Prints the String S in Reverse d. None of the above

4. For checking the palindrome of a string using slice, which of the following is correct?

   `Text = "MalayalaM"`

   a. `text[:]==text[-1]` b. `text[:]==text[:-1]`

   c. `text[:]==text[::-1]` d. `None of the above`

5. Which function is used to convert each word in a string into capital letter and the rest of them in small?

   a. `title()` b. `capitalize()` c. `capitalise()` d. `capital()`

6. `s = "The most important thing is to respect"`

   `x = s.split()`

   `print(x[-3] + " " + x[-1] + " " + x[2] )`

   a. respect is important b. important is respect

   c. is respect important d. thing is to

7. `string = 'We must ask madam'`

   `print(string[-5:],end="#")`

   `print(string[0:-14],end="#")`

   `print(string[5:2:-1],end="#")`

   a. madam We sum# b. madam# sum#We

   c. #madam#We #sum# d. madam#We #sum#

8. What will be the output of the following Python statement?

   `>>>"Coolday"[2:]`

   a. olday b. Cool c. day d. oold

9. `'It is a great work'.split(' ',3)`
   a. `['It', 'is', 'a', 'great work']`
   b. `['It is', 'a', 'great work']`
   c. `['It', 'is a', 'great work']`
   d. `['It', 'is', 'a', 'great', 'work']`
10. What will be the output of the following Python code?

```
Ex = "snow world"
    Ex[3] = 's'
    print(Ex)
```

   a. snow b. snow world c. Error d. snos world
11. What will be the output of the following Python code?

```
Data = "Well Done"
    print(Data.find("e"))
```

   a. -1 b. 1 c. 0 d. Error
12. What will be the output of the **"hello" +1+2+3?**
   a. hello123 b. hello c. Error d. hello6
13. Say **Data="Good Day"** what will be the return value of **type(Data)**?
   a. int b. bool c. str d. String
14. What will be the output of the following Python code?

```
print("United NATION S".capitalize())
```

   a. `UNITED NATION S` b. `uNITED nATION s`
   c. `United Nation S` d. `United nation s`
15. What will be the output of the following Python code?

```
print("MALAYALAM".count('LA'))
```

   a. 2 b. 0 c. 1 d. None of the mentioned
16. What will be the output of the following Python code?

```
print("MALAYALAM".count('LA',-7,-2))
```

   a. 2 b. 0 c. 1 d. Error
17. What will be the output of the following Python code?

```
print('TRUE'.isalnum())
```

   a. True b. False c. None d. Error
18. What will be the output of the following Python code snippet?

```
print('\n'.isspace())
```

   a. True b. False c. None d. Error
19. What will be the output of the following Python code?

```
print('XMas is coming'.partition('g'))
```

a. `('XMas is comin', 'g')`
b. `('XMas', 'is coming')`
c. `('XMas' 'g',is comin')`
d. `('XMas is comin', 'g', '')`

20.
```
s1 = "Good"
s2 = "Good"
print(id(s1) == id(s2),s1>s2)
```

a. `True False`
b. `True True`
c. `False False`
d. `False True`

10 Lists

Introduction to List

List is another iterable object in python which can store multiple values of various data types. We will understand lists by first knowing the important features of a list.

1. List is a heterogeneous collection of data, which can store data of all types.
2. The values of Lists are enclosed within a square bracket.

```
#List declaration
L=[]
L1=[10,30,60]
L2=["Python","C","Java","HTML"]
L3=["Primary",200,98.9]
```

3. Duplicate values are allowed in a list.

```
L1=[10,30,10,30,10,10]
```

4. Each value in a list is called an element and each element of a list can be extracted using its index number. The index number starts from 0.

```
L1=[10,30,60]
print(L1[0])
print(L1[2])
```

```
10
60
```

5. List is a mutable Python object, where the values are allowed to change.

```
L1=[10,30,60]
print(id(L1))
L1[1]+=100
print(id(L1))
print(L1)
```

```
140663120432320
140663120432320
[10, 130, 60]
```

6. To know the total number of elements in a list, len() function is used.

```
L2=["Python","C","Java","HTML"]
print(len(L2))
#4
```

7. The elements of a list can be any other data structure like string/tuple/list/dictionary etc

```
L=[[0,2,4],[1,3,5],['a','b','c']]
L=[(1,2,3),"data",{1:12,2:23}]
```

List indexing

Since a list is an iterable object, each element in a list has an index number using which it can be extracted.

```
L=[1,'Python',3.9.5,'Language',17]
```

0	1	2	3	4
1	**Python**	**3.9.5**	**Language**	**17**
-5	-4	-3	-2	-1

Each element in the list has a positive index as well as negative index number, using which the element can be extracted. The index number is provided in a square brackets as shown below:

```
>>>print(L)         # [1,'Python',3.9.5,'Language',17]
>>>print(L[3])      # Language
>>>print(L[-4])     # Python
```

Operations in Lists

Following operations are possible in this iterable object:

a. **Concatenation :** Concatenation means combining 2 or more lists. Concatenation is possible using '+' (plus) sign. Here, the second list is combined with the first to get a new list. The length of the new list will therefore be the sum of length of list 1 and list 2. Following example illustrate concatenation in lists:

Example 1

```
L1=[34,13,90,56] #Length: 4
L2=[16,89,16]    #Length: 3
L3=L1+L2 #concatenation
print (L3,len(L3),sep="\n")     #Length: 4+3=7
[34, 13, 90, 56, 16, 89, 16]
7
```

Note: Concatenation in list is possible **only** between lists.

Example 2

```
B=[5,6,7]
C=23
print(B+C)
#Error
TypeError: can only concatenate list (not "int") to list
```

Example 3

```
L1=["Mango","orange","Pineapple"]
L2=[120,60,54]
L3=L2+L1
print(L3)
[120, 60, 54, 'Mango', 'orange', 'Pineapple']
```

b. **Repetition:** Repetition in a list means repeating the element of a list specific number (N) of times. Repetition is possible when the list object is multiplied with an integer. We can repeat a list using asterisk (*). The final result is also a list. See the following example to understand repetition:

Example 1

```
L1=["Mango","orange","Pineapple"]
print(L1*2) #The list is repeated 2 times
['Mango', 'orange', 'Pineapple', 'Mango', 'orange', 'Pineapple']
```

Note that the two lists cannot be multiplied. Repetition is possible when a list is multiplied with an integer

Example 2

```
L1=["Mango","orange","Pineapple"]
print(L1*L1)
TypeError: can't multiply sequence by non-int of type 'list'
```

c. **Membership:** There are two membership operators 'in' and 'not in'. They are used to find an element in a given list.

in : The 'in' operator results True if the given value/element is found in the given list

Example 1

```
a=12
L=[1,2,12,45,12]
if a in L:
  print('Present')
else:
  print('Not Present')
```

Explanation: In the above example, the value 12 is to be searched which is present at index number 3. So the condition is True and hence Present displayed.

Output

```
Present
```

not in: Evaluates to true if the given value/element is not found in the given list

Example 2

```
A=input("Enter a character")
L=['a','e','i','o','u','A','E','I','O','U']
if A in L:
  print('It is a Vowel')
else:
  print('It is not a Vowel')

Enter a characterT
It is not a Vowel

Enter a charactere
It is a Vowel
```

a. **Slicing:** It is a feature which allows you to extract element/ elements from a list using the index numbers. The final result is also a list. To understand slicing we will refer to the following list

```
L1=[10,23,10,56,11,23,13,56]
```

0	1	2	3	4	5	6	7
10	23	10	56	11	23	13	56
-8	-7	-6	-5	-4	-3	-2	-1

There are 3 parameters which can be provided in slicing.

`List[start:end:step]`

start → specifies the beginning index number. If not provided, then it's 0.

end → specifies the ending index. If it's not provided, then it takes the length of the list (which is the count of the total number of elements in the list). The last index taken is always **end-1**

step → It is also optional. If not provided then it's taken as 1. It specifies that by how many steps the index should be jumped to display the next element. If the step provided is positive then the direction of display of the element is from left to right. If the step is negative, then the direction of display of the element is from right to left. Also, if step is negative, then start becomes len(list)-1 by default while end goes till the first element on left.

Examples with reference to above list 'L1', with explanation:

```
>>> print(L1) #List printed
```

0	1	2	3	4	5	6	7
10	23	10	56	11	23	13	56
-8	-7	-6	-5	-4	-3	-2	-1

```
>>> print(L1[:]) #Start is default 0 and end is default < len(L1)
```

0	1	2	3	4	5	6	7
10	23	10	56	11	23	13	56
-8	-7	-6	-5	-4	-3	-2	-1

```
>>> print(L1[::]) #Start is default 0 and end is default < len(L1)
```

0	1	2	3	4	5	6	7
10	23	10	56	11	23	13	56
-8	-7	-6	-5	-4	-3	-2	-1

```
>>> print(L1[1:4]) #start is 1 and end is <4, step=1 (default)
[23,10,56]
```

0	1	2	3	4	5	6	7
10	23	10	56	11	23	13	56
-8	-7	-6	-5	-4	-3	-2	-1

```
>>> print(L1[6:]) #Start is 6, end is < len(a)
[13,56]
```

0	1	2	3	4	5	6	7
10	23	10	56	11	23	13	56
-8	-7	-6	-5	-4	-3	-2	-1

```
>>>print(L1[::2]) #Start and end default, but step is 2
[10,10,11,13]
```

0	1	2	3	4	5	6	7
10	23	10	56	11	23	13	56
-8	-7	-6	-5	-4	-3	-2	-1

```
>>>print(L1[::-1])
[56,13,23,11,56,10,23,10]
```

0	1	2	3	4	5	6	7
10	23	10	56	11	23	13	56
-8	-7	-6	-5	-4	-3	-2	-1

#As step is negative, the direction of printing element is from right to left, hence reverse list printed

```
>>> print(L1[::-3])
[56, 11, 23]
```

0	1	2	3	4	5	6	7
10	23	10	56	11	23	13	56
-8	-7	-6	-5	-4	-3	-2	-1

#The step is negative, so direction is right to left. Also, every third element is printed from right to left as step=-3

```
>>> print(L1[1:8:3])
```

[23, 11, 56]

0	1	2	3	4	5	6	7
10	23	10	56	11	23	13	56
-8	-7	-6	-5	-4	-3	-2	-1

#Start =1, while end<8. step=3 will print every third element starting from index 1.

```
>>> print(L1[1:8:-1])
```

#This won't print anything as direction of printing of elements should be right to left, but the values of start and end indicate left to right direction

```
>>> print(L1[-1:-6:-1])
[56, 13, 23, 11,56]
```

0	1	2	3	4	5	6	7
10	23	10	56	11	23	13	56
-8	-7	-6	-5	-4	-3	-2	-1

#Here negative indexing is specified, so according to the index number as shown in the picture we see elements from -1 till -5 from right to left direction

```
>>> print(L1[2:-2])
[10,56,11,23]
```

0	1	2	3	4	5	6	7
10	23	10	56	11	23	13	56
-8	-7	-6	-5	-4	-3	-2	-1

#In this example, there is a combination of positive and negative indexing. Start is 2, end one less than -2 position and since the step is 1 by default and the direction of index is also from left to right, the elements as per the index are printed.

```
>>> print(L1[-4:-8:-1])
[11,56,10,23]
```

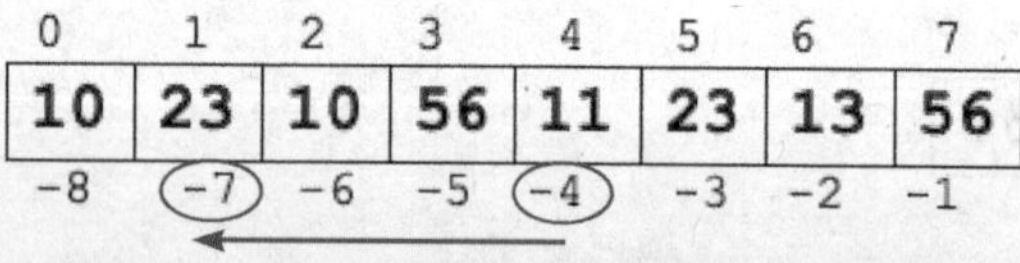

Traversing a list using loops

Since a List is an iterable object, we can reach each and every element of the list one after the other in a sequence using loops.

Two ways to traverse a list

#Here element is taken from the list L and given to i, which is printed	#Here the index is extracted using the range function and to display the element, the index is specified in square brackets with list object.

L2=["Python","C","Java","HTML"]
for i in L2:
    print(i,end='**')
 	
Python**C**Java**HTML**
	L2=["Python","C","Java","HTML"]
	for i in range(len(L2)):
	    print(i,L2[i],sep='**')
	
	0**Python
	1**C
	2**Java
	3**HTML

List Comprehension

It is another way to create a list from the existing list or create a new list based on a criteria. It is considered a faster as well as smart way to use loops to create lists. Following example will make it more clear:

```
>>> a=[i for i in range(1,10,2)]
>>> print(a)
[1, 3, 5, 7, 9] #List of odd numbers created
```

```
#creating a list of all multiples of 7 from an existing list L
>>>L=[67,3,66,72,49,35,12,14,90,84,91,51]
>>>S=[i for i in L if i%7==0]
>>>print(S)
[49, 35, 14, 84, 91]
```

```
#Creating  a list of vowels present in the Name N
N=input("Enter a name")
S=[i for i in N if i in "AEIOUaeiou"]
print(S)
```

```
Enter a nameShabana Azmi
['a', 'a', 'a', 'A', 'i']
```

Interesting thing to know:

You can accept elements in a list using list comprehension also in the following manner:

```
x = [int(x) for x in input("Enter multiple value separated by space: ").split()]
print("List elements are: ", x)
```

Output:

```
Enter multiple value separatd by space: 45
List elements are:  [45]
>>>
======== RESTART: /Users/sarikakaushal/Documents/tr
Enter multiple value separatd by space: 23 55 12 78
List elements are:  [23, 55, 12, 78]

Enter multiple value separatd by space: 45
List elements are:  [45]
>>>
======== RESTART: /Users/sarikakaushal/Documents/tr
Enter multiple value separatd by space: 23 55 12 78
List elements are:  [23, 55, 12, 78]
```

Note: If the conditions are too long and complicated, then we should avoid using list comprehension else the code appears complicated.

Example 1: To find the minimum and maximum element from the list.

```
A=[3,6,12,56,90,23,2]
Ma=Mi=A[0]
for i in range(1,len(A)):
    if Ma<A[i]:
        Ma=A[i]
    if Mi>A[i]:
        Mi=A[i]
print("Maximum : ",Ma, "Minimum :",Mi)
```

```
Maximum :  90 Minimum : 2
```

Example 2: To find and display the mean of numeric values stored in a list L.

```
L=[3,6,12,56,90,23,2]
Mean=0
for i in range(len(L)):
  Mean+=L[i]
print("Mean :",Mean/len(L))
```

```
Mean : 27.428571428571427
```

Note:

1. It is important to note that if we copy a list in another object, then the changes made in the original list will be seen in another object also. This is because when we duplicate a list then it means the two objects with different names point to the same address where the elements of the list are stored. So, changes are reflected back. In other words a clone if original list is made

```
>>> L=[45,67,90]
>>> L1=L                #List L copied to L1
>>> print(id(L))
140535619898624
```

```
>>> print(id(L))
140535619898624
>>> L[1]+=34           #Second element of List L changed
>>> print(L)
[45, 101, 90]
>>> print(L1)          #Changes are seen when L1 is accessed
[45, 101, 90]
```

2. If you make a copy of the list using the list function, then the exact copy is made but will be independent of each other. This is shown in the example below:

```
>>> L=[45,67,90]
>>> L1=list(L)            #List L copied to L1 using list()
>>> print(id(L))          #id different
140535619904000

>>> print(id(L1))         #id different
140535619904320

>>> L[1]+=100
>>> print(L)
[45, 167, 90]

>>> print(L1)
[45, 67, 90]              #Changes are not reflected in L1, when L is changed
```

Another way to make exact copy but independent of the original List, we can use copy() function as shown below:

```
L=[45,67,90]
L1=L.copy()        #List L copied to L1 using copy()
print(id(L))
print(id(L1))           #id different
L[1]+=100
print(L)
print(L1)
```

Built in Functions

<table>
<tr><th></th><th>Function</th><th>Description</th><th>Syntax</th></tr>
<tr><td>1</td><td>len()</td><td>This function finds the length of the list, which means it returns the total number of elements in a list.</td><td>len(List)</td></tr>
<tr><td></td><td>Example:</td><td colspan="2">L=[12,23,44,"One"]
print(len(L))
4
print(len([2,2,4,5,7,9]))
6
S=len(L)+ 2
print(S)
6

W=len(L*3)
print(W)
12 #Here L*3 will first result in
[12, 23, 44, 'One', 12, 23, 44, 'One', 12, 23, 44, 'One']
Hence the length 12</td></tr>
<tr><td>2</td><td>list()</td><td>It converts an iterable object into a list. If no parameter is provided then a blank list is created</td><td>list(iterable)</td></tr>
<tr><td></td><td>Example:</td><td colspan="2">>>> S="Hello"
>>> L=list(S)
>>> print(L)
['H', 'e', 'l', 'l', 'o'] #Each character in a string becomes an element of list

>>> T=("Y","R","G8")
>>> L1=list(T)
>>> print(L1)
['Y', 'R', 'G8'] #Tuple can be converted to a list

>>> D={"Y":"you","R":"are","G8":"great"}
>>> L2=list(D)
>>> print(L2)
['Y', 'R', 'G8'] #By default only the key becomes the elements of the list

>>> L3=list()
>>> print(L3)
[ ] #Blank list created</td></tr>
</table>

<table>
<tr><td></td><td></td><td colspan="2"><code>>>> L=list(12)</code>
<code>TypeError: 'int' object is not iterable</code></td></tr>
<tr><td>3</td><td>append()</td><td><ul><li>This function is used to insert an element in a list.</li><li>There is no other way to insert an element in the list.</li><li>Single element is inserted using this function and thus every time this function is used, the length of the list is increased by one.</li></ul></td><td>list.append(-object)</td></tr>
<tr><td></td><td>Example</td><td colspan="2"><code>>>> L=[]</code>
<code>>>> L.append(10)</code>
<code>>>> L.append("Value")</code>
<code>>>> L.append(78.90)</code>
<code>>>> print(L)</code>
<code>[10, 'Value', 78.9] #One value at a time is inserted</code>

<code>>>> L.append(['*','&'])</code>
<code>>>> print(L)</code>
<code>[10, 'Value', 78.9, ['*', '&']] #list is passed as a single element</code>

<code>>>> L.append((1,2))</code>
<code>>>> print(L)</code>
<code>[10, 'Value', 78.9, ['*', '&'], (1, 2)] #Tuple can also be passed as a single element</code>

<code>>>> L.append(11,34)</code>
<code>TypeError: list.append() takes exactly one argument (2 given)</code></td></tr>
<tr><td>4</td><td>extend()</td><td>This function is used to extend the list by adding the iterable provided as a parameter. The list with which this function is used is modified. The length of the modified list is increased by the count of elements in the iterable.</td><td>list.extend(iterable)</td></tr>
<tr><td></td><td>Example</td><td colspan="2"><code>>>>L=[10,12,15]</code>
<code>>>> L.extend("DATA")</code>
<code>>>> print(L)</code>
<code>[10, 12, 15, 'D', 'A', 'T', 'A']</code>
<code>#string is an iterable and each character is stored as an element. Length of the list L is increased by 4 and hence the length of L becomes 7.</code>

<code>>>> L=[10,12,15]</code>
<code>>>> L.extend([89,98])</code>
<code>>>> print(L)</code></td></tr>
</table>

		`[10, 12, 15, 89, 98]`
		#List is an iterable and thus 2 elements are added to the list L, thus elements increased from 3 to 5.
		
		`>>> L=[10,12,15]`
		`>>> L.extend((89,98))`
		`>>> print(L)`
		`[10, 12, 15, 89, 98]`
		#Tuple is an iterable and thus 2 elements are added to the list L, thus elements increased from 3 to 5.
		
		`>>> L=[10,12,15]`
		`>>> L.extend({"G":1,"O":2,"D":3})`
		`>>> print(L)`
		`[10, 12, 15, 'G', 'O', 'D']`
		#Dictionary is an iterable and by default its keys are added as elements, thus elements increased from 3 to 6.
		
		`>>> L=[10,12,15]`
		`>>> L.extend(10)`
		`TypeError: 'int' object is not iterable`
		#The parameter allowed is iterable not object.	

5	insert()	This function is used to insert an element at a given index number. ***Note:*** ▪ If the index is positive but beyond the range, then the element is inserted at the end of the list ▪ If the index is negative but beyond the range, then the element is inserted at the beginning of the list. ▪ insert( ) function inserts one lament at a time and thus the length of the list is increased by 1.	List.insert(index-,Value)

	Example	`>>> L=[10,30,50,22,78,89]`
		`>>> L.insert(100,2)`
		`>>> print(L)`
		`[10, 30, 50, 22, 78, 89, 2]`
		#index 100 is out of range and since 100 is a positive number, 2 is inserted at the end of the list.
		
		`>>> L.insert(-100,13)`	

		>>> print(L)
		[13, 10, 30, 50, 22, 78, 89, 2]
		#index -100 is out of range and since -100 is a negative number, 13 is inserted in the beginning of the list.
		>>> L=[12,14,16,18,20,22,24]
		>>> L.insert(-12,100)
		>>> print(L)
		[100, 12, 14, 16, 18, 20, 22, 24]
		#index -12 is out of range and since -12 is a negative number, 100 is inserted in the beginning of the list.
		
		>>> L.insert(100,90)
		>>> print(L)
		[100, 12, 14, 16, 18, 20, 22, 24, 90]
		#index 100 is out of range and since 100 is a positive number, 90 is inserted at the end of the list.
		
		>>> L.insert(2,"one")
		>>> print(L)
		[100, 12, 'one', 14, 16, 18, 20, 22, 24, 90]
		#string "one" is inserted at index 2 and all the elements from index 2 till the end are shifted to the right side.
		
		>>> L.insert(-1,"two")
		>>> print(L)
		[100, 12, 'one', 14, 16, 18, 20, 22, 24, 'two', 90]
		#string "two" is inserted at index -1 and the element 90 which was at -1 index is therefore shifted to the right.
		
		>>> L.insert(-4,"three")
		>>> print(L)
		[100, 12, 'one', 14, 16, 18, 20, 'three', 22, 24, 'two', 90]
		#string "three" is inserted at index -4 and all the elements from -4 index onwards (i.e 22, 24, 'two',90) are therefore shifted to the right.
		
		>>> L=[10,30,50,22,78,89]
		>>> L.insert(2,("abra","dabra"))
		>>> print(L)

		[10, 30, ('abra', 'dabra'), 50, 22, 78, 89] #Tuple is inserted as a single element at index number 2 and all the elements from index 2 till the end are shifted to the right.	
6	count()	This function returns the number of occurrences of a value in a list. If the value is absent in the list then 0 is returned. This function takes only one parameter	List. count(value)

		>>> L=[12,13,14,15,(12,13),14,13,15]
		>>> print(L.count(12))
		1
		# 12 appears once. The second 12 at index 5 is not a single element, it's a tuple (12,13), so it's not included.
		>>> print(L.count(13))
		2
		# 13 appears twice. 13 at index 5 is not a single element, it's a tuple (12,13), so it's not included.
		>>> print(L.count(10))
		0
		#10 is not present in the list and hence 0.
		>>> print(L.count((12,13)))
		1
		#(12,13) appears at index 5 as a single element and is present only once. Hence the function returns 1.
		>>> print(L.count([12,13]))
		0
		#(12,13) appears at index 5 as a single element but it is a tuple not a list. Hence the function returns 0.
		>>> print(L.count(12,13))
		TypeError: **list.count() takes exactly one argument (2 given)**	

7	index()	▪ index( ) function returns the beginning index of the first occurrence of value found in the list. ▪ Generates 'ValueError' exception if the value is not found. ▪ The start and the end index number of the elements for search can be provided. ▪ If not provided then the whole list is searched.	List. index(Value, start,end) #The searching is from start index till end-1 index

<table>
<tr><td></td><td>Example:</td><td colspan="2">

```
>>> L=[1,2,3,5,2,11,6,5]
>>> print(L.index(5))
3
#5 is present at two locations, 3 and at 7. But the first occurrence is 3 and hence the result.
>>> print(L.index(5,0,3))
ValueError: 5 is not in list
>>> print(L.index(5,0,4))
3
#5 is present at once at location 3 from index 0 and 4-1. Hence the result.

>>> print(L.index(6))
6
#6 is present at location 6.
```

</td></tr>
<tr><td>8</td><td>remove()</td><td>Removes the first occurrence of the value, if found. If the value is not found then the function raises ValueError. The parameter it takes is value.</td><td>List.
remove(value)</td></tr>
<tr><td></td><td></td><td colspan="2">

```
>>> L=[1,2,3,5,2,11,6,5,(8,9)]
>>> L.remove(5)
>>> print(L)
[1, 2, 3, 2, 11, 6, 5, (8, 9)]
# The first occurrence of 5 is at location 3, so it is removed.

>>> L.remove(66)
ValueError: list.remove(x): x not in list

>>> L.remove((8,9))
>>> print(L)
[1, 2, 3, 2, 11, 6, 5]
#The element to be removed is a Tuple and is removed


>>> L.remove(2)
>>> print(L)
[1, 3, 2, 11, 6, 5]
# The first occurrence of 2 was at index 1, which is removed and hence the result.
```

</td></tr>
</table>

<table>
<tr><td>9</td><td>pop()</td><td><ul><li>Removes the value at the provided index number and returns the value, if found.</li><li>If the index number doesn't exist then the function raises IndexError.</li><li>The parameter it takes is index.</li><li>Note, if the index is not provided then the last element is deleted and its value is returned.</li><li>Index provided can be positive or negative</li></ul></td><td>List.
pop(index)</td></tr>
<tr><td></td><td>Example</td><td>>>> L=[67,34,"Python",888.99,"Programs",(10,11)]
>>> print(L.pop(3))
888.99
#Value at index 3 is 888.99, which is returned and printed

>>> T=L.pop()
>>> print(T)
(10, 11)
#Since no parameter is provided, the last index is deleted and its value is stored in the object T, which is further printed.

>>> print(L.pop(8))
IndexError: pop index out of range

>>> print(L)
[67, 34, 'Python', 'Programs']
>>> print(L.pop(-2))
Python
#Second element from the right is deleted and printed

>>> print(L)
[67, 34, 'Programs']</td><td></td></tr>
<tr><td>10</td><td>re-
verse()</td><td>This function is used to reverse the elements of the list. The original list is modified. The function doesn't take any parameter.</td><td>List.re-
verse()</td></tr>
<tr><td></td><td></td><td>>>> L=[67,"one",55,12,"two",98.4,"three"]
>>> print(L)
[67, 'one', 55, 12, 'two', 98.4, 'three']
>>> print(id(L))</td><td></td></tr>
</table>

		140315847811776
		
		`>>> L.reverse()`
		`>>> print(L)`
		['three', 98.4, 'two', 12, 55, 'one', 67]
		`>>> print(id(L))`
		140315847811776
		#id is same indicating that the List is mutable object
		
		`>>> L=[67,(1,2),[6,33,88],"two"]`
		`>>> L.reverse()`
		`>>> print(L)`
		['two', [6, 33, 88], (1, 2), 67]	

11	sort()	▪ This function arranges the elements of the list either in ascending or in descending order. ▪ By default, the list is sorted in ascending order. ▪ To sort the list in descending order, `reverse=True` parameter is used. ▪ The original List is modified. ▪ Note that the sort function will work with data of similar type, i.e. all numbers or all strings. For heterogeneous data, function will generate error	List.sort(reverse=True)

	Example	`>>> L=[56,23,78,44,90,12]`
		`>>> L.sort()`
		`>>> print(L)`
		`[12, 23, 44, 56, 78, 90]`
		#numeric values are sorted in ascending order by default
		
		`>>> L.sort(reverse=True)`
		`>>> print(L)`
		`[90, 78, 56, 44, 23, 12]`
		#numeric values are sorted in descending order
		
		`>>> L=["Bhavna","Manya","Anika","Charu"]`
		`>>> L.sort()`
		`>>> print(L)`
		`['Anika', 'Bhavna', 'Charu', 'Manya']`	

		#Values are sorted in alphabetical order. Note that the ASCII values of uppercase letters are smaller than of lowercase letters. So
		>>> L=['Anika', 'anika','Bhavna', 'Charu', 'Manya','charu']
		>>> L.sort()
		>>> print(L)
		['Anika', 'Bhavna', 'Charu', 'Manya', 'anika', 'charu']
		
		>>> L=['three', 98.4, 'two', 12, 55, 'one', 67]
		>>> L.sort()
		TypeError: '<' not supported between instances of 'float' and 'str'
		
		>>> L=[67,(4,2,6),(2,67,1),90]
		>>> L.sort()
		TypeError: '<' not supported between instances of 'tuple' and 'int'
		
		>>> L=[(6,7.4),(4,2,6),(2,67,1),(9,0,8)]
		>>> L.sort()
		>>> print(L)
		[(2, 67, 1), (4, 2, 6), (6, 7.4), (9, 0, 8)]
		#Since all elements are tuples, they can be sorted. The first element in each tuple is compared and sorted. If two tuples have the same first element then the second element is compared and sorted and so on.
		>>> L=[(2,5,3),(2,3),(2,5),(3,2,5),(3,2,4)]
		>>> L.sort()
		>>> print(L)
		[(2, 3), (2, 5), (2, 5, 3), (3, 2, 4), (3, 2, 5)]
		
		>>> L=[(6,7.4),(4,2,6),[2,67,1],(9,0,8)]
		>>> L.sort()
		TypeError: '<' not supported between instances of 'list' and 'tuple'	

12	sorted()	▪ This function returns a new list, which contains elements arranged in ascending order by default. ▪ To sort in descending order, reverse=True parameter is used. ▪ The original List is **not** modified.	sorted(iterable,reverse=True)

		▪ Note that the sorted function will work with data of similar type, i.e. all numbers or all strings. For heterogeneous data, function will generate error	

		`>>> L=[78, 45, 90.56, 22]`
		`>>> print(sorted(L))`
		`[22, 45, 78, 90.56]`
		
		`>>> L=[(2, 67, 1), (4, 2, 6), (6, 7.4), (9, 0, 8)]`
		`>>> print(sorted(L,reverse=True))`
		`[(9, 0, 8), (6, 7.4), (4, 2, 6), (2, 67, 1)]`
		
		`>>> A=(67,23,56,77)`
		`>>> print(sorted(A))`
		`[23, 56, 67, 77]`
		
		`>>> A={23:8,5:34,6:67}`
		`>>> print(sorted(A))`
		`[5, 6, 23]`
		`#The keys are taken from dictionary to form the sorted list`
		
		`>>> A=(67,23,56,77)`
		`>>> print(sorted(A,reverse=True))`
		`[77, 67, 56, 23]`
		
		`>>> A="SCHOOL"`
		`>>> print(sorted(A))`
		`['C', 'H', 'L', 'O', 'O', 'S']`
		`# If the iterable is a string then the each character becomes the element of the list, sorted alphabetically in ascending order, by default`	

13	`min()`	It returns the minimum value from a given list. The data type of elements in the list should be same.	`min(iterable)`

		`>>> L=['Anika', 'anika','Bhavna', 'Charu', 'Manya','charu']`
		`>>> print(min(L))`
		`Anika`
		`# This is because the ASCII value of "A" is smallest amongst all`
		
		`>>> L=[67,34,61,35,12,90]`	

		>>> print(min(L))
		12
		
		>>> L=[(2, 67, 1), (4, 2, 6), (6, 7.4), (9, 0, 8)]
		>>> print(min(L))
		(2, 67, 1)
		#The first element is smallest in all the tuples in the list
		
		>>> L=[67,"one",55,12,"two",98.4,"three"]
		>>> min(L)
		TypeError: '<' not supported between instances of 'str' and 'int'	

14	max()	It returns the maximum value from a given list. The data type of elements in the list should be the same.	max(iterable)

		>>> L=['Anika', 'anika','Bhavna', 'Charu', 'Manya','charu']
		>>> print(max(L))
		charu
		# This is because the ASCII value of "c" is largest amongst all
		
		>>> L=[67,34,61,35,12,90]
		>>> print(max(L))
		90
		
		>>> L=[(2, 67, 1), (4, 2, 6), (6, 7.4), (9, 0, 8)]
		>>> print(max(L))
		(9,0,8)
		#The first element is smallest in all the tuples in the list
		
		>>> L=[67,"one",55,12,"two",98.4,"three"]
		>>> max(L)
		TypeError: '<' not supported between instances of 'str' and 'int'
		
		#We can also provide multiple values to find the maximum
		>>> max(12,78,45,22)
		78	

15	sum()	▪ It returns the sum of numbers in the List. It works only for numeric values. ▪ It has two parameters, iterable and start ▪ It returns the sum of start value + sum of elements of iterable. ▪ If start is not provided, then it's taken as 0.	sum(iterable,start)

		>>> L=[78,45,90.56,22]
		>>> print(sum(L))
		235.56
		
		>>> print(sum(L,10))
		245.56
		#235.56 added with 10
		
		>>> print(sum(L,40))
		275.56
		#235.56 added with 40
		
		>>> print(sum(L,10.5))
		246.06
		#235.56 added with 10.5
		
		>>> print(sum(L,[23,45]))
		#Error	

Nested list

When a list has many other sublists as its elements, it is called a nested list. We need to understand how each element in a nested list can be accessed and modified too as the list is an iterable object.

A=[[4,1,7,1],[3,11,21],[8,33,9],99,88]

To access each element of the list, if we use the loop, we will get the following result:

```
A=[[4,1,7,1],[3,11,21],[8,33,9],99,88]
for i in range(len(A)):
  print("A[",i,"]=",A[i])
```

Output:

```
A[ 0 ]= [4, 1, 7, 1]
A[ 1 ]= [3, 11, 21]
A[ 2 ]= [8, 33, 9]
A[ 3 ]= 99
A[ 4 ]= 88
```

To understand the output further, let us understand it diagrammatically.

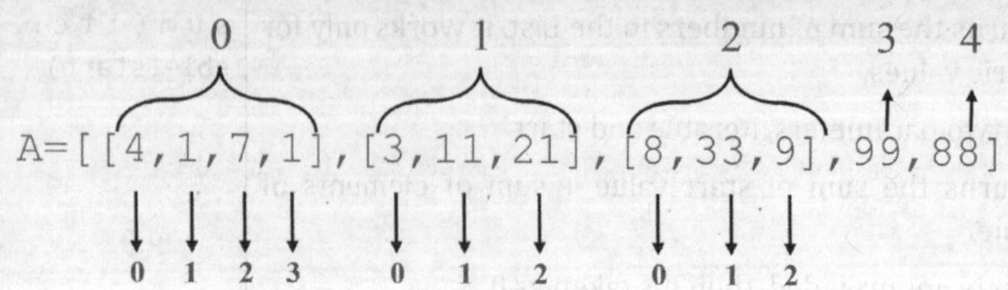

The above list has 5 elements from 0 to 4.

The first element is [4,1,7,1]

The second element is [3,11,21]

The third element is [8,33,9]

Fourth and fifth elements are 99 and 88 respectively

Each element of the first element can further be accessed using its respected index number.

A

0				1			2			3	4
0	1	2	3	0	1	2	0	1	2	99	88
4	1	7	1	3	11	21	8	33	9		

So A[0][0] → 4

A[0][1] → 1

A[0][2] → 7

A[0][3] → 1

A[1][0] → 3

A[1][1] → 11

A[1][2] → 21

A[2][0] → 8

A[2][1] → 33

A[2][2] → 9

A[3] → 99

A[4] → 88

#Program to store elements in a nested list and print then using a single loop. (Assuming each sublist further has 3 elements)

```
L=[[3,1,2],[2,7,8],[9,4,5],[6,8,9]]
for i,j,k in L:
  print(i,j,k,sep=' , ')
```

If a nested list has same number of element in the sub list, then this is another way to access the element. Three variables i,j,k as three elements in the sublist

```
3 , 1 , 2
2 , 7 , 8
9 , 4 , 5
6 , 8 , 9
```

#Program to display the type of each element of a list

```
L=[10,34,[12,90],(90,56,12),"Hello",["one","two","three"]]
for i in L:
  print(i, "is a",type(i))
```

```
10 is a <class 'int'>
34 is a <class 'int'>
[12, 90] is a <class 'list'>
(90, 56, 12) is a <class 'tuple'>
Hello is a <class 'str'>
['one', 'two', 'three'] is a <class 'list'>
```

#Program to sort each sublist of a given list in descending order and display the final result.

```
L=[[45,78,12],[7,14,2],[9,56,2],[3,5,6]]
for i in L:
  i.sort(reverse=True)
print(L)
```

```
[[78, 45, 12], [14, 7, 2], [56, 9, 2], [6, 5, 3]]
```

Note: In a nested list, note that the changes were made in i but were reflected in L. This is because each sublist in a list is referenced through the address and not the value. So changes made in the child list/sublist are reflected back in the main list.

Example 1: Program to search a number from the list of numbers, using Linear search.

```
L=[56,2,15,112,56,89,90,32,56]
N=int(input("Enter the number to be searched in a list"))
for i in L:
  if N==i:
    print("Number",N,"found")
    break
else:
  print("Number",N,"not present in the list")
```

Output:

```
Enter the number to be searched in a list33
Number 33 not present in the list
>>>
=============== RESTART: /Users/sarikakausha
Enter the number to be searched in a list56
Number 56 found

Enter the number to be searched in a list33
Number 33 not present in the list
>>>
=============== RESTART: /Users/sarikakausha
Enter the number to be searched in a list56
Number 56 found
```

#Python method to do the above program:

```
L=[56,2,15,112,56,89,90,32,56]
N=int(input("Enter the number to be searched in a list"))
if L.count(N)==0:
  print("Number",N,"not present in the list")
else:
  print("Number",N,"found")
```

Example 2: Program to accept 5 numbers and store them in a list. Find the sum of numbers stored.

```
L=[]
S=0
for i in range(5):
  L.append(int(input("Enter a number")))
print("Sum is :",sum(L))

Enter a number23
Enter a number56
Enter a number1
Enter a number23
Enter a number8
Sum is : 111
```

Example 3: Program to count the frequency of elements in a list.

```
L=[12,67,13,45,89,67,12,12,13,45]

F=[]

F1=[]

for i in L:

  if i not in F:

    F.append(i)

    F1.append(L.count(i))


print("In list ",L)
```

```
for i in range(len(F)):
  print(F[i],"occurs",F1[i],"Times")
```

```
In list  [12, 67, 13, 45, 89, 67, 12, 12, 13, 45]
12 occurs 3 Times
67 occurs 2 Times
13 occurs 2 Times
45 occurs 2 Times
89 occurs 1 Times
```

Example 4: Program to find max and min value in a List.

```
A=[3,6,12,56,90,23,2]
Ma=Mi=A[0]
for i in range(1,len(A)):
    if Ma<A[i]:
        Ma=A[i]
    if Mi>A[i]:
        Mi=A[i]
print("Maximum : ",Ma, "Minimum :",Mi)
```

#Python method to do the program:

```
A=[3,6,12,56,90,23,2]
print(max(A),min(A))
```

Example 5: Program to find mean of numeric values stored in list.

```
A=[3,6,12,56,90,23,2]
M=0
for i in range(len(A)):
  M+=A[i]
print("Mean :",M/len(A))
```

#Python method to do the program:

```
A=[3,6,12,56,90,23,2]
print("Mean is : ",sum(A)/len(A))
```

Example 5: Program to accept elements in a list and swap element at the even location with the elements at the odd location.

```
L=[]
while True:
  L.append(int(input("Enter no")))
  ch=input("More elements : Y/N")
  if ch in ['n','N']:
```

```
    break
N=len(L) if len(L)%2==0 else len(L)-1
print("Original List",L)
for i in range(0,N,2):
  L[i],L[i+1]=L[i+1],L[i] #Note that swapping occurs simultaneously
print("Modified List",L)
```

```
Enter no45
More elements : Y/Ny
Enter no78
More elements : Y/Ny
Enter no12
More elements : Y/Ny
Enter no90
More elements : Y/Ny
Enter no44
More elements : Y/Ny
Enter no90
More elements : Y/Ny
Enter no8
More elements : Y/Nn
Original List [45, 78, 12, 90, 44, 90, 8]
Modified List [78, 45, 90, 12, 90, 44, 8]
```

Example 6: Create a list of pair of two consecutive numbers from 1 to 20

```
#List comprehension method is used
S=[(i,i+1) for i in range(1,21,2)]
print(S)
[(1, 2), (3, 4), (5, 6), (7, 8), (9, 10), (11, 12), (13, 14), (15, 16), (17, 18), (19, 20)]
```

OR

```
S=[]
for i in range(1,21,2):
  S.append((i,i+1))
print(S)
```

Can you guess what will be the output if we modify the above code to...?

```
S=[]
for i in range(1,21,2):
   S+=((i,i+1))
print(S)
```

Summary

1. List is a heterogeneous collection of data, which can store data of all types. The values of Lists are enclosed within a square bracket.
2. The operations allowed in a list are concatenation, and repetition.
3. Concatenation is possible using '+' (plus) sign. [3,4,5]+[1,2,3] → [3,4,5,1,2,3]
4. Repetition in a list means repeating the element of a list specific number (N) of times. [5,6,"one"]*3 → [5, 6, 'one', 5, 6, 'one', 5, 6, 'one']
5. The 'in' membership operator results True if the given value/element is found in the given list while 'not in' membership operator results True if the given value/element is not found in the given list.
6. Reaching each and every element of the list one after the other in a sequence using loops is called Traversing.
7. List comprehension is used to create a list from the existing list or create a new list based on a criteria.
8. `len()` function finds the length of the list, which means it returns the total number of elements in a list.
9. `list()` function converts an iterable object into a list.
10. `append()` function is used to insert an element in a list. The function accepts only 1 parameter and adds only 1 element at the end of the list.
11. `extend()` function is used to extend the list by adding the iterable provided as a parameter. The length of the modified list is increased by the count of elements in the iterable, which is passed as a parameter.
12. `insert(L,N)` function is used to insert an element N at a given index number L. If the index number is much beyond the range and is positive then the element is inserted at the end of the list. If the index number is much beyond the range and is negative then the element is inserted in the beginning of the list.
13. `count()` function returns the number of occurrences of a value in a list. If the number doesn't exist then 0 is returned.
14. `index()`function returns the beginning index of the first occurrence of value found in the list. 'ValueError' exception is generated if the value is not found.
15. `remove()` function removes the first occurrence of the value, if found. If the value is not found then 'ValueError' exception is raised.
16. `pop()` function removes the value at the provided index number and returns the value, if found. If the index number doesn't exist then the function raises IndexError.
17. `reverse()` function modifies the original list by reversing the elements of the list.
18. `sort()` function arranges the elements of the list either in ascending or in descending order. The default is ascending order. `reverse=True` parameter is used to arrange the list is descending order

19. `sorted(L)` function returns a new list, which contains elements of the list L arranged in ascending order by default. `reverse=True` parameter is used to arrange the list in descending order.
20. `min(L)` function returns the minimum value from a given list L. The elements must be homogenous.
21. `max(L)`function returns the maximum value from a given list L. The elements must be homogenous.
22. `sum(L)`function returns the sum of values from a given list L. The elements must be numeric.

List Questions

1. Choose correct option/options

```
L= ["Data", [1 8, 2, 16]]
print(L[0][1])
print(L[1][3])
```

1. 16,a 2. D,16 3. t, 16 4. a,16

2.
```
A = [7, 10, 95, 25]
print(A[::-2])
```

1. [25, 10] 2. [95, 10] 3. [10, 25] 4. [25, 25]

3.
```
L= [10, 20, 30, 40, 50, 60, 70, 80]
print(L[2:3],end="**")
print(L[::4],end="**")
print(L[5:])
```

1. [30] [10, 50] [60, 70, 80]** 2. [30]**[10, 50]**[60, 70, 80]
3. [20,30]**[10, 50]**[70, 80] 4. [30]**[50,10]**[80, 70, 60]

4.
```
L = [10, 80, 30, 70, 50]
L.append(60*2)
print(L)
```

1. [10, 80, 30, 70, 50, 120] 2. [10, 70, 50, 120]
3. [10, 80, 30, 70, 60, 120] 4. [10, 80, 30, 70, 60, 60]

5.
```
L = [4, 8, 12, 16,90,56,87]
L[1:4] = [20, 24, 28]
print(L)
```

1. [20, 24, 28, 90, 56, 87] 2. [4, 28, 90, 56, 87]
3. [4, 20, 24, 28] 4. [4, 20, 24, 28, 90, 56, 87]

6.
```
L = [89, 56, 10, 20, 30, 40]
del L[1:4]
print(L)
```

1. [89] 2. [89, 30, 40] 3. [89, 40, 30] 4. [56, 10, 20]

7. Which of the following commands will create a list?

   1. `list1 = list()`
   2. `list1 = []`
   3. `list1 = list([1, 2, 3])`
   4. all of the mentioned

8. `L=[245,133,124,123]`, what is `max(L)`?

   1. 245
   2. 133
   3. 124
   4. 123

9. `L=[2, 33, 222, 14, 25]`, What is `L[-1]`?

   1. Error
   2. None
   3. 25
   4. 2

10. `L=[2, 33, 222, 14, 25]`, What is `list1[:-1]`?

    1. [2, 33, 222, 14]
    2. Error
    3. 25
    4. [25, 14, 222, 33, 2]

11.
```
L=[13, 4, 1, 5, 70, 3]
L.extend([4, 8])
print(L)
```

    1. [13, 4, 1, 5, 70, 3, 4, 8]
    2. [13, 4, 1, 5, 70, 3]
    3. [4, 8, 13, 4, 1, 5, 70, 3]
    4. [8, 4, 4, 1, 5, 70, 3, 4]

12.
```
L=[3, 4, 5, 20, 5, 25, 1, 3]
L.pop(-2)
print(L)
```

    1. [3, 4, 5, 20, 5, 1, 3]
    2. [3, 4, 5, 20, 5, 25, 3]
    3. [3, 4, 5, 20, 5, 25, 1]
    4. [3, 4, 5, 20, 5, 5, 3]

13.
```
Data= [[1, 2, 3, 4],
       [4, 5, 6, 7],
       [8, 9, 10, 11],
       [12, 13, 14, 15]]
for i in range(0, 4):
    print(Data[i][2], end = " ")
```

    1. 1 4 8 12
    2. 2 5 9 13
    3. 3 6 10 14
    4. 4 7 11 15

14.
```
points - [[5, 12], [5, 9.9], [4.9, 2.5]]
points.sort()
print(points)
```

    1. [[5, 9.9], [9.9, 2.5], [5, 12]]
    2. [[4.9, 2.5], [5, 9.9], [5, 12]]
    3. [[5, 12]], [5, 9.9],[4.9, 2.5]]
    4. [[4.9, 2.5], [5, 12], [5, 9.9]]

15.
```
a=[1,2,3]
a.append((4,8))
print(a)
```

1. [1, 2, 3, 4, 8] 2. [1, 2, 3, 8, 4]
3. [1, 2, 3, (4, 8)] 4. [1, 2, 3, (8, 4)]

16. ```
a=[14,52,7]
b=a.copy()
print(b is a)
```
1. True  2. False  3. None  4. Error

17. ```
a=list((45,)*4)
print((45)*4,end='&')
print(a)
```
1. 180&(45, 45, 45, 45) 2. 180&[45, 4]
3. 180&[45, 45, 45, 45] 4. 180&[4, 4, 4, 45]

18. ```
a= [1, 2, 3, 4, 5]
for i in range(1, 5):
    a[i-1] = a[i]
for i in range(0, 5):
    print(a[i],end = " ")
```
1. 1 2 4 5 5  2. 2 3 4 5 5
3. 2 3 3 4 5  4. 3 3 4 4 5

19. ```
L1 = ["Homi", "Kevin", "Nikita"]
L1.insert(2, "Uma")
print(L1)
```
a. ['Homi', 'Kevin', 'Uma', 'Nikita'] b. ['Homi', 'Uma','Kevin', 'Nikita']
c. ['Nikita', 'Uma','Kevin', 'Homi'] d. ['Kevin', 'Uma','Nikita', 'Homi']

20. ```
No = [6,3]
Data = ["TV", "PS5"]
for x in Data:
    for y in No:
        print(y, x, sep=" are the ")
```
a.
```
6 TV are the
3 TV are the
6 PS5 are the
3 PS5 are the
```
b.
```
6 are the TV
3 are the TV
6 are the PS5
3 are the PS5
```
c.
```
TVare the6
TVare the3
PS5are the6
PS5are the3
```
d. Syntax Error
```

21. Write a Python program that accepts 5 elements in a list and find the largest number from a list.
22. Write a Python program that accepts 5 elements in a list and find the smallest number from a list.
23. Write a Python program that accepts N elements in a list. Remove the duplicate elements from the list, if any.
24. Write a Python program to accept a number. Remove the number from a given list, if it is present.
25. Write a Python program that accepts N elements in a list. Remove all the values except integer values from the list.
26. Write a Python program to convert a given list of strings into a list of lists.

    For example,if the original list of string is:

    ```
    S=["Jack","and","Jill"']
    ```

    The final result should be:

    ```
    [['J', 'a', 'c', 'k'], ['a', 'n', 'd'], ['J', 'i', 'l', 'l']]
    ```

27. Write a Python program to add two given lists of different lengths from right to left.

    For example,if

    ```
    L1=[2, 9, 7, 10, 5, 8]

    L2=[13, -3, 2, -7]

    L=[2, 9, 20, 7, 7, 1]
    ```

    ```
    #Sample Solution
    L2=[2, 9, 7, 10, 5, 8]
    L1=[13, -3, 2, -7]
    L=[]
    x,y=len(L1),len(L2)
    if x<y:
      L1,L2=L2,L1

    t=len(L1)-len(L2)
    L.extend(L1[:t])
    for i in range(len(L2)):
      L.append(L1[t]+L2[i])
      t+=1
    print(L)
    ```

28. Write a Python program to find the maximum and minimum values in a given list within specified index range.

Original list:

```
L=[4, 3, 0, 5, 3, 0, 2, 3, 4, 2, 4, 3, 5]
```

Index range:

```
2 to 7
```

Maximum and minimum values of the said given list within index range:

```
(5, 0)
```

29. Write a Python program to compute the sum of digits of each number of a given list separately.

For example, if

```
L=[110, 223, 156]
```

Output generated :

```
2,612
```

30. Write a Python program to reverse each sub list in a given list of lists.

For example, if

```
L=[[1, 2, 3, 4], [5, 6, 7, 8], [9, 10, 11, 12], [13, 14, 15, 16]]
```

Output:

```
L=[[4, 3, 2, 1], [8, 7, 6, 5], [12, 11, 10, 9], [16, 15, 14, 13]]
```

31. Write a Python program to find common element(s) in a given nested lists.

For example, if

```
L=[[12, 18, 23, 25, 45], [7, 12, 18, 24, 28], [1, 5, 8, 12, 15, 16, 18]]
```

Output:

Common Elements:

```
[18, 12]
```

32. Write a Python program to find the sum of all the numeric values in a given heterogenous list.

For example, if

```
L=["Data",89,2.7,"77","numbers",6]
```

Output:

```
97.7
```

31. Write a Python program to swap the first half of the element of the list with the second half.

Original List

```
L=[45,78,12,55,88,90]
```

Modified List

```
L=[55,88,90,45,78,12]
```

32. Write a Python program to display the count along of all those elements which are multiple of 7. Also display the elements

33. Give the output for the python codes below:

`X= 8`
`B = [0] * X`
`W= 1.0 / X`
`for i in range(X):`
`    low = i * W`
`    high = low + W`
`    B[i] = 3*i+1`
`print (B)`
	`a = [1, 3, 5, 7]`
	`b = a`
	`print(b)`
	`for i in range(len(a)):`
	`    b[i]+=(i+1)*a[i]`
	`print(a)`

`X=[34,78,1,2,56,77,9]`
`for i in range(0,len(X),2):`
`    print(X[i:len(X)])`
	`L=[]`
	`Y=(2,6,25,9,3)`
	`L.extend(Y)`
	`L.insert(2,7)`
	`L.insert(-3,4)`
	`L.append(45)`
	`print(L)`
	`L.sort()`
	`print(L)`

34. Write single line statements for the following:

a. Create a blank list LT.

b. Add the elements 6,4,3 in it.

c. Insert 89 at the 2nd position

d. Insert 7 at the last position

e. Print the elements at the even position

f. Remove the element at the last position

g. Remove the value 4 from the list.

h. Print the final list

35. Write a program to accept three values each in two lists L1 and L2. Find the sum of elements of the two lists and store the resultant sum in the third list L3 in the manner given below:

```
L1=[9,5,7]  L2=[4,6,5]
Sum=957+465=1422
L3=[1,4,2,2]
```

36. Write a program to accept a number N from the user. Store the odd numbers from 1 to N in the list followed by even numbers in the reverse order from 1 to N in the same list in the following manner:

```
if N=9 then the resultant list should be
L=[1,3,5,7,9,8,6,4,2]
```

37. Write a program to accept N elements in a list such that they are either 0, 1 or 2. Display the list and then arrange it in such a manner that the list is sorted according to 0, 1 and 2. Note that the sort function should not be used. For example

```
if L=[0,2,1,0,1,0,0,1] (if N=8)
Resultant List : L=[0,0,0,0,1,1,1,2]]
```

38. Store elements in two lists L1 and L2. Sort them in ascending order. Merge the two lists and store the elements in the third list L3 in the following manner:

```
if L1=[1,4,6,8,10], L2=[2,4,9,10,15],
then the resultant list should be
L3=[1,2,4,4,6,8,9,10,10,15]
```

11 Tuples

Introduction to Tuple

Tuple is also an iterable object in python which can store multiple values of various data types. We will understand tuple by understanding it's important features:.

1. Tuple is a heterogeneous collection of data, which can store data of all types.
2. The values of a Tuple are enclosed within a round bracket.

```
#Tuple declaration
T=()
T1=(10,"XII",60,"XI")
T2=(78,98.5,12)
T3=("Primary","secondary","Sr Secondary")
```

3. Duplicate values are allowed in a Tuple.

```
T=(10,30,10,30,10,10)
```

4. Each value in a Tuple is called an element and each element of a Tuple can be extracted using its index number. The index number starts from 0.

```
T=(10,30,60)
print(T[0])
print(T[2])
10
60
```

5. Tuple is an immutable Python object, where the values are not allowed to get changed.

```
T=(10,30,60)
print(id(T))
140398952728192

T[1]+=100 #Error
TypeError: 'tuple' object does not support item assignment
```

6. To know the total number of elements in a tuple, len() function is used.

```
T=("Python","C","Java","HTML")
print(len(T))
#4
```

7. The elements of a Tuple can be any other data structure like string/tuple/list/dictionary etc

```
T=((0,2,4),(1,3,5),('a','b','c'))
T=([1,2,3],"data",{1:12,2:23})
```

8. A tuple with single element is created in the following manner:

```
T=(12) # It creates an integer object
print(type(T))
T=(12,)   # It creates a Tuple with single element
print(type(T))
>>> T=(12)
>>> print(type(T))
<class 'int'>
>>> T=(12,)
>>> print(type(T))
<class 'tuple'>
```

9. Packing and unpacking in Tuples: In packing, insert the values into a tuple, but in unpacking, we extract all those values stored in the tuples into variables as shown in the following example:

```
X,Y,Z=67,"33Km/H","90Km"
T=X,Y,Z
print(T)                        #(67, '33Km/H', '90Km') → Packing
Y=("Neha",90,"XII")
(Name,per,Class)=Y              # →  Unpacking
print("Name:",Name)             #Name: Neha
print("Percentage:",per)        #Percentage: 90
print("Class:",Class)           #Class: XII
```

Tuple indexing

Since a tuple is also an iterable object, each element in a tuple has an index number using which it can be extracted.

```
T=(1,'Python',3.9.5,'Language',17)
```

0	1	2	3	4
1	**Python**	**3.9.5**	**Language**	**17**
-5	-4	-3	-2	-1

Each element in the tuple has a positive index as well as negative index number, using which the element can be extracted. The index number is provided in a square brackets as shown below:

```
>>>print(T)        # [1,'Python',3.9.5,'Language',17]
>>>print(T[3])     # Language
>>>print(T[-4])    # Python
```

Operations in Tuple

Following operations are possible in this iterable object:

a. **Concatenation :** Concatenation means combining 2 or more tuples. Concatenation is possible using '+' (plus) sign. Here, the second tuple is combined with the first to get a new tuple. The length of the new tuple will therefore be the sum of length of tuple 1 and tuple 2. Following example illustrate concatenation in tuple:

Example 1

```
T1=(44,43,90,56) #Length: 4

T2=(166,19,16)     #Length: 3

T3=T1+T2 #concatenation

print (T3,len(T3),sep="\n")     #Length: 4+3=7
(44, 43, 90, 56, 166, 19, 16)
7
```

Note: Concatenation in list is possible only between lists.

Example 2

```
B=(5,6,7)

C=23

print(B+C)

#Error
TypeError: can only concatenate tuple (not "int") to tuple
```

Example 3

```
T1=("Red","Yellow","Black")

T2=(1,2,3,4,5)

T3=T2+T1

print(T3)
(1, 2, 3, 4, 5, 'Red', 'Yellow', 'Black')
```

b. **Repetition:** Repetition in a tuple means repeating the element of a tuple specific number (N) of times. Repetition is possible when the tuple object is multiplied with an integer. We can repeat a tuple using asterisk (*). The final result is also a tuple. See the following example to understand repetition:

Example 1

```
T1=("Tic","Tac","Toe")

print(T1*3) #The tuple is repeated 3 times
('Tic', 'Tac', 'Toe', 'Tic', 'Tac', 'Toe', 'Tic', 'Tac', 'Toe')
```

Note that the two tuples cannot be multiplied. Repetition is possible when a tuple is multiplied with an integer

Example 2

```
T1=("Mango","orange","Pineapple")
print(T1*T1)
```

```
TypeError: can't multiply sequence by non-int of type 'tuple'
```

c. **Membership:** There are two membership operators 'in' and 'not in'. They are used to find an element in a given tuple.

in : The 'in' operator results True if the given value/element is found in the Given tuple

Example 1

```
a=12
T=(1,2,12,45,12)
if a in T:
  print('Present')
else:
  print('Not Present')
```

Explanation: In the above example, the value 12 is to be searched which is present at index number 3. So the condition is True and hence Present displayed.

Output

```
Present
```

not in: Evaluates to true if the given value/element is not found in the given tuple

Example 2

```
even=(2,4,6,8)
odd=(1,3,5,9)
T=(2,5,6,1,56,2,3,9,10,8,7)
for i in T:
  if i in even:
    print(i,"in even list")
  elif i in odd:
    print(i, "in odd list")
  else:
    print(i, "not in the list")
```

```
2 in even list
5 in odd list
6 in even list
1 in odd list
56 not in the list
2 in even list
3 in odd list
9 in odd list
10 not in the list
8 in even list
7 not in the list
```

a. **Slicing:** It is a feature which allows you to extract element/ elements from a tuple using the index numbers. The final result is also a tuple. To understand slicing we will refer to the following tuple

`T=(1,2,0,5,11,23,3,6)`

0	1	2	3	4	5	6	7
1	**2**	**0**	**5**	**11**	**23**	**3**	**6**
-8	-7	-6	-5	-4	-3	-2	-1

There are 3 parameters which can be provided in slicing.

`Tuple[start:end:step]`

start→ specifies the beginning index number. If not provided, then it's 0.

end→ specifies the ending index. If it's not provided, then it takes the length of the tuple (which is the count of the total number of elements in the tuple). The last index taken is always end-1

step→ It is also optional. If not provided then it's taken as 1. It specifies that by how many steps the index should be jumped to display the next element. If the step provided is positive then the direction of display of the element is from left to right. If the step is negative, then the direction of display of the element is from right to left. Also, if step is negative, then start becomes len(list)-1 by default while end goes till the first element on left.

Examples with reference to above list 'L1', with explanation:

```
>>> print(T) #Tuple printed
```

0	1	2	3	4	5	6	7
1	**2**	**0**	**5**	**11**	**23**	**3**	**6**
-8	-7	-6	-5	-4	-3	-2	-1

```
>>> print(T[:]) #Start is default 0 and end is default < len(L1)
```

0	1	2	3	4	5	6	7
1	**2**	**0**	**5**	**11**	**23**	**3**	**6**
-8	-7	-6	-5	-4	-3	-2	-1

```
>>> print(T[::])#Start is default 0 and end is default < len(L1)
```

0	1	2	3	4	5	6	7
1	2	0	5	11	23	3	6
-8	-7	-6	-5	-4	-3	-2	-1

```
>>> print(T[1:4]) #start is 1 and end is <4, step=1 (default)
(2,0,5)
```

0	1	2	3	4	5	6	7
1	2	0	5	11	23	3	6
-8	-7	-6	-5	-4	-3	-2	-1

```
>>> print(T[6:]) #Start is 6, end is < len(a)
(3,6)
```

0	1	2	3	4	5	6	7
1	2	0	5	11	23	3	6
-8	-7	-6	-5	-4	-3	-2	-1

```
>>>print(T[::2]) #Start and end default, but step is 2
(1,0,11,3)
```

0	1	2	3	4	5	6	7
1	2	0	5	11	23	3	6
-8	-7	-6	-5	-4	-3	-2	-1

```
>>>print(T[::-1])
(6, 3, 23, 11, 5, 0, 2, 1)
```

0	1	2	3	4	5	6	7
1	2	0	5	11	23	3	6
-8	-7	-6	-5	-4	-3	-2	-1

#As step is negative, the direction of printing element is from right to left, hence reverse tuple printed

```
>>> print(T[::-3])
(6, 11, 2)
```

0	1	2	3	4	5	6	7
1	2	0	5	11	23	3	6
-8	-7	-6	-5	-4	-3	-2	-1

#The step is negative, so direction is right to left. Also, every third element is printed from right to left as step=-3

```
>>> print(T[1:6:2])
(2, 5, 23)
```

0	1	2	3	4	5	6	7
1	2	0	5	11	23	3	6
-8	-7	-6	-5	-4	-3	-2	-1

#Start =1, while end<6. step=2 will print every second element starting from index 1.

```
>>> print(T[1:8:-1])
```

#This won't print anything as direction of printing of elements should be right to left, but the values of start and end indicate left to right direction

```
>>> print(T[-1:-6:-1])
(6, 3, 23, 11, 5)
```

0	1	2	3	4	5	6	7
1	2	0	5	11	23	3	6
-8	-7	-6	-5	-4	-3	-2	-1

#Here negative indexing is specified, so according to the index number as shown in the picture we see elements from -1 till -5 from right to left direction

```
>>> print(T[2:-2])
(0, 5, 11, 23)
```

0	1	2	3	4	5	6	7
1	2	0	5	11	23	3	6
-8	-7	-6	-5	-4	-3	-2	-1

#In this example, there is a combination of positive and negative indexing. Start is 2, end one less than -2 position and since the step is 1 by default and the direction of index is also from left to right, the elements as per the index are printed.

```
>>> print(T[-4:-8:-1])
(11, 5, 0, 2)
```

0	1	2	3	4	5	6	7
1	2	0	5	11	23	3	6
-8	-7	-6	-5	-4	-3	-2	-1

Traversing a Tuple using loops

Since a List is an iterable object, we can reach each and every element of the list one after the other in a sequence using loops.

Two ways to traverse a Tuple

#Here element is taken from the tuple T and given to i, which is printed
 	
T=("India","UK","China","USA")
for i in T:
   print(i,end="**\n")
 	
India**
UK**
China**
USA**
	#Here the index is extracted using the range function and to display the element, the index is specified in square brackets with tuple object.
	
	T=("India","UK","China","USA")
	for i in range(len(T)):
	   print(T[i],end="*\n*")
	
	India*
	UK
	China
	USA
	*

Example1: To find the minimum and maximum element from the Tuple.

```
A=(3,6,12,56,90,23,2)
Ma=Mi=A[0]
for i in range(1,len(A)):
    if Ma<A[i]:
        Ma=A[i]
    if Mi>A[i]:
        Mi=A[i]
print("Maximum : ",Ma, "Minimum :",Mi)

Maximum :  90 Minimum : 2
```

Example 2: To find and display the mean of numeric values stored in a tuple.

```
A=(3,6,12,56,90,23,2)
M=0
for i in range(len(A)):
  M+=A[i]
print("Mean :",M/len(A))

Mean : 27.428571428571427
```

Built in Functions used with Tuple

	Function	Description	Syntax
1	len()	This function finds the length of the tuple and returns the total number of elements in a tuple.	len(Tuple)
	Example:	T=(22,13,100,"Tuple") print(len(L)) 4 print(len((2,2,4,5,9)))	

<table>
<tr><td></td><td></td><td colspan="2">5
S=len(T)* 2
print(S)
8

W=len(T*3)
print(W)
12 #Here T*3 will first result in
(22, 13, 100, 'Tuple', 22, 13, 100, 'Tuple', 22, 13, 100, 'Tuple')
Hence the length 12</td></tr>
<tr><td>2</td><td>tuple()</td><td>It converts an iterable object into a tuple. If no parameter is provided then a blank tuple is created</td><td>tuple(iterable)</td></tr>
<tr><td></td><td>Example:</td><td colspan="2">>>> S="TUPLE"
>>> T=tuple(S)
>>> print(T)
('T', 'U', 'P', 'L', 'E') #Each character in a string becomes an element of the tuple

>>> T=["RR","GG","BB"]
>>> T1=Tuple(T)
>>> print(T1)
('RR', 'GG', 'BB') #List can be converted to a Tuple

>>> D={"Y":"you","R":"are","G8":"great"}
>>> T=tuple(D)
>>> print(T)
('Y', 'R', 'G8') #By default only the key becomes the elements of the Tuple

>>> T=list()
>>> print(T)
( ) #Blank Tuple created

>>> L=tuple(12)
TypeError: 'int' object is not iterable</td></tr>
<tr><td>3</td><td>count()</td><td>This function returns the number of occurrences of a value in a list. If the value is absent in the tuple then 0 is returned. This function takes only one parameter</td><td>tuple.count(value)</td></tr>
</table>

		>>> T=(12,13,14,15,(12,13),14,13,15)
		>>> print(T.count(12))
		1
		# 12 appears once. The second 12 at index 5 is not a single element, it's a tuple (12,13), so it's not included.
		
		>>> print(T.count(13))
		2
		# 13 appears twice. 13 at index 5 is not a single element, it's a tuple (12,13), so it's not included.
		
		>>> print(T.count(10))
		0
		#10 is not present in the tuple and hence 0.
		
		>>> print(T.count((12,13)))
		1
		#(12,13) appears at index 5 as a single element and is present only once. Hence the function returns 1.
		
		>>> print(T.count([12,13]))
		0
		#(12,13) appears at index 5 as a single element but it is a tuple not a list. Hence the function returns 0.
		
		>>> print(T.count(12,13))
		TypeError: tuple.count() takes exactly one argument (2 given)	

4	index()	▪ index( ) function returns the beginning index of the first occurrence of value found in the tuple ▪ Generates 'ValueError' exception if the value is not found. ▪ The start and the end index number of the elements for search can be provided. ▪ If not provided then the whole tuple is searched.	Tuple.index(Value, start,end) #The searching is from start index till end-1 index

	Example:	>>> T=(45,11,78,90,"Kite","rope",78,56,12,11)
		>>> print(T.index(78))
		2
		#78 is present at two locations, 2 and at 6. But the first occurrence is 2 and hence the result.	

		>>> print(T.index(15,0,3))
		ValueError: tuple.index(x): x not in tuple
		>>> print(T.index(11,3))
		9
		#11 is present at once at location 9 from index 3 and len(T)-1. Hence the result.
		>>> print(T.index("rope"))
		5
		#"rope" is present at location 5.	

5	sorted()	■ This function returns a new list, which contains elements arranged in ascending order by default. ■ To sort in descending order, reverse=True parameter is used. ■ Note that the sorted function will work with data of similar type, i.e. all numbers or all strings. For heterogeneous data, function will generate error	sorted(iterable,reverse=True)

		>>> T=(4,1,8,5,9,0,3,6,9,2,5)
		>>> print(sorted(T))
		[0, 1, 2, 3, 4, 5, 5, 6, 8, 9, 9]
		
		>>> T=([2, 67, 1], [4, 2, 6], [6, 7.4], [9, 0, 8])
		>>> print(sorted(T,reverse=True))
		[[9, 0, 8], [6, 7.4], [4, 2, 6], [2, 67, 1]]
		
		>>> T=(67,23,56,77)
		>>> print(sorted(T))
		[23, 56, 67, 77]
		
		>>> D={3:"Grade 3",1:"Grade 1",12:"Senior Secondary",10:"Secondary"}
		>>> print(sorted(D))
		[1, 3, 10, 12]
		#The keys are taken from dictionary to form the sorted list
		
		>>>A=(67,23,56,77)
		>>> print(sorted(A,reverse=True))
		[77, 67, 56, 23]
		
		>>> A="TERRIBLE"	

		>>> print(sorted(A)) **[‘B’, ‘E’, ‘E’, ‘I’, ‘L’, ‘R’, ‘R’, ‘T’]** **# If the iterable is a string then the each character becomes the element of the list, sorted alphabetically in ascending order, by default**	
6	min()	It returns the minimum value from a given tuple. The data type of elements in the tuple should be same.	min(iterable)

		>>> colors=(“Orange”,”Red”,”Purple”,”Green”,”Black”,”White”)
		>>> min(colors)
		‘Black’
		# This is because the ASCII value of “B” is smallest amongst all
		>>> No=(67.5,34.32,61.9,67.55,67.4,90)
		>>> print(min(No))
		34.32
		
		>>> T=((2, 67, 1), (4, 2, 6), (6, 7.4), (9, 0, 8))
		>>> print(min(T))
		(2, 67, 1)
		#The first element is smallest in all the tuples in the tuple
		
		>>> L=(67,”one”,55,12,”two”,98.4,”three”)
		>>> min(L)
		TypeError: ‘<’ not supported between instances of ‘str’ and ‘int’	

7	max()	It returns the maximum value from a given tuple. The data type of elements in the list should be same.	max(iterable)

		>>> T=(‘Anika’, ‘anika’,’Bhavna’, ‘Charu’, ‘Manya’,’charu’)
		>>> print(max(T))
		charu
		# This is because the ASCII value of “c” is largest amongst all
		
		>>> T=(67/99,34,61,35,12,90.67)
		>>> print(max(T))
		90.67
		
		>>> T=([2, 67, 1], [4, 2, 6], [6, 7.4], [9, 0, 8])
		>>> print(max(T))
		[9,0,8]	

<table>
<tr><td></td><td></td><td colspan="2">

```
#The first element is smallest in all the lists in the tuple

>>> T=(67,"one",55,12,"two",98.4,"three")
>>> max(T)
TypeError: '<' not supported between instances of 'str' and 'int'
```

</td></tr>
<tr><td>15</td><td>sum()</td><td>

- It returns the sum of numbers in the tuple. It works only for numeric values.
- It has two parameters, iterable and start
- It returns the sum of start value + sum of elements of iterable.
- If start is not provided, then it's taken as 0.

</td><td>sum(iterable,start)</td></tr>
<tr><td></td><td></td><td colspan="2">

```
>>> T=(78,45,90.56,22)
>>> print(sum(T))
235.56

>>> print(sum(T,10))
245.56
#235.56 added with 10
>>> print(sum(T,40))
275.56
#235.56 added with 40
>>> print(sum(T,10.5))
246.06
#235.56 added with 10.5

>>> print(sum(T,(23,45)))
#Error
```

</td></tr>
</table>

Nested Tuple

When a tuple has many other iterables as its elements, it is called a nested tuple. We need to understand how each element in a nested tuple can be accessed.

T=((14,3,1,9,1),(13,5,11,21),(1,8,33,9),(99,88)]

To access each element of the list, if we use the loop, we will get the following result:

```
T=((14,3,1,9,1),(13,5,11,21),(1,8,33,9),(99,88))
for i in range(len(T)):
  print("T[",i,"]=",T[i])
```

Output:

```
T[ 0 ]= (14, 3, 1, 9, 1)
T[ 1 ]= (13, 5, 11, 21)
T[ 2 ]= (1, 8, 33, 9)
T[ 3 ]= (99, 88)
```

To understand the output further, let us understand it diagrammatically.

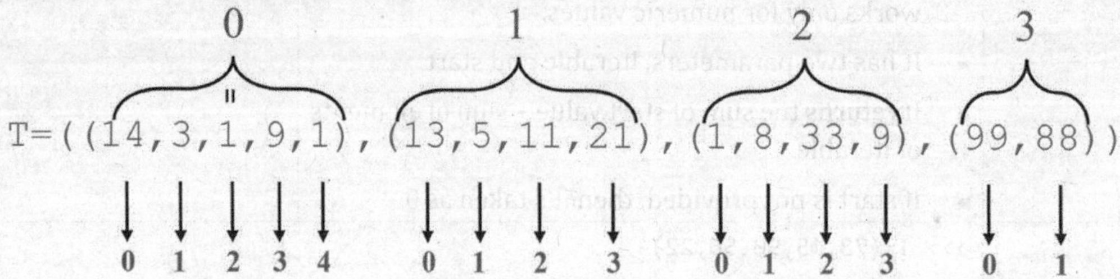

The above list has 4 elements from 0 to 3.

The first element is (14,3,1,9,1)

The second element is (13,5,11,21)

The third element is (1,8,33,9)

The fourth element is (99,88)

Each element of the first element can further be accessed using its respected index number.

T

0					1				2				3	
0	1	2	3	4	0	1	2	3	0	1	2	3	0	1
14	3	1	9	1	13	5	11	21	1	8	33	9	99	88

So T[0][0] → 14

T[0][1] → 3

T[0][2] → 1

T[0][3] → 9

T[0][4] → 1

T[1][0] → 13

T[1][1] → 5

T[1][2] → 11

T[1][3] → 21

T[2][0] → 1

T[2][1] → 8

T[2][2] → 33

T[2][3] → 9

T[3][0] → 99

T[3][1] → 88

#Program to display the type of each element of a tuple

```
T=((14,3,1,9,1),[3,5,11],(1,8,33,9),"Strange",99.45)
for i in T:
  print("Type of",i,"is",type(i))
```

```
Type of (14, 3, 1, 9, 1) is <class 'tuple'>
Type of [3, 5, 11] is <class 'list'>
Type of (1, 8, 33, 9) is <class 'tuple'>
Type of Strange is <class 'str'>
Type of 99.45 is <class 'float'>
```

#Program to display the elements of a tuple in separate lines. Each sub element should be separated by '*', if it's an iterable object.

```
T=((14,3,1,9,1),[3,5,11],(1,8,33,9),"Strange",99.45)
for i in T:
  if type(i)in [int,float]:
    print(i)
  else:
    for j in i:
      print(j,end='*')
  print()
```

```
14*3*1*9*1*
3*5*11*
1*8*33*9*
S*t*r*a*n*g*e*
99.45
```

Tuple Assignment

It is one of the important and unique features in Python in Tuple, where the tuple of variables can be assigned values from the tuple on the right side of the assignment.

For example

```
(a,b,c)=(10,20,30)
print("a=",a,"b=",b,"c=",c)

a= 10 b= 20 c= 30
```

Another way to do the above program:

```
T=(10,20,30)
(a,b,c)=T
print("a=",a,"b=",b,"c=",c)
```

Note that the number of variables and the assignment values should be the same.

```
>>>(a,b,c)=(10,20)
    (a,b,c)=(10,20)
ValueError: not enough values to unpack (expected 3, got 2)
```

Interesting thing about Tuple!

We know that a tuple is an immutable object but if any element of a tuple is a mutable object, then all the functions applicable to a mutable object will be applicable to that mutable element. Following example illustrate it

#Program to sort the element of the list stored in a tuple T

```
T=([14,3,1,9,1],(3,5,11),[11,8,33,9])
print("Original Tuple",T)
for i in range(len(T)):
  if type(T[i])==list:
    T[i].sort()

print("Changed Tuple",T)

Original Tuple ([14, 3, 1, 9, 1], (3, 5, 11), [11, 8, 33, 9])
Changed Tuple ([1, 1, 3, 9, 14], (3, 5, 11), [8, 9, 11, 33])
```

Similarly we can update or delete the elements of mutable elements of a tuple too.

#Program to increase the even number by 10 and odd number by 20 for mutable elements of a tuple. Also 0 is present in the mutable element, make it 100.

```
T=((5,22,89),[9,0,34,1],[67,11,0,0],78)
print("Original Tuple",T)
for i in range(len(T)):
  if type(T[i])==list:
    for j in range(len(T[i])):
      if T[i][j]==0:
        T[i][j]=100
      elif T[i][j]%2==0:
        T[i][j]+=10
      else:
        T[i][j]+=20

print("Changed Tuple",T)
```

```
Original Tuple ((5, 22, 89), [9, 0, 34, 1], [67, 11, 0, 0], 78)
Changed Tuple ((5, 22, 89), [29, 100, 44, 21], [87, 31, 100, 100], 78)
```

Solved Examples

Example 1: Program to search a number from the tuple of numbers, using Linear search.

```
T=(56,2,15,112,56,89,90,32,56)
N=int(input("Enter the number to be searched in a Tuple"))
for i in T:
  if N==i:
    print("Number",N,"found")
    break
else:
  print("Number",N,"not present in the tuple")
```

Output:

```
Enter the number to be searched in a Tuple112
Number 112 found
>>>
======== RESTART: /Users/sarikakaushal/Documer
Enter the number to be searched in a Tuple100
Number 100 not present in the tuple
...
Enter the number to be searched in a Tuple112
Number 112 found
>>>
======== RESTART: /Users/sarikakaushal/Documer
Enter the number to be searched in a Tuple100
Number 100 not present in the tuple
...
```

#Python method to do the above program:

```
T=(56,2,15,112,56,89,90,32,56)
N=int(input("Enter the number to be searched in a Tuple"))
if T.count(N)!=0:
  print("Number",N,"found")
else:
  print("Number",N,"not present in the tuple")
```

Example 2: Program to store 5 numbers in a tuple. Find the sum of numbers stored.

```
T=(45,12,3,89,8)
S=0
print("sum is :",sum(T))
```

```
sum is : 157
```

Example 3: Program to count the frequency of elements in a tuple.

```
T=(12,67,13,45,89,67,12,12,13,45)
F=()
F1=()
for i in T:
  if i not in F:
    F+=(i,)
    F1+=(T.count(i),)

print("In Tuple ",T)
for i in range(len(F)):
  print(F[i],"occurs",F1[i],"Times")
```

```
In Tuple  (12, 67, 13, 45, 89, 67, 12, 12, 13, 45)
12 occurs 3 Times
67 occurs 2 Times
13 occurs 2 Times
45 occurs 2 Times
89 occurs 1 Times
```

Example 4: Program to find max and min value in a tuple.

```
A=(3,6,12,56,90,23,2)
Ma=Mi=A[0]
for i in range(1,len(A)):
    if Ma<A[i]:
        Ma=A[i]
    if Mi>A[i]:
        Mi=A[i]
print("Maximum : ",Ma, "Minimum :",Mi)
```

#Python method to do the program:

```
A=(3,6,12,56,90,23,2)

print(max(A),min(A))
```

Example 5: Program to find mean of numeric values stored in list.

```
A=(3,6,12,56,90,23,2)

M=0

for i in range(len(A)):

  M+=A[i]

print("Mean :",M/len(A))
```

#Python method to do the program:

```
A=(3,6,12,56,90,23,2)

print("Mean is : ",sum(A)/len(A))
```

Example 6: Program to accept 5 numbers and store in a Tuple

#We know that tuple is an immutable object so we will use a technique to redeclare tuple with the loop.

```
T=()
for i in range(5):
  X=int(input("enter a number"))
  T+=(X,) #converting value in tuple and using concatenation
  print("Tuple Address",id(T))
print(T)
```

```
enter a number12
Tuple Address 140592950837056
enter a number67
Tuple Address 140592977066688
enter a number3
Tuple Address 140592971593664
enter a number90
Tuple Address 140592977094112
enter a number1
Tuple Address 140592977124064
(12, 67, 3, 90, 1)
```

Summary

1. Tuple is an immutable iterable object in python which can store multiple values of various data types. Since it's immutable, changes are not allowed.
2. The elements of the tuple are stored in round brackets.
3. The operations allowed in a tuple are concatenation, and repetition.
4. Concatenation is possible using '+' (plus) sign. (3,4,5)+(1,2,3) → (3,4,5,1,2,3)
5. Repetition in a tuple means repeating the element of a tuple specific number (N) of times. ("A","E","I")*3 → ("A","E","I","A","E","I","A","E","I")
6. The 'in' membership operator results True if the given value/element is found in the given tuple while 'not in' membership operator results True if the given value/element is not found in the given tuple.
7. Reaching each and every element of the tuple one after the other in a sequence using loops is called Traversing.
8. `len()` function finds the length of the tuple, which means it returns the total number of elements in a tuple.
9. `tuple()` function converts an iterable object into a tuple.
10. `count()` function returns the number of occurrences of a value in a tuple. If the number doesn't exist then 0 is returned.
11. `index()`function returns the beginning index of the first occurrence of value found in the tuple. 'ValueError' exception is generated if the value is not found.

12. `sorted(T)` function returns a new list, which contains elements of the tuple T arranged in ascending order by default. `reverse=True` parameter is used to arrange the tuple in descending order.
13. `min(T)` function returns the minimum value from a given tuple T. The elements must be homogenous.
14. `max(T)`function returns the maximum value from a given tuple T. The elements must be homogenous.
15. `sum(T)`function returns the sum of values from a given tuple T. The elements must be numeric.

Questions

1. Write a Python program to store 4 elements in a tuple
2. Write a Python program to find the sum of all the elements of a tuple.
3. Write a Python program to find the largest element in a tuple.
4. Write a Python program to find the smallest element in a tuple.
5. Write a Python program to find the second largest element in a tuple.
6. Write a Python program to find the second smallest element in a tuple.
7. Write a Python program to print the reverse of a tuple.
8. Write a python program to accept the Name, Brand and price of a car in three variables. Pack the three values into a tuple T.
9. Given a list `L=[5,7,1,2,5]`. Write python code to convert it into a tuple.
10. Find and correct the syntax errors in the code given below. Underline the corrections also.

```
T1 = (12,5,6,13,9,56,3)
print T1*T1
print(2+T1)
print(len[T1] * 2)
```

11. Write two differences between Tuple and List. also give an example for each one of them.
12. Choose the functions which will work with a tuple from the given set of built in functions. Also specify the reason for the functions not chosen.
    `count(), append(), insert(), index(), len(), sort(), sorted(), sum()`
13. Give output for the following python codes:

<table>
<tr>
<td><pre>T = ()
for item in range(5):
    T = T + (item,)
print(T)</pre></td>
<td><pre>T = X=("Python", [12,6.4, 6], (4, 5.6,
"Objects"))
print(T[0][1])
T[1].sort()
print(T)
print(sorted(X[0]))</pre></td>
</tr>
</table>

P=(3,5,7,11,13,11,7); print(P.count(11)) print(P.index(11)) print (3 in P, 43 in P)	S =("South",) W=("West",) print(S) print(type(W)) print((S+W)*2)

14. Choose the correct way to access value 56 from the following tuple

    `T = ("Colors", [34,56,78], (5, 15, 25))`

    1. `print(T[1:2][1])`
    2. `print(T[1:2](1))`
    3. `print(T[1:2][1])`
    4. `print(T[1][1])`

15. What is the type of the variable T

    ```
    T = ("Calculator")
    print(type(T))
    ```

    1. list
    2. tuple
    3. array
    4. str

16. If `T = (1, 2, 4, 3)`,which of the following is incorrect?

    1. print(T[3])
    2. T[3] = 45
    3. print(max(T))
    4. print(len(T))

17. ```
    T=(78,34,66,12,78)
    print(T[1:3])
    ```

    1. (78, 34)
    2. (34, 66)
    3. (66, 12)
    4. (34, 66, 12)

18. ```
    T = (1, 2, 4, 3, 8, 9)
    R=[T[i] for i in range(0, len(T), 2)]
    print(R)
    ```

    1. [1, 4, 8]
    2. [1, 2, 4]
    3. [1, 4, 9]
    4. [1, 2, 9]

19. ```
    T = (6,5)
    print(2 * T)
    ```

    1. (11, 11)
    2. (5, 6, 5, 6)
    3. (6, 5, 6, 5)
    4. (12, 10)

20. ```
    t1 = (1, 2, 4, 3)
    t2 = (1, 2, 3, 4)
    print(t1 == t2)
    ```

    1. True
    2. False
    3. None
    4. Error

21. If `a=(1,2,3,4)` then `print(a[1:-1])` is ____________

    1. (2, 3)
    2. (1,2,3)
    3. (2, 3,4)
    4. (1,2,3,4)

22. ```
    a=(1,3,5)
    print(sum(a,10))
    ```

    1. 16
    2. 17
    3. 18
    4. 19
    ```

23. (a,b,c)=(1,2,3)

```
print( a,b,c)
```

Will print....

1. [1,2,3]   2. (1,2,3)   3. 1 2 3   4. Syntax Error

24. a=(1,3)

```
b=(2,4)
c=a+b
print(c)
```

1. (1, 2, 3, 4)   2. (1, 3, 1, 3)   3. (4, 3, 2, 1)   4. (1, 3, 2, 4)

25. a,b=1,3

```
a,b=b,a
print(a,b)
```

1. 3 1   2. 1 3   3. 3 3   4. 1 1

26. a=[(4,9),(4,6),(4,8)]

```
a.sort()
print(a)
```

1. [(4, 9), (4, 6), (4, 8)]   2. [(4, 8), (4, 6), (4, 9)]

3. [(4, 9), (4, 8), (4, 9)]   4. [(4, 6), (4, 8), (4, 9)]

12 Dictionary

Introduction to Dictionary

Dictionary is another iterable object which stores not only values but their respective keys also. Let us understand dictionary through its important features:

1. It is a mutable object. Changes are allowed in a dictionary object.
2. It is a collection of items enclosed in curly brackets. Each item is a key value pair separated by a colon.

   Syntax:

   ```
   <Obj Name>={'key1':'Value1','key2':'Value2',...}
               \_____________/  \_____________/
                   Item 1           Item 2
   ```

   Following are the examples which show the declaration of the dictionary object.

   ```
   >>> D={}
   >>> print(D)
   {} #Blank dictionary object created

   >>> D={12:"Twelve",4:"Four",7:"Seven"}
   >>> print(D)
   {12: 'Twelve', 4: 'Four', 7: 'Seven'}
   #Three items are stored in dictionary D. item_1 is 12: 'Twelve', item_2 is 4: 'Four', item_3 is 7: 'Seven'
   ```

3. The values are accessed using the respective keys. So a dictionary object doesn't have predefined keys (0,1,2..) unlike lists and tuples.

   ```
   >>> D={12:"Twelve",4:"Four",7:"Seven"}
   >>>print(D[12]) #Accessing value of item 1
   Twelve

   >>> print(D[7]) #Accessing value of item 3
   Seven

   >>> print(D[1])#There is no key '1'
   #KeyError as key 1 doesn't exist in the dictionary.
   ```

4. The key can be any immutable object, like integer, float, string or tuple. The value can be any object. Moreover keys in a dictionary cannot be repeated while values can be.

```
>>> D={12:"Class Twelve",(12,13):"Numbers","Value":99.99,True:"Yes"}
#Key in item 1 is integer 12 => allowed
#Key in item 2 is tuple (12,13) => allowed
#Key in item 3 is string 'Value' => allowed
#key in item 4 is Boolean True => allowed

>>> D={[12,13]:"Numbers",67:90}
#Key in item 1 is list [12,13] => NOT allowed as the key can only be an immutable object
TypeError: unhashable type: 'list'
```

5. The key must be unique, while the values may be repeated.

```
>>>D={1:11,2:22,3:33,4:11,5:22}
#Note that the value of D[1] and D[4] both is 11. Same way D[2] and D[5] value is 22. This is allowed
```

But, if the key is repeated in a dictionary, then it takes the last value assigned to the same key. For example

```
>>>D={1:11,1:22,3:33,4:11,1:29,3:56}
```

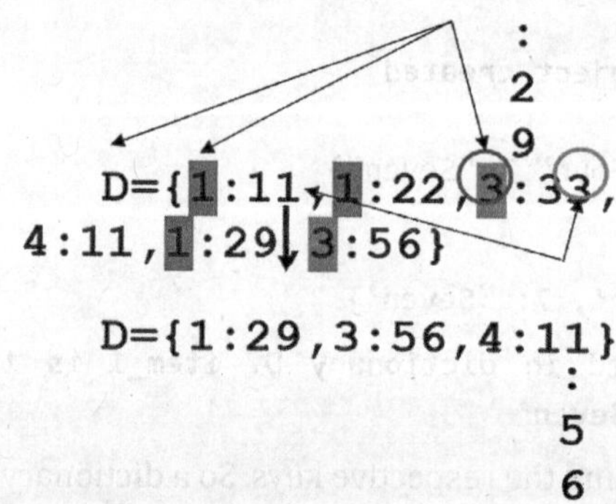

Last value for key '1' is 29, '3' is 56. Hence the last values are taken.

```
>>>print(D)
{1: 29, 3: 56, 4: 11}
```

Accessing the items in a dictionary

The item is accessed using a key. For example, in the given dictionary declaration,

```
>>>D={56:'strength',89:'average'}
```

We need to use the key in square brackets to get the value

```
>>> print(D[89])
average
>>> print(D[56])
strength
>>> print(D[0])
KeyError: 0
```

We can also get the items using a loop.

```
#Printing Keys of items
for i in D:
    print(i)
56
89
#Printing Values from Keys of items
for i in D:
    print(D[i])
strength
average
#Printing Keys and values both
for i in D:
    print(i, D[i],sep='-->')
56-->strength
89-->average
```

Why is dictionary a Mutable Object?

Mutability means ability to modify or change and that's what a dictionary object also allows. We can change the value and key (in an indirect way) of the dictionary Object. Adding and modifying an item in a dictionary is very easy.

```
D={"Roll":11,"Name":"Jatin","Class":12} #Dictionary object created print(D)
D['Age']=17  #'Age' key doesn't exist so its created
D['Roll']=10 #'Roll' key already present so its value is changed from 11 to 10
print(D)     # Modified Dictionary object
{'Roll': 11, 'Name': 'Jatin', 'Class': 12}              #Original Dictionary
{'Roll': 10, 'Name': 'Jatin', 'Class': 12, 'Age': 17}   #Changed Dictionary
```

Traversing a dictionary object

Since, keys are specified in a dictionary declaration, there are various ways to access the items of the dictionary.

To access each item of a dictionary object using a loop, we can use the name of the dictionary as shown in the example below:

```
#Simple way to access each item in a dictionary
D={"Roll":11,"Name":"Jatin","Class":12}
for i in D:        #By default keys are accessed when dictionary name is used in loop
  print(i,"has value",D[i])
```

```
Roll has value 11
Name has value Jatin
Class has value 12
```

```
#using List comprehension to display the items of a dictionary
D={"Roll":11,"Name":"Jatin","Class":12}
R=[(i,D[i]) for i in D]
print(R)
[('Roll', 11), ('Name', 'Jatin'), ('Class', 12)]
```

There are exclusive functions to access only keys or only values or items of the dictionary which we will study in the later part of the chapter.

Using membership operator with Dictionary Object

We can use 'in' and 'not in' membership operators to check whether a key is present in the dictionary or not.

```
#Program to accept a key and check whether it exists in the dictionary D or not.
D={'PID': 12, 'Name': 'Paste', 'Qty': 200, 'Price': 20, 'Code': '001'}
N=input("Enter the key to be searched")
if N in D:
  print(N,"Key found")
else:
  print(N,"Key not found")
```

```
Enter the key to be searchedQty
Qty Key found
>>>
================================== R
Enter the key to be searchedPaste
Paste Key not found
```

```
Enter the key to be searchedQty
Qty Key found
>>>
==================================== R
Enter the key to be searchedPaste
Paste Key not found
```

Built in functions used with Dictionary

	Function	Description	Syntax
1	len()	This function finds the length of the dictionary and returns the total number of items in it.	len(dictionary)
	Example:	D={"Roll":11,"Name":"Jatin","Class":12} print(len(D)) 3 print(len({1:6,2:7,3:8,4:9}) 4	
2	dict()	It is used to create a dictionary object, either blank or from a key value pair, given through an iterable.	dict() dict(iterable) dict(mapping)

		>>>D=dict() **# Blank Dictionary created**
		>>>print(D)
		{}
		
		#Dictionary can be created by providing the value to reactive keys. You don't have to provide the keys in quotes as it will be taken as an expression.
		>>>D=dict(A=22,B=994,C='N')
		>>>print(D)
		{'A': 22, 'B': 994, 'C': 'N'}
		>>>D=dict(RollNo=12,Name='Nisha',Class='XI')
		>>>print(D)
		
		#Dictionary can be created using mapping of (key, value) pairs, provided within iterable.
		>>> D=dict((('A',22),('B',994),('C','N')))
		>>> print(D)
		{'A': 22, 'B': 994, 'C': 'N'}
		OR
		>>> D=dict([('A',22),('B',994),('C','N')])
		>>> print(D)
		{'A': 22, 'B': 994, 'C': 'N'}	

		OR
		>>> D=dict(([‘A’,22],[‘B’,994],[‘C’,’N’]))
		>>> print(D)
		{‘A’: 22, ‘B’: 994, ‘C’: ‘N’}
		OR
		>>> D=dict([[‘A’,22],[‘B’,994],[‘C’,’N’]])
		>>> print(D)
		{‘A’: 22, ‘B’: 994, ‘C’: ‘N’}
		
		>>>D=dict(((‘RollNo’,12),(‘Name’,’Nisha’),(‘Class’,’XI’)),Age=17)
		>>>print(D)
		{‘RollNo’: 12, ‘Name’: ‘Nisha’, ‘Class’: ‘XI’, ‘Age’: 17}	

3	keys()	It is used to extract the list of available keys from the given Dictionary Object.	dictionary.keys()

		>>>D={‘RollNo’:12,’Name’:’Anna’,’per’:89}
		>>>print(D.keys())
		dict_keys([‘RollNo’, ‘Name’, ‘per’])
		
		#Using the keys() function with loop
		D={‘RollNo’:12,’Name’:’Anna’,’per’:89}
		for i in D.keys():
		    print(i, “=”, D[i])
		RollNo = 12
		Name = Anna
		per = 89
		
		Note that the above program can also be done without using the keys( ) function.
		D={‘RollNo’:12,’Name’:’Anna’,’per’:89}
		for i in D:
		    print(i, “=”, D[i])	

4	values()	It is used to extract the values of items from the given Dictionary Object.	dictionary.values()
		>>>D={‘RollNo’: 12, ‘Name’: ‘Nisha’, ‘Class’: ‘XI’, ‘Age’: 17} >>>print(D.values()) **dict_values([12, ‘Nisha’, ‘XI’, 17])** **#Using the values() function with loop** D={‘RollNo’: 12, ‘Name’: ‘Nisha’, ‘Class’: ‘XI’, ‘Age’: 17} for i in D.values(): print(i,end=’ , ‘) **12 , Nisha , XI , 17 ,**	

<table>
<tr><td></td><td></td><td colspan="2">

The above program can also be done without using the values( ) function.

```
D={'RollNo': 12, 'Name': 'Nisha', 'Class': 'XI', 'Age': 17}
for i in D:
    print(D[i],end=' , ')
```

```
#Program which accepts a number and checks whether it exists in the value or not.
D={12:90,22:100,67:23,45:700}
N=int(input("Enter the value to be searched"))
if N in D.values():
  print(N,"Value found")
else:
  print(N,"Value not found")

Enter the value to be searched100
100 Value found
```

</td></tr>
<tr><td>5</td><td>items()</td><td>It returns a copy of the dictionary's list of (key, value) pairs where the key value pairs are in the form of tuples.</td><td>dictionary.items()</td></tr>
<tr><td></td><td></td><td colspan="2">

```
#item() returns the list of tuples of key value pair
D={'RollNo': 12, 'Name': 'Nisha', 'Class': 'XI', 'Age': 17}
print(D.items())
dict_items([('RollNo', 12), ('Name', 'Nisha'), ('Class', 'XI'), ('Age', 17)])
```

```
#D.items generates list of tuples which are printed using loop
D={'RollNo': 12, 'Name': 'Nisha', 'Class': 'XI', 'Age': 17}
for i in D.items():
print(i)
('RollNo', 12)
('Name', 'Nisha')
('Class', 'XI')
('Age', 17)
```

```
#Another way of printing key value pair
D={'RollNo': 12, 'Name': 'Nisha', 'Class': 'XI', 'Age': 17}
for i,j in D.items():
print(i, " : ",j)
RollNo  :  12
Name  :  Nisha
Class  :  XI
Age  :  17
```

</td></tr>
<tr><td>6</td><td>get()</td><td>This function returns the value of the key if it exists in a dictionary otherwise returns "default value". If default is not provided, it returns "None"</td><td>Dictionary.get(key, default)</td></tr>
</table>

		P={"PID":12,"Name":"Brush","Qty":200,"Price":20} print(P.get("Pname")) **None #Pname key is not present in dictionary hence None returned** print(P.get("Pname","Not Present")) **Not Present #Pname key is not present in dictionary hence default value 'Not Present' returned** print(P.get("Name")) **Brush #The value 'Brush' returned as the key 'Name' is found** print(P.get("Name","Not Present")) **Brush #The value 'Brush' returned as the key 'Name' is found and hence the default value is ignored** P={"PID":[12,13],"Pname":["Brush","Pencil"],"Qty":[200,100],"-Price":[20,50]} print(P.get("Pname")) **['Brush', 'Pencil']#The value is returned as the key 'Pname' is found.** print(P.get("Pname","Not Present")) **['Brush', 'Pencil'] #The value is returned as the key 'Pname' is found and hence default is ignored** print(P.get("Quantity"))**#Quantity key is not present in dictionary hence None returned as no default value is specified.** **None**	
7	update()	It is used to update the dictionary object with either key/value pair or with another dictionary object. If the key exists, then its value is replaced in the dictionary otherwise the dictionary is updated by adding a new item.	Dictionary.update(key=value /dictionary/iterable)
		P={"PID":12,"Name":"Brush","Qty":200,"Price":20} print(P)**#Dictionary printed** **{'PID': 12, 'Name': 'Brush', 'Qty': 200, 'Price': 20}** P={"PID":12,"Name":"Brush"} P.update([("Qty",200),("Price",20)])**#Updating using elements provided in a list** print(P) **{'PID': 12, 'Name': 'Brush', 'Qty': 200, 'Price': 20}** P.update(Name="Pasta") print(P)**#Name exists in the object D, so its value is updated to 'Pasta'** **{'PID': 12, 'Name': 'Pasta', 'Qty': 200, 'Price': 20}**	

		P.update(Code="001") print(P)**#Code doesn't exist in the object so its added as the last item in the object** **{'PID': 12, 'Name': 'Paste', 'Qty': 200, 'Price': 20, 'Code': '001'}** D1={"Country":"India","State":"New Delhi"} D2={"Population":10909012,"State":"Delhi"} D1.update(D2)**#State changed from 'New Delhi' to 'Delhi', 'Population' added to D1** print(D1) **{'Country': 'India', 'State': 'Delhi', 'Population': 10909012}**	
8	del	del command is used to delete either the item by providing the key if it exists or it raises a KeyError, if the key doesn't exist. It can also delete the complete Object.	del <mutable object/key>
		P={'PID': 12, 'Name': 'Brush', 'Qty': 200, 'Price': 20} del P['Name']**#Name key deleted** print(P) **{'PID': 12, 'Qty': 200, 'Price': 20}** del P['Name']**#Name key was already deleted so error will occur** **KeyError: 'Name'** del P print(P)**#Since the object P was deleted, it doesn't exist anymore** **NameError: name 'P' is not defined**	
9	clear()	This function is used to remove all the items from a dictionary and it becomes blank. Note that this function doesn't remove or delete the object. It just makes its empty	dictionary.clear()
		P={'PID': 12, 'Name': 'Brush', 'Qty': 200, 'Price': 20} P.clear()**#Dictionary becomes empty as all items are deleted** print(P) **{}**	
10	fromkeys()	It is used to create a new dictionary with a given set of keys. Default value provided to the keys is 'None'. Though a value can be provided to the keys, but it will be the same for all the keys.	dict.fromkeys(iterable, value=None)
		#Keys are taken from the existing dictionary P for a new object S. But its values are not taken so, the default values for all keys become null P={"PID":12,"Name":"Brush","Qty":200,"Price":20} S=dict.fromkeys(P) print(S) **{'PID': None, 'Name': None, 'Qty': None, 'Price': None}**	

		#Keys are taken from the existing dictionary P for a new object S. But this time the value from the ‘Val’ object is assigned to all the keys of new dictionary S. P={“PID”:12,”Name”:”Brush”,”Qty”:200,”Price”:20} Val=”Data” S=dict.fromkeys(P,Val) print(S) **{‘PID’: ‘Data’, ‘Name’: ‘Data’, ‘Qty’: ‘Data’, ‘Price’: ‘Data’}** **#In this example, the keys are taken from the list. The values of all keys are taken from the object Val** Key=[‘a’,’e’,’i’,’o’,’u’] Val=’Vowel’ S=dict.fromkeys(Key,Val) print(S) **{‘a’: ‘Vowel’, ‘e’: ‘Vowel’, ‘i’: ‘Vowel’, ‘o’: ‘Vowel’, ‘u’: ‘Vowel’}** **#Here the keys are taken from the tuple (iterable object) and each of them have value taken from Val object (which is a tuple)** Key=(‘a’,’e’,’i’,’o’,’u’) Val=(‘Alphabet’,’Vowel’) S=dict.fromkeys(Key,Val) print(S) **{‘a’: (‘Alphabet’, ‘Vowel’), ‘e’: (‘Alphabet’, ‘Vowel’), ‘i’: (‘Alphabet’, ‘Vowel’), ‘o’: (‘Alphabet’, ‘Vowel’), ‘u’: (‘Alphabet’, ‘Vowel’)}** **#Here also the keys are taken from the list(iterable object) but each key is assigned the value None)** Key=[‘a’,’e’,’i’,’o’,’u’] S=dict.fromkeys(Key,None) print(S) **{‘a’: None, ‘e’: None, ‘i’: None, ‘o’: None, ‘u’: None}**	
11	copy()	It creates a shallow copy of the object. This means it makes a duplicate copy of the object. So any modification in the object will not be reflected in the copy. It doesn’t have any parameter	dictionary.copy()

		>>> E={“EID”:100,”Ename”:”Vinayak”,”Dept”:1}
		>>> F=E.copy() #Copy created
		>>> E[‘Sal’]=1200000 **#Original dictionary object modified**
		>>> print(E)
		{‘EID’: 100, ‘Ename’: ‘Vinayak’, ‘Dept’: 1, ‘Sal’: 1200000}	

<table>
<tr><td></td><td></td><td colspan="2">

```
>>> print(F) #Copy is not affected
{'EID': 100, 'Ename': 'Vinayak', 'Dept': 1}
```

Note: If we directly copy the object without any function, then the new object will refer to the same address where the original object points. So any changes made in either of the objects will be seen in both.

```
>>>E={'EID': 100, 'Ename': 'Vinayak', 'Dept': 1, 'Sal': 1200000}
>>> F=E
>>> F['GradePay']=4500

>>> print(F)
{'EID': 100, 'Ename': 'Vinayak', 'Dept': 1, 'Sal': 1200000, 'GradePay': 4500}

>>> print(E)
{'EID': 100, 'Ename': 'Vinayak', 'Dept': 1, 'Sal': 1200000, 'GradePay': 4500}
#Changes are reflected in E and F both whenever any changes are done either in E or F
```

</td></tr>
<tr><td>12</td><td>pop()</td><td>It is used to remove the item whose key is provided and its value is returned. If the key doesn't exist, it returns the default value else a KeyError is raised. Unlike in list, this function cannot be used with a parameter.</td><td>Dictionary.pop (Key,default=-None)</td></tr>
<tr><td></td><td></td><td colspan="2">

```
P={"PID":12,"PName":"Pen","Qty":200,"Price":20}
print(P.pop("PName","No such Key"))
Pen #Key PName exist so its value is returned

P={"PID":12,"PName":"Pen","Qty":200,"Price":20}
print(P.pop("NAme"))
KeyError: 'NAme' (as NAme doesn't Exist)
#KeyError raised as the the default value is not specified
And the key 'NAme' doesn't exist

P={"PID":12,"PName":"Pen","Qty":200,"Price":20}
print(P.pop("NAme","No Such Key"))
No Such Key

#We can use pop( ) to change the key in the dictionary. The code below changes the key from 'Qty' to 'Quantity'
P={"PID":12,"PName":"Pen","Qty":200,"Price":20}
P["Quantity"]=P.pop("Qty")
print(P)
{'PID': 12, 'PName': 'Pen', 'Price': 20, 'Quantity': 200}
```

</td></tr>
<tr><td>13</td><td>popitem()</td><td>It removes the last item inserted in the dictionary. It returns the key and value of the item deleted as a tuple. Will show KeyError if the dictionary is empty. It doesn't take any parameter.</td><td>dictionary.popitem()</td></tr>
</table>

<table>
<tr><td></td><td></td><td colspan="2">>>> Code={"R":1,"G":2,"B":3}
>>> Code.popitem()
('B', 3)
#the last item is removed and returned as key value pair
>>> Code.clear()**#Making the dictionary object empty**
>>> Code.popitem() **#Error as there is no key to delete**
KeyError: 'popitem(): dictionary is empty'</td></tr>
<tr><td>14</td><td>setdefault()</td><td>This function returns the value of the key provided as the attribute. If the key doesn't exist, then it is added in the dictionary with the default value. If no default value is provided, then 'None' is added as a value.</td><td>dictionary.setdefault(key,default=None)</td></tr>
<tr><td></td><td></td><td colspan="2">>>>Code={"R":1,"G":2,"B":3}
>>> Code.setdefault("G")
2 #The key 'G' exist in the dictionary, so its value is returned, which is 2
>>> Code.setdefault("g")
>>> print(Code)
{'R': 1, 'G': 2, 'B': 3, 'g': None} #The key 'g' doesn't exist so its inserted in the dictionary. Since its value is not provided, the default 'None' is taken as the value
>>> print(Code.setdefault("g",4))
None #Since the key 'g' was inserted in the previous command, so None returned.
>>> Code.setdefault("G","X"))
2 #Since the key 'G' exists, 2 returned and the value 'X' is ignored
>>>Code.setdefault("b",33))
33 #The key 'b' doesn't exist so it's inserted in the dictionary with the value 33.
>>> print(Code)
{'R': 1, 'G': 2, 'B': 3, 'g': None, 'b': 33}</td></tr>
<tr><td>15</td><td>max()</td><td>It returns the maximum 'key' or 'value' in the Dictionary. Note that the data type of all keys or all values must be same</td><td>max(iterable)</td></tr>
<tr><td></td><td></td><td colspan="2">>>> N={7:"Seven",4:"Four",9:"Nine",3:"Three"}
>>> max(N)**#By default, the maximum of key values is returned, if not explicitly specified**
9
OR
>>> max(N.keys())**#Same result as above generated**
9</td></tr>
</table>

		>>> max(N.values())
		'Three'#Returns the minimum value from the values in the dictionary. For strings, the search is done as per the alphabet's ASCII code.
		
		>>> max(N.items())#It returns the tuple which has a key-value pair. But the max value returned is with respect to the key. So the item returned is the one which has the largest key
		(9, 'Nine')	

16	min()	It returns the minimum 'key' or 'value' in the Dictionary. Note that the data type of all keys or all values must be same	min(iterable)

		>>> N={7:"Seven",4:"Four",9:"Nine",3:"Three"}
		>>> min(N)#By default, the minimum of key values is returned, if not explicitly specified
		3
		OR
		>>> min(N.keys())#Same result as above generated
		3
		
		>>> min(N.values())
		'Four'#Returns the minimum value from the values in the dictionary. For strings, the search is done as per the alphabet's ASCII code.
		
		>>> min(N.items())#It returns the tuple which has a key-value pair. But the min value returned is with respect to the key. So the item returned is the one which has the smallest key
		(3, 'Three')	

17	sorted()	It returns a sorted list of the specified iterable. Default sorting is in ascending order	sorted(iterable,reverse=True)
		>>>a={'p':12,'s':13,'a':55,'b':23,'n':11} >>>print(sorted(a))#returns the sorted list of keys ['a', 'b', 'n', 'p', 's'] >>>print(sorted(a.values())) #returns the sorted list of values [11, 12, 13, 23, 55] >>>print(sorted(a.items()))#returns the sorted list of tuple of items with respect to keys [('a', 55), ('b', 23), ('n', 11), ('p', 12), ('s', 13)] >>>print(sorted(a.items(),reverse=True)) #returns the sorted list of tuple of items in reverse order [('s', 13), ('p', 12), ('n', 11), ('b', 23), ('a', 55)]	

Example1: Program to accept Name and Salary of an employee and store it in a dictionary.

```
D={}
D['Name']=input("Enter Name")
D['Sal']=float(input("Enter Salary"))
print(D)
```

```
Enter NameJohn
Enter Salary34567
{'Name': 'John', 'Sal': 34567.0}
```

Example 2: Program to accept Names and Salaries of employees and store in a dictionary in the format {Name: [Name 1, Name 2.....], Sal:[Sal1, Sal2...]}. Do it for N number of employees

```
D={}
N=[]
S=[]
while True:
   N.append(input("Enter Name"))
   S.append(float(input("Enter Salary")))
   Ch=input("More records")
   if Ch in ['n','N']:
      D['Name']=N
      D['Salary']=S
      break
print(D)
Enter NameJack
Enter Salary4567
More recordsy
Enter NameHarry
Enter Salary9054
More recordsY
Enter NamePrick
Enter Salary5426
More recordsN
{'Name': ['Jack', 'Harry', 'Prick'], 'Salary': [4567.0, 9054.0, 5426.0]}
```

Example 3: Program to combine two dictionaries by adding the values of common key. The dictionary D1 should be modified. For example

D1={“Data1”:100,”Data2”:200,”Data3”:600}

D2={“Data1”:500,”Data4”:800,”Data3”:100}

The modified dictionary D1 should be

D1={‘Data1’: 600, ‘Data2’: 200, ‘Data3’: 700, ‘Data4’: 800}

```
D1={"Data1":100,"Data2":200,"Data3":600}
D2={"Data1":500,"Data4":800,"Data3":100}
#Desired Result {'Data1': 600, 'Data2': 200, 'Data3': 700, 'Data4': 800}
for i in D2: #Keys of D2 extracted
  if i in D1: #Checked whether the key extracted is present in D1
     D1[i]+=D2[i] #If yes then values are added
  else:
     D1[i]=D2[i] #If not then its inserted
print(D1)
```

```
{'Data1': 600, 'Data2': 200, 'Data3': 700, 'Data4': 800}
```

Example 4: Program to find min, max and sum all the values in a dictionary.

```
R={5:23,9:44,88:12,90:45,4:26,7:44}
print("Minimum Value:",min(R.values()))
print("Maximum Value:",max(R.values()))
print("Sum of Values:",sum(R.values()))
```

```
Minimum Value: 12
Maximum Value: 45
Sum of Values: 194
```

Example 5: Program to create a dictionary of items in the form (N, N*N), for N numbers where N is accepted by the user. For example

If N=3

D={1:1,2:4,3:9}

```
D={}
N=int(input("Enter the number of terms"))
for i in range(1,N+1):
  D[i]=i**2
print("Dictionary Content: ",D)
```

```
Enter the number of terms6
Dictionary Content:  {1: 1, 2: 4, 3: 9, 4: 16, 5: 25, 6: 36}
```

Example 6: Program to accept a key and remove it from a dictionary

```
R={5:23,9:44,88:12,90:45,4:26,7:44}
N=int(input("Enter key to be searched"))
if N in R:
  print(N, "removed with value",R.pop(N))
  print("Modified dictionary",R)
else:
  print("Key not found")
```

```
Enter key to be searched90
90 removed with value 45
Modified dictionary {5: 23, 9: 44, 88: 12, 4: 26, 7: 44}
```

Example 7: Program to sort the items of the dictionary as per the key in ascending order.

```
a={'p':12,'s':13,'a':55,'b':23,'n':11}
print("Original Dictionary :",a)
L=sorted(a.items())
a=dict(L)
print("Sorted dictionary",a)
```

```
Original Dictionary : {'p': 12, 's': 13, 'a': 55, 'b': 23, 'n': 11}
Sorted dictionary {'a': 55, 'b': 23, 'n': 11, 'p': 12, 's': 13}
```

Example 8: Program to sort the items of the dictionary as per the value in ascending order.

```
R={5:23,9:44,88:12,90:45,4:26,7:44}
print("Original Dictionary",R)
T=sorted(R.items(),key=lambda x:x[1])
R=dict(T)
print("Sorted Dictionary",R)
```

```
Original Dictionary {5: 23, 9: 44, 88: 12, 90: 45, 4: 26, 7: 44}
Sorted Dictionary {88: 12, 5: 23, 4: 26, 9: 44, 7: 44, 90: 45}
```

Example 9: Program to count the occurrence of each character in a string and store it in a dictionary D

```
D={}
N=input("Enter a string")
for i in N:
  if i not in D:
    D[i]=N.count(i)
print(D)
```

```
Enter a stringTHIS IS A TRUE STORY
{'T': 3, 'H': 1, 'I': 2, 'S': 3, ' ': 4, 'A': 1, 'R': 2, 'U': 1, 'E': 1, 'O': 1, 'Y': 1}
```

Example 10: Program to display unique values from a dictionary D

```
#Method 1
D={5:23,9:44,88:12,90:45,4:26,7:44,6:23}
T=list(D.values())
print("Unique values",list(set(T)))

#Method 2
D={5:23,9:44,88:12,90:45,4:26,7:44,6:23}
U=dict.fromkeys(D.values())
print("Unique Values",list(U.keys()))
```

```
Unique values [44, 45, 12, 23, 26]
Unique Values [23, 44, 12, 45, 26]
```

Example 11: Create a dictionary with the roll number, name and marks of n students in a class and display the rollno and names of students who have scored marks above 75.

```
D={}
while True:
  Roll=input("Enter Roll No")
  Name=input("Enter Name")
  mks=float(input("Enter Mks"))
  D[Roll]=[Name,mks]
  ch=input("More Records")
  if ch in ['n','N']:
    break
print("The details of students who have scored marks above 75 are")
for x,y in D.items():
  if y[1]>75:
    print("Roll No:", x,"Name:",y[0])
```

```
Enter Roll No12
Enter NameNisha
Enter Mks78
More Recordsy
Enter Roll No2
Enter NameUrvashi
Enter Mks75.5
More Recordsy
Enter Roll No8
Enter NamePriyesh
Enter Mks67
More Recordsy
Enter Roll No40
Enter NameTanushree
Enter Mks98
More Recordsy
Enter Roll No3
Enter NameRiya
Enter Mks66
More Recordsn
The details of students who have scored marks above 75 are
Roll No: 12 Name: Nisha
Roll No: 2 Name: Urvashi
Roll No: 40 Name: Tanushree
```

Note: if the format for storing the data is not specified then the program can be done in variety of ways

Summary

1. Dictionary is a mutable iterable object which stores not only values but their respective keys also.
2. Keys in a dictionary are unique and can be any immutable object while values can be repeated and can be of any data type.
3. Each key-value pair in a dictionary is called an item. The items are enclosed in curly brackets.
4. `len()` function finds and returns the length of the dictionary.
5. `dict()` function is used to create a dictionary object.
6. `keys()` function is used to extract the list of available keys from the given Dictionary Object.
7. `values()` function is used to extract the values of items from the given Dictionary Object.
8. `items()` function returns a copy of the dictionary's list of (key, value) pairs where the key value pairs are in the form of tuples.
9. `get()` function returns the value of the key if it exists in a dictionary otherwise returns "default value". If default is not provided, it returns "None"
10. `update()` used to update the dictionary object with either key/value pair or with another dictionary object.
11. `del` command is used to delete either the item by providing the key if it exists or it raises a KeyError, if the key doesn't exist. It can also delete the complete Object.

12. `clear()` function is used to remove all the items from a dictionary and it becomes blank. Note that this function doesn't remove or delete the object.
13. `fromkeys()` is used to create a new dictionary with a given set of keys. Default value provided to the keys is 'None'.
14. `copy()` function creates a shallow copy of the object.
15. `pop()` function is used to remove the item whose key is provided and its value is returned. It must have a parameter
16. `popitems()` function is used to remove the last item inserted in the dictionary. It doesn't have any parameters.
17. `setdefault()` function returns the value of the key provided as the attribute. If the key doesn't exist, then it is added in the dictionary with the default value.
18. `max()` returns the maximum 'key' or 'value' in the Dictionary. If a dictionary object is passed without any function , like keys() or values(), then it returns the maximum of key values.
19. `min()` returns the minimum 'key' or 'value' in the Dictionary. If a dictionary object is passed without any function, like keys() or values(), then it returns the maximum of key values.
20. `sorted()` function returns a sorted list of the specified iterable. If the dictionary object is passed as a parameter without keys(), values(), items() functions, then the list of sorted keys is returned.

Questions

1. Given two dictionary objects D1 and D2. Create a third dictionary object by merging both the objects as shown below:

```
D1={1:11, 2:22}
D2={3:33, 4:44}
NewD : {1: 11, 2: 22, 3: 33, 4: 44}
```

2. Write a Python code to accept the Pcode and Pname for a few products and store them in dictionary D. Accept a code and check if it's existing in the Dictionary D and print the product name.

```
D={"P11":"Mobile","P2":"Blanket","P45":"Table"}
Accept Code: P2
Product Name: Blanket
```

3. Write a Python code to accept a number N and generate a dictionary that contains items in the form of num, num* num from 1 and N.

```
If N=5, then the dictionary created should be
D={1:1,2:4,3:9,4:16,5:25}
```

4. Accept N elements in two lists L1 and L2, such that L1 contains the names of the cricketers and L2 contains their best score in One Day match. Create a dictionary object such that the elements of L1 become the key and the elements of L2 become their value and print the result.

```
If
L1=["Rahul Dravid","Dhoni","Sachin"]
```

```
L2=[177,183, 200]
Then
D={"Rahul Dravid":177,"Dhoni":183,"Sachin":200}
```

5. Write a python code to store N items as "JeweleryName":"Price" in a dictionary object D. Arrange the Dictionary object by their keys in alphabetical order. For example, if

```
D={"earrings":100,"bracelet":250,"necklace":8000}
Then the sorted result should be:
{'bracelet': 250, 'earings': 100, 'necklace': 8000}
```

6. Given a dictionary object D, accept a key which should be removed.
7. Write a Python code to combine two dictionary adding values for common keys.

```
If D1 = {'a': 100, 'b': 200, 'c':300}
D2 = {'a': 300, 'b': 200, 'd':400}
R={'a': 400, 'b': 400, 'd': 400, 'c': 300}
```

8. Write a python program to accept a string from the user and create a dictionary object which stores the vowels as keys and their count in the string as their values. For example:

```
Enter a string welcome to the world of magic
{'a': 1, 'e': 3, 'i': 1, 'o': 4, 'u': 0}
```

9. Write a python program to find the name of the Item with maximum quantity from the dictionary D which stores items as keys and their quantity as value.

   For example

```
D={'item1':67,'item2':55,'item3':77}
Result: item3
```

10. Write a Python Code to represent the data of the list Buses and tuple Mileage in the dictionary Transport. Dictionary Transport should contain each value from Buses as key and corresponding value from tuple Mileage.

```
Buses=["Ashok Leyland","Tata Starbus","Mahindra Cruzio"]
Mileage=(100,90,110)
```

   Find the following from the dictionary Transport

   Maximum and Minimum mileage, Average Mileage, Total Mileage and the Bus name with maximum and minimum mileage

   For example:

```
Transport
{"Ashok Leyland":100,"Tata Starbus":90,"Mahindra Cruzio:110"}
Maximum mileage - 110 Minimum mileage - 90
Average mileage - 100 Total mileage - 300
Bus name with maximum mileage - Mahindra Cruzio
Bus name with minimum mileage - Tata Starbus
```

11. Give the output

a.
```
A ="GREAT WORK";
D={True:1,False:0}
for I in A:
    print(D[I not in "AEIOU"],end='#')
```

b.
```
A={1:"X",2:"Y",3:"Z"}
for i,j in A.items():
    print(i,j,end="*")
```

c.
```
d={"name":"Ravi","DOB":"22-04-2007","Per":77}
d1={"Name":"Rahul"}
d1=d.copy()
print("d1 :",d1)
```

d.
```
d={"name":"Ravi","DOB":"22-04-2007","Per":77}
d1={"Name":"Rahul"}
d.update(d1)
print("d :",d)
print("d1 :",d1)
```

12. MCQ

A. If a is a dictionary with some key-value pairs, what does a.popitem() do?

  a. It will removes all the key-value pairs

  b. It will removes the key-value pair for the key given as an argument

  c. It will remove the last item from the dictionary but doesn't return it

  d. It will remove and return the last item from the dictionary

B. Which of the statement(s) is/are correct.

  a. Dictionary is an iterable object.

  b. Python dictionary is a mapping of unique keys to values

  c. Dictionary is mutable.

  d. All the above.

C. Keys of the dictionary must be

  a. Same b. Unique

  c. can be similar or unique d. All of these

D. The function used to remove all items from a dictionary object.

  a. clear( ) b. pop( ) c. del d. keys( )

E. The function which will return key-value pair of the dictionary

  a. key( ) b. values( ) c. items( ) d. dict( )

F. To create a dictionary , key-value pairs are separated by................

a. Semicolon (;) b. Comma (,) c. Colon (:) d. Slash (/)

G. Which of the following statements create a dictionary?

a. `d = { }` b. `d = {"john":40, "peter":45}`

c. `d = {40 : "john", 45 : "peter"}` d. `All of the mentioned above`

13. Differentiate between Dict.setdefault() and Dict1.update()functions used with a data type dictionary with suitable examples of each.

14. Name the function which can be used to perform the following on the python dictionary object

    a. Returns list of values of dictionary Dict

    b. Removes all the items from a dictionary

    c. Returns a list of (key, value) tuple pairs

5. To create a dictionary, key-value pairs are separated by................

   a. Semicolon (;) b. Comma (,) c. Colon (:) d. Slash (/)

6. Which of the following statements create a dictionary?

   a. d = {} b. d = {"john":40, "peter":45}

   c. d = {40:"john", 45:"peter"} d. All of the mentioned above.

13. Differentiate between Dict.setdefault() and Dict.update() functions used with a data type dictionary with suitable examples of each.

14. Name the function which can be used to perform the following on the python dictionary object:

    a. Returns list of values of dictionary Dict

    b. Removes all the items from a dictionary

    c. Returns a list of (key,value) tuple pairs

13 Sorting Techniques

Sorting techniques

Arranging the elements of an object in increasing or decreasing order is called sorting. Though sorting is very easily possible in Python and can be implemented by using the sort() function, we still need to understand the techniques behind the concept of sorting. There are a variety of sorting techniques which are used on the basis of data and efficiency. Some of them are Bubble Sort., Selection Sort. Merge Sort, Insertion Sort, Quick Sort and Heap Sort. in this section we will understand two very commonly used sorting techniques:

1. Bubble Sort
2. Insertion Sort

Bubble sort is a technique where two consecutive elements are compared and the largest of the two is shifted to the right. The process is repeated depending on the number of elements in the list.

Let us understand the method diagramatically:

In Task-1, the largest element is moved to the right side. So 97 is shifted to the right and becomes the last element. The same task is to be repeated for second largest, third largest and so on.

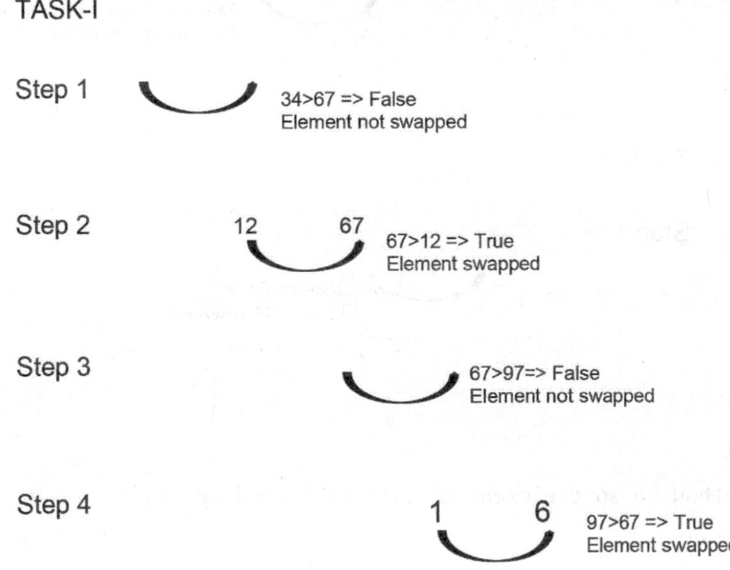

In Task 2 the same process is repeated but till the second last index number as the appropriate value has already reached the last index number.

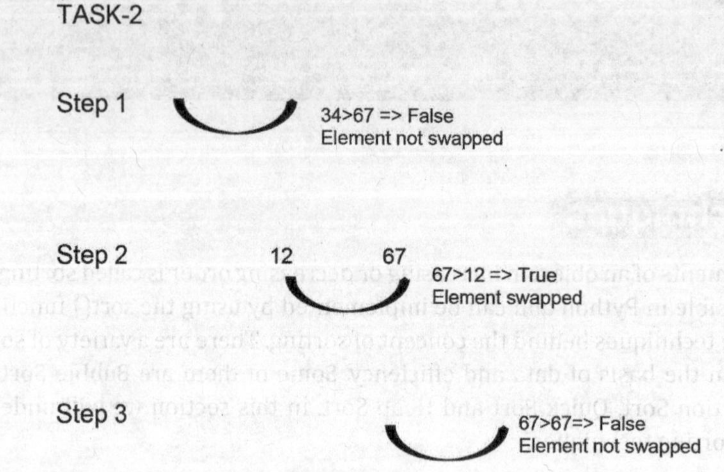

Task 3 and 4 are performed in the similar manner

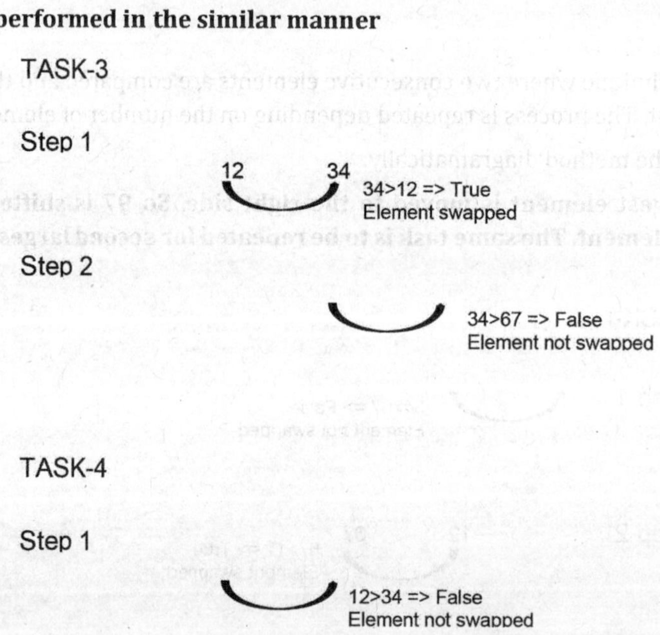

Elements

Final Program-1

```
#Bubble Sort method to sort element of list in ascending order
L=[34,12,67,97,67]
   for i in range(len(L)-1):
      for j in range(len(L)-i-1):
         if L[j]>L[j+1]:
```

```
            L[j],L[j+1]=L[j+1],L[j]
print(L)
```

#Output

[12, 34, 67, 67, 97]

Program-2

```
#Bubble Sort method to sort element of list in descending order
L=[34,12,67,97,67]
for i in range(len(L)-1):
    for j in range(len(L)-i-1):
        if L[j]<L[j+1]:
            L[j],L[j+1]=L[j+1],L[j]
print(L)
```

[97, 67, 67, 34, 12]

Insertion Sort is the method, where we assume that the list is divided into two parts, the left side sorted with one element and right side with the rest of the elements which are unsorted. The logic is that one element at a time is picked from the unsorted part and shifted to a sorted area.

Original List

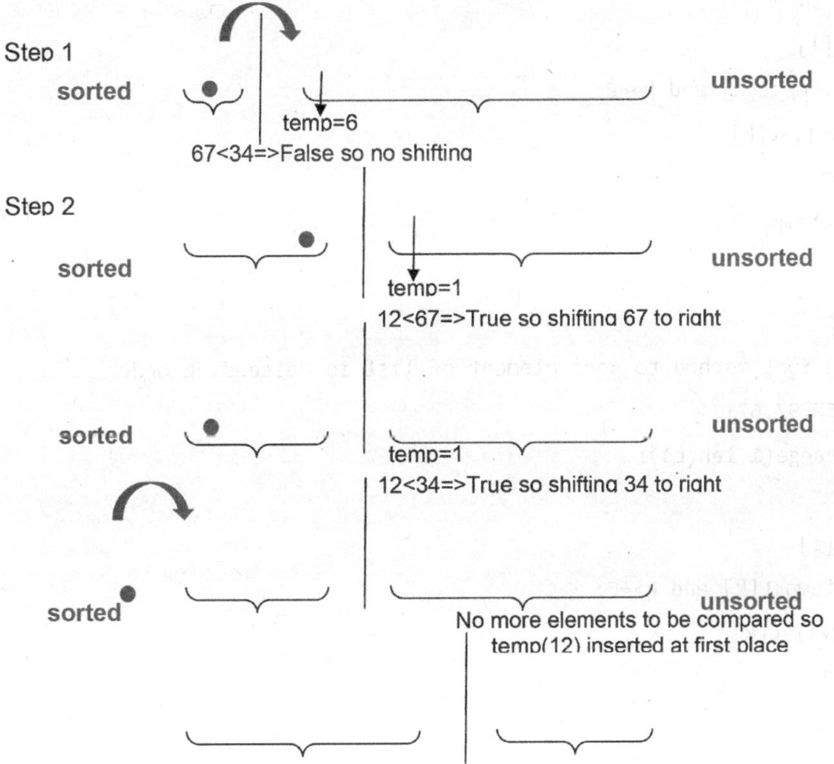

Program-1

```
#Insertion Sort method to sort element of list in ascending order
```

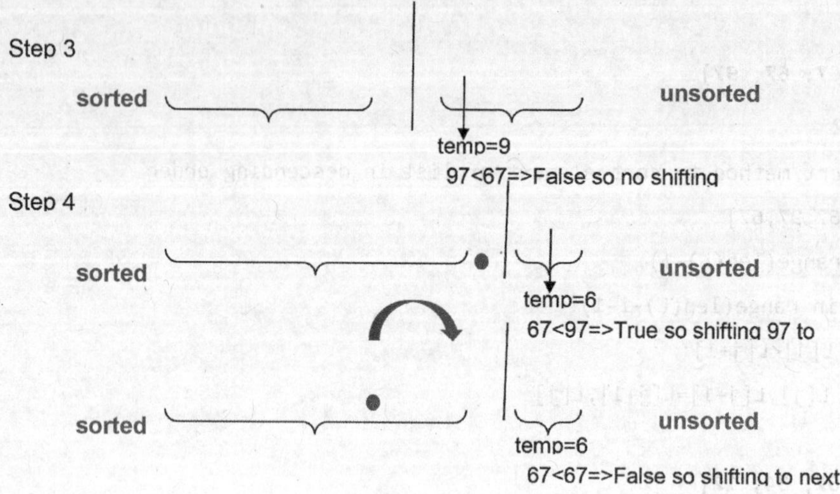

List Sorted

```
L=[34,12,67,97,67]
for i in range(1,len(L)):
    k=i-1
    temp=L[i]
    while temp<L[k] and k>=0:
        L[k+1]=L[k]
        k-=1
    L[k+1]=temp
print(L)
```

Program-2

```
#Insertion Sort method to sort element of list in descending order
L=[34,12,67,97,67]
for i in range(1,len(L)):
    k=i-1
    temp=L[i]
    while temp<L[k] and k>=0:
        L[k+1]=L[k]
        k-=1
```

```
    L[k+1]=temp
print(L)
```

Summary

1. Arranging the elements of an object in increasing or decreasing order is called sorting. Some of the types of sorting are Bubble Sort., Selection Sort. Merge Sort, Insertion Sort, Quick Sort and Heap Sort.
2. Bubble sort is a technique where two consecutive elements are compared and the largest of the two is shifted to the right.
3. Insertion Sort is the method, where we assume that the list is divided into two parts, the left side sorted with one element and right side with the rest of the elements which are unsorted.

Questions

1. Write a program to accept 5 elements in a list L and arrange them in descending order using the bubble sort method.
2. Write a program to accept 7 names of flowers in a list L and arrange them in ascending order as per their length using any sorting method.

   For example:

   `L=[Lavender, Rose, Lotus, Jasmine, Sunflower, Daisy, Magnolia]`

   Sorted List:

   `[Rose, Lotus, Daisy, Jasmine, Lavender, Magnolia, Sunflower]`
3. Write a program to accept names of your 5 friends in a list L and arrange them in descending order as per their last letter in the name using the insertion sort method.

   For example:

   `L=['Angel', 'Prisha', 'Nidhi', 'Jasmine', 'Rajiv']`

   Sorted List:

   `['Prisha', 'Jasmine', 'Nidhi', 'Angel', 'Rajiv']`
4. The following program will sort all the elements of the given list in descending order, if all the blanks are filled in correctly.

   ```
   L=[55,12,89,34,9]
   for i ____ range(______):
       for ____ in range(______):
           if L[j]_____L[j+1]:
               L[j],L[j+1]______L[_____],L[j]
   ```

5. The following program will sort all the modes of transportation stored in the given list in ascending order using the insertion sort method, if all the blanks are filled in correctly.

```
L=["bus", "car", "bike", "rikshaw", "scooter", "plane"]
for i in ____(1,len(L)):
    k=i-1
    temp=______
    while _______<len(L[k]) and k____0:
        L[k+1]=L[k]
        k=______
    L[____]=temp
print(L)
```

14 Python Modules

Introduction to Python modules

When you write python programs, there is always a possibility where you need to use few of the already written program tasks in other programs too. But as soon as you close a program, the commands written inside it cannot be accessed by other programs and you need to write them again. Similarly when your program becomes too long, it is always convenient to break the task into various files as this will allow easy modification and reusability. To accomplish this task, python allows you to make files with some commonly used functions or scripts so that they can be accessed as and when needed. They are called modules. So, we can say that a python module contains definitions of tasks and commands which can be used as and when needed in other programs.

For example, you can create a module which can find the square root and cube root of a number and use them as per the program requirement. As said earlier, the modules are also Python programs, so their file extension is .py. You will learn to create modules in class XII.

To use the module in your python program, you have two options:

1. Using import keyword
2. Using from statement.

Importing module using 'import'

You can use import <module name> either in the interpreter or script mode to start accessing the functions inside it.

`>>>import math` #will allow your program to access the functions in the math module

When using this method, you need to prefix the name of the module to the name of the function.

```
>>>math.sqrt(10)
3.1622776601683795
```

Also, you can access all the functions defined inside the module

You can also temporarily change the name of the module using this method of accessing module functions

`>>>import math as M` #Math module will be referred as 'M' in the current program

```
>>>M.sqrt(10)
```

Importing module using 'from' statement

Syntax:

```
>>>from <module name> import *
```

When using this method, you don't have to prefix the module name to the function name. Using this method, all functions can be imported except those beginning with an underscore(_).

```
>>>from math import *
>>>sqrt(8)
2.8284271247461903
```

If you do not wish to import all the functions of a module, then you can specify the names of the functions to be imported.

```
>>>from math import sqrt
>>sqrt(8)
2.8284271247461903
>>>ceil(4)
NameError: name 'ceil' is not defined
```

Importing math module : We will study the following mathematical related functions available in the math module.

functions/ commands in math module	Purpose	Example	Output
pi	It provides the value for π = 3.141592..., to available precision.	import math r=5 print("Area of circle :",math.pi*r*r)	Area of circle : 78. 53981633974483
e	It provides the value for mathematical constant e = 2.718281..., to available precision.	import math print("e=",math.e)	e= 2.71 8281828459045
sqrt(x)	This function returns the square root of x. It returns float answer	import math print(math.sqrt(2)) print(math.sqrt(6.2)) print(math.sqrt(4.0)) print(math.sqrt(-2))	 1.41421.... 2.48997.. 2.0 ValueError

ceil(x)	This function returns the smallest integer greater than or equal to x.	`import math`
		`print(math.ceil(4))`
		`print(math.ceil(4.0))`
		`print(math.ceil(4.9))`
		`print(math.ceil(0.4))`
			
			4
			4
			5
			1

floor(x)	This function returns the largest integer less than or equal to x.	`import math`
		`print(math.floor(4))`
		`print(math.floor(3.7))`
		`print(math.floor(4.9))`
		`print(math.floor(0.4))`
			
			4
			3
			4
			0

pow(x,y)	This function returns x raised to power y. The answer returned is a float value as it converts both arguments x and y to float.
	Note that if x is negative and y is float, then the function raises ValueError.
	It is different from ** (Exponentiation) operator as it generates float result while ** generates integer result if both x and y are integers
		`import math`
		`print(math.pow(2,4))`
		`print(math.pow(2.1,2))`
		`print(math.pow(1.1,2.2))`
		`print(math.pow(2,-1))`
		`print(math.pow(2,1/2))`
		`print(math.pow(-2,3))`
		`print(math.pow(2,0))`
		`print(math.pow(0,3))`
		`print(math.pow(-2,3.1))`
		`#ValueError`
			
			16.0
			4.41
			1.2332...
			0.5
			1.41421...
			-8.0
			1.0
			0.0
			ValueError

fabs(x)	This function returns the absolute value of x. The answer returned is a floating point answer.	`import math`
		`print(math.fabs(-4))`
		`print(math.fabs(4.0))`
		`print(math.fabs(4.9))`
		`print(math.fabs(-0.4))`
			
			4.0
			4.0
			4.9
			0.4

sin(x)	This function returns the sine of x radians.	`import math`
		`for i in range(1,10):`
		`  print(math.sin(i))`
		0.8414709848078965
		0.9092974268256817
		0.1411200080598672
		-0.7568024953079282
		-0.9589242746631385
		-0.27941549819892586
		0.6569865987187891
		0.9893582466233818
		0.4121184852417566	

cos(x)	This function returns the cosine of x radians.	import math for i in range(1,10): print(math.cos(i)) 0.5403023058681398 -0.4161468365471424 -0.9899924966004454 -0.6536436208636119 0.2836621854632263 0.9601702866503661 0.7539022543433046 -0.14550003380861354 -0.9111302618846769
tan(x)	This function returns the tangent of x radians.	import math for i in range(1,5): print(math.tan(i)) 1.557407724654902 -2.185039863261519 -0.1425465430742778 1.1578212823495775

Importing random module

This module is used to generate random numbers on various criterias.

functions/ commands in random module	Purpose	Example	Output
random	It generates a floating point random number in the range from 0.0 to 1.0, where 1.0 is not included	import random for i in range(1,6): print(random.random()) 0.8324776635009212 0.8819136587417624 0.5945430308758748 0.5728661800999074 0.8560473420149999	
randint(x,y)	It generates an integer random number between x and y, where both x and y can be included	import random for i in range(1,5): print(random.randint(1,10)) 7 8 8 2	

randrange(start,end,-step)	It generates an integer random number between start and end-1 (both included), the interval of random number depends on step value.
	Default step value is 1 if not provided. Default start value is 0, if not provided
		For example :
		randrange(1,7) can have possible random numbers as (1,2,3,4,5,6)
		randrange(1,7,2) can have possible random numbers as (1,3,5)
		randrange(10,2,-2) can have possible random numbers as (10,8,6,4)
		randrange(-5,1) can have possible random numbers as (-5,-4,-3,-2,-1,0)
		`import random`
		`for i in range(1,5):`
		` print(random.randrange(1,20), end=',')`
		2,1,14,15,

Importing statistics module

This module is used for calculating mathematical statistics of numeric data.

functions/ commands in statistics module	Purpose	Example	Output

mean(data)	▪ It is used to calculate the average of numeric data provided in the form of an iterable or a sequence.
	▪ It takes only one argument.
	▪ The numeric data can be integer or float, positive or negative.
	▪ The result is always a float value.
		`>>> from statistics import *`
		`>>> a=[4,7,8,1,2]`
		`>>> b=(44,6.7,3)`
		`>>> d={1:89,5.5:99}`
		`>>> mean(a)`
		4.4 #mean->(4+7+8+1+2)/5
		
		`>>> mean(b)`
		17.9 #mean->(44+6.7+3)/3
		`>>> mean(d)`
		3.25 #mean->(1+5.5)/2
		
		`>>> mean([12,56,89])`
		52.333333333333336	

Median (data)	■ It returns the middle value of the numeric data provided in the form of an iterable.
	■ If there are even data values, then the median is calculated by taking the average of the middle two values.
	■ Note that if the data items are provided in an unsorted manner then they are first arranged in ascending order and then median is calculated.
	■ The numeric data provided can be positive, negative, integer or float data.
	■ If the data is empty, then StatisticsError is raised
		`>>> from statistics import *`
		`>>> X=[45,12,5,1,8]`
		`>>> median(X)`
		`8 #[1,5,8,12,45]`
		`>>> Y=[1,4,7,9]`
		`>>> median(Y)`
		`5.5#(4+7)/2=5.5`
		`>>> Z=(1.1,6,6.2,7,7.5)`
		`>>> median(Z)`
		`6.2 #(1.1,6,6.2,7,7.5)`
		`>>> median((-9,-3,-4))`
		`-4 #(-9,-4,-3)`
		`>>>median(())`
		`StatisticsError: no median for empty data`

mode(data)	■ It returns the single most common data from the given data values.
	■ If there is no common data, then the first one in the list is returned.
	■ If there are multiple modes with the same frequency, then the first one in the list is returned.
	■ It can take non numeric parameters also.
	■ If the data is empty, then StatisticsError is raised
		`>>> A=[1,2,3,4,5]`
		`>>> mode(A)`
		`1` `#No common value so the first value 1 is returned`
		`>>> A=[7,4,2,6,3]`
		`>>> mode(A)`
		`7` `#No common value so the first value 7 is returned`
		`>>> A=[3,3,2,3,5,6]`
		`>>> mode(A)`
		`3` `#Common/repeated value is 3 so 3 is returned`
		`>>> A=[3,3,2,2,5,6]`
		`>>> mode(A)`
		`3``#Common/repeated value is 3 and 2 both and they both occur 2 times. But the first occurrence is of 3 so 3 is returned`

		>>>A=["one","-three","two","one","-three","three"]
		>>> mode(A)
		'three'#As three is occurring most number of times
		
		>>> A=()
		>>> mode(A)
		StatisticsError: no median for empty data

Summary

1. Modules are python files which contain a set of functions or objects that you want to include in your program. There are two ways to use modules in a python program. One is using 'import' keyword and other is using 'from <module> import <function/object names>'
2. Some of the functions/commands in math module are `pi`, `e`, `sqrt()`, `ceil()`, `floor()`, `pow()`, `fabs()`, `sin()`, `cos()`, `tan()`
3. `pi` returns the value for $\pi = 3.141592$
4. e returns the value for mathematical constant $e = 2.718281$
5. `sqrt(x)` function returns the square root of x.
6. `ceil(x)` function returns the smallest integer greater than or equal to x.
7. `floor(x)` function returns the largest integer less than or equal to x.
8. `pow(x,y)` function returns x raised to power y.
9. `fabs(x)` function returns the absolute value of x.
10. `sin(x)` function returns the sine of x radians.
11. `cos(x)` function returns the cosine of x radians.
12. `tan(x)` function returns the tangent of x radians.
13. Some of the functions/commands in the random module are `random()`, `randrange()`, `randint()`.
14. `random()` function generates a floating point random number in the range from 0.0 to 1.0, where 1.0 is not included
15. `randint(x,y)` function generates an integer random number between x and y, where both x and y can be included.
16. `randrange(X,Y,Z)` function generates an integer random number between X and Y-1 (both included), with a step interval of Z. default step is 1.
17. Some of the functions/commands in the statistics module are `mean()`, `median()`, `mode()`
18. `mean(L)` function is used to calculate the average of numeric data provided in the form of an iterable or a sequence L.

19. `median(L)` function returns the middle value of the numeric data provided in the form of an iterable L.

20. `mode(L)` function returns the single most common data from the given data values.

Questions

1. Name the module required to import to use the following functions in python. Also explain each one of them with examples

   a. `cos()` b. `random()` c. `median()` d. `ceil()`

2 For the given program, what are the possible random values that can be generated:

```
import random
for i in range(10):
    print(random.randrange(-3,2))
```

3 Give the output for the following commands:

```
print(math.pow(2,3))
print(math.pow(3, 2))
print(math.ceil(7.99))
print(math.floor(7.99))
print(math.sqrt(256))
```

4 Choose the incorrect option:

   a. from math import % b. from math import *

   c. import math d. import math as M

5 What will be the output of the following Python code?

   print(random.randrange(0,100,5))

   a. 56 b. 3 c. 75 d. 91

6 Given the following program, what could be the possible values for X and Y both

```
import random
X=random.randint(1,3)
Y=random.randint(1,4)
for i in range(X+1):
    for j in range(i,Y+1):
        print(i,j)
```

7 Choose the possible output/outputs for the program given below. Also tell the maximum and the minimum values for both X and Y

```
import random
X = random.random()
Y= random.randrange(0,4)
print(int(x),":", y+int(x))
```

   a. `0:1` b. `0:4` c. `1:3` d. `1:0`

8. Give the output for the commands given below:

```
import math
print(abs(math.sqrt(49)))
print(abs(math.sqrt(49.0)))
print(math.ceil(3.4))
print(math.floor(-9.9))
```

9. Write all the possible output for the python code given below:

```
import random
L= ["glass","water","milk","tumbler","shake"]
for i in range(2):
    X=random.randrange(-1,-4,-2)
    print(L[X],end=" ")
```

10. Differentiate between the following built in functions along with the examples in the form of a python code along with the output

    a. `mode()` and `median()`
    b. `ceil()` and `floor()`
    c. `pow()` and `sqrt()`
    d. `randint()` and `randrange()`

11. Rahul wrote the following python program to generate 4 digit OTP.

```
import random
otp=""
i=0
while True:
    otp+=str(random.randint(0,9))
    i+=1
    if i==4:
        break
print(otp)
```

You need to modify the above program in such a manner that the otp generated should have only even digits excluding 0. Can you help think of another way to redo the above program? Pls suggest

12. Write a program to fill the empty list `L[]` with 5 elements making sure that each element is of three digits.

13. Fill in the blanks:

    a. The module used to find the mean of given numbers stored in a list is ________.
    b. random module has a function which allows you to generate a random 2 digit odd number. Can you name the function? ________
    c. A function which generates a floating point number between 0 and 1 is ________ and it is accessed using ________ module.
    d. The `pow(a,b)` function which comes under ________ module returns ab and the result is never an integer but ________

e. ____________ function of the random module takes no argument.

f. While using the function `mode(X)`, if X is empty then __________ exception is raised. This function is used under _________ module.

g. `print(random.random()*900 + 100)` will always generate a _______ digit number.

14. Read the program given below carefully:

```
import statistics
L=[1,2,3,4,5]
s=0
for i in L:
    s+=i
print(s//len(L))
```

What is the above program generating? Can you suggest a simpler way to do the above program? You can use any built in function.

15 Society, Law and Ethics

Digital Footprints

How do you express your presence on the internet.? When you feel happy or you want to share something with your friends you upload either the picture or the text on social networking sites like Facebook or Instagram. Every time you share something on the digital platform like some write up or some pictures you leave an impression of yours in the online world. The posts which are shared by you online leave an impression about you which is visible to the virtual world. This not only includes the posts shared by you, the sites you searched or visited or the comments you make on a post but also the information available online about you.

Digital footprint is the information shared by you or is about you available online. Digital footprint is used by the apps or the companies to know more about you. Have you ever noticed that when you search for a particular product online then you start receiving similar suggestions whenever you surf the net. Your login credentials and your preferences are stored by the cookies. Though these cookies are not harmful, they do keep track of your preferences to make your search fast.

You should keep in mind that anything you share online, whether text or images, has the potential to be available online forever.

So you should decide about the 'Your Digital' footprints in this virtual world. The way you mark your presence in the real world through your actions and create an impression about yourself with full consciousness, same way you should be very carefully making an impression about yourself in the virtual world through the posts you share or the searches you do or the comments you make. You can take advantage of the online platform to represent your best qualities which can help you to excel in your academic and professional life.

To check and manage your digital footprint:

- You can search your name on various search engines and see the result.
- You must also separate your professional account with your personal account.
- You should be aware of the privacy settings of your social networking platform.
- You must monitor your linked accounts (facebook, instagram, twitter etc)

Digital society and Netizen

Digital technologies have permeated our everyday tasks and interactions as they have changed the way we learn, work and socialise. Every aspect of our lives is affected by the digitalisation of data. With access to the internet, digital services have become an essential part of people's lives. Today, people have easy access to information sources and technologies which have enabled them to get involved in a lot of online activities including social, educational and political fields too.

This technological revolution has given rise to a new term called 'Digital Society'. Digital society is the society where everything is paperless and runs on digital technology. And this is due to the adoption of ICT(Information and Communication Technologies) in all areas including home, education, workplace etc Today, The commonly used terms in digital society are 5g, IoT (Internet of Things), Cloud computing, Big Data etc.

The people who use digital tools on the internet are known as Netizens. It is a combination of two words, Inter**net** and Ci**tizens**. Hence, Netizens are also known as digital citizens. We all are netzens as we all use the internet. As a netizen we must follow some etiquettes. The etiquettes practiced in the digital world is categorized in the following categories:

- Net etiquettes
- Communication etiquettes
- Social media étiquettes

Net etiquettes

When we interact with our friends physically we follow some etiquette and rules. Similarly, when we meet a stranger we know whether to talk to him or not, whether or not to reveal our personal information. Same way when we are online we should follow certain rules and behavior. This is important for our safety and security. The rules we should follow when we are online are called net etiquettes. We must follow these basic net etiquettes as an ethical netizen whenever we are online::

- We should always be aware of what we post online. We must respect the privacy of our friends and family before sharing any mail or content on the social networking platform. Also while forwarding the mail, we must use BCC (blind carbon copy) rather than CC (carbon copy) if we are sending something out to more than one person. This will avoid the email addresses of others to get publicized.
- Never say untrue things about anyone on the public forum. Sharing of fake news must be avoided.
- We often use audio, video or images from various sources. As an ethical netizen, we must give credit to the source if we use someone's content.
- The Internet was created to share meaningful information and spread awareness and knowledge. We must do the same on the online platform as a responsible netizen.
- We must respect different cultures and the opinions of others.
- We must act responsible by making sure that we do not harass, or provoke anyone. Threatening online, posting personal information about someone else, expressing deliberately offensive opinions about someone etc come under cyberbullying. Cyberbullying or stealing someone's identity is a serious crime and we must not engage or involve ourselves in it.

Communication etiquettes

In the digital world, we communicate using text (through mails and chats), audio and video conferencing, live chats on social networking sites etc. We need to follow certain rules when communication is done via digital mode.

The following communication etiquettes must be practiced:

- We should be precise in delivering the message. Long emails should be avoided as we need to respect everyone's time. At the same time mails with bulky attachments should not be sent. This can consume a lot of bandwidth while opening the attachment.
- We should be polite while communicating, especially during audio and video chats. Everyone's viewpoint should be respected and listened to. Suggestions, if any, should be made with politeness and cordial behavior should be shown.
- Our behaviour is judged by the etiquettes we show and the comments we make on the online platform. Similarly, we judge the other person on the basis of the comments he/she receives. So we need to be very responsible while sharing anything in writing on the digital platform about anyone.

Social media étiquettes

Today, people from every age group are active on social media. Facebook has more than a billion users. There are a million active accounts on Twitter, Instagram and LinkedIn. People communicate with others on social media and share their videos and build their audience too, like on youtube. So you need to follow some basic etiquettes while handling social media platform:

- Be very cautious while posting or tagging someone. While posting a group picture, it is advisable to post the photo with the caption "Tag yourself" to encourage others to take the initiative.
- Be careful in providing the passwords to your social media accounts as these accounts are vulnerable to hacking.
- Do not accept the friend invitation from anyone and everyone as we don't come to know who is hiding behind the screens.
- We should never chat with online strangers.
- Never share personal details like name, address, contact details etc online on social media platforms. It can be misused.
- Unless you're sending a private message, your social media posts should have well-placed, appropriate and respectful sense of humor as what humour for you might be a serious matter for others.
- Avoid getting into your own social media arguments. If you tag things on social media related to any argument then your words and actions can be saved and can be provocative too.
- It is unethical to misrepresent yourself by taking the credit of others.
- Before you become an active user of a new social media platform, read up on its best practices as different platforms have their own set of rules they follow.

Data protection

In this digital world when everything from a small not so important to highly confidential data is stored and maintained on the cloud, it becomes really important to protect it from getting misused or leaked. Examples of sensitive data include biometric information, company's financial records, or other personal documents, images,audios,videos, health related data etc. Data protection thus is a very important concept to prevent and protect your important information. It provides tools and policies to actually restrict access to the data. The purpose of data protection is to define when and on what conditions personal data can be accessed or processed. It is important to know that the data protection and privacy laws and regulations vary from country to country. Some of the commonly used practices and technologies to protect data include

- Firewalls- which will ensure that only authorized users are allowed to access or transfer data
- data Encryption- which protects your data from unauthorized access even if data is stolen as the data can only be accessed with the right encryption key
- Authentication which allows you to verify credentials and give access accordingly.

Intellectual Property Right

People do startups, use their ideas to promote their business. They give an exclusive name to their company, get a logo designed for it. But what if the name or the logo they design is used by someone else? Or what if their original idea is used by another person or company pretending to be theirs? Is there any way to preserve their rights and protect their original inventions which includes expressions, designs, symbols, names, logos etc. The rights which protect an individual or a company and prevent their original content and invention to be used by others without their permission are called Intellectual Property Rights. It allows people to seek legal advice. Intellectual Property Rights are legal rights governing the use of creations of the human mind.

For example, in the case of Movies the producers are the owner of the movie as they finance it. It is their " intellectual property" and they have the right to decide whether they want to allow others to reproduce, translate, remake, copy or adapt their intellectual property.

In India, three important Intellectual Property Rights recognised under statute are

- The Patents Act, 1970
- The Trade Marks Act, 1999
- The Copyright Act, 1957

Note that the IPRs are exclusive rights and therefore there is always a challenge to strike a balance between the interests of innovators and the interests of the society at large.

Copyright

Copyright is an intellectual property right which protects the literary and artistic creations of authors, artists, musicians etc. A copyright can give its owner exclusive rights to their original work. Works covered by copyright range from books, music, paintings, sculpture, and films, to computer programs, databases, advertisements, maps, and technical drawings. Copyright protection extends only to expressions, and not to ideas, procedures, methods of operation. In the majority of countries copyright protection is obtained automatically without the need for registration. Copyright in a work is considered as infringed only if a substantial part is made use of unauthorizedly. For example, if a lyricist copies a phrase from another lyricist's song, there is likely to be infringement even if that phrase is very short and that is covered under copyright.

Patent

A patent is an exclusive right granted for a new invention or discoveries. "New invention" means any invention or technology which has not been anticipated by publication in any document or used in the country or elsewhere in the world before the date of filing of patent application with complete specification. A patent provides protection for the invention to the owner of the patent and gives full control to the patentee to decide whether or how the invention can be used by others. A patent is a limited-duration protection.

Trademark

A trademark includes a name, logo, word, or sign that differentiates goods from the goods of other enterprises. Trademark symbolizes the value or goodwill associated with the goods and its specific source and it distinguishes one company from others. It is due to the trademark which helps consumers identify and purchase a product. It would be difficult to distinguish the duplicates if there are no trademarks. For example, the BPB symbol bpb which nearly all could easily recognize and identify–is an example of trademark. While patents and copyrights can expire, trademark rights come from the use of the trademark, and therefore can be held indefinitely. Registration of a trademark is not required.

Violation of IPR

Intellectual property rights can be violated in many ways. Some are listed below:

Plagiarism

The word "plagiarism" is derived from the Latin term "plagiare". It means to copy or take ideas from someone else's work. When someone's work is copied and used or falsely claimed of authorship then this act is called Plagiarism. It may be intentional or unintentional. Based on the type of copy, plagiarism is categorized as Ghost Writer, Photocopy, Potluck Paper, Self Stealer. In Ghost copy the entire content is copied as it is without making any modifications. In photocopy the part of the text is copied and used without making any changes. In Potluck Paper the material is copied from various resources and presented after making very minor alterations. Self Stealer is an interesting plagiarism where the author copies his or her own content and reuses it again. To prevent plagiarism, either quote the original work and indicate the source.

Copyright Infringement

In Plagiarism, the original idea is copied and used irrespective of the fact whether the actual source is protected by copyright or not. But in copyright infringement the laws of the copyright holder are violated. This is because in copyright infringement the source which is copied is protected by copyrights and in spite of that the material is copied and reused. An example was given in the previous section where the producer of the movie can decide whether the others can reproduce, translate, remake or copy his movie as he has copyright on his movie. But if someone without taking permission remakes the movie then it will become an act of copyright infringement. Copyright infringement is a criminal offense.

Trademark infringement

Trademarks are given the status of intellectual property across the globe. There are many organisations, both international and national, that endeavour to protect intellectual properties such as trademarks. When a person who is not authorised by the holder of a registered trademark to use the name, logo, sign etc but he violates it by using it, then this is called Trademark infringement.

OpenSource Softwares and licensing

Open Source software is computer software which is available for people to use freely, to access and modify the source code and to distribute the modified version of the software. The word Open means 'collaboration is open to all' and Source means source code is freely shared. One of the main advantages of open source is its visibility, which makes it easy to troubleshoot problems.

There are a variety of open source softwares available starting from Operating system to Open office presentation softwares to open office Browser and so on. Some of the commonly used operating system software are

- Operating Systems (all Linux distributions)
- Wordpress- Free web software to create websites or blogs
- GIMPShop-Image editor similar to Adobe Photoshop
- Web Browser-Mozilla Firefox
- open office (word processing, spreadsheet and presentation software available in 21 different languages http://www.openoffice.org)
- WebServer Software-Apache
- Database-MySQL
- Perl, PHP, Python (scripting languages)

When we say that the open source softwares is free to use and modify, it doesn't mean that they are free to be used and modified without any specific guidelines and permissions. A clear set of permissions and guidelines are documented and shared between the creator of the software and its users, which governs how the software can be used, modified, reused and reshared. This document is called a license. The license will determine whether you are allowed to make changes in the original source code and fix issues, if you find. The license indicates how the software may be used. OSS is unique in that it is always released under a license that has been certified to meet the criteria of the Open Source definition. There are many open source license, some of them are discussed below:

GNU General Public License: It is one of the most popular open source licenses. It was written by Richard Stallman. According to it, any software that is written based on any GPL component must be released as open source. A popular example of software that uses GPL is WordPress. Features of GNU GPL are:

1. The program governed by the GPL license, even if modified, must be subject to the GPL again.
2. It gives freedom to run the program. It also gives freedom to study how the program works and modify it to suit the needs. One needs to have access to the source code for doing any modification. The license allows distribution in source code

3. It gives freedom to redistribute copies and distribute modified versions of the program, so that the community can benefit from your improvements.
4. You can also charge for the software but the copy of the GNU GPL has to be given. This will make the person aware that the same software is available for free too.
5. You can copy the software and there is no limit to that. It can be copied either on your or your client's server.
6. Software that uses any GPL-licensed component has to release its full source code and all rights to modify and distribute the entire code.

Linux is available under the GPL license

Creative Commons licenses are for all kinds of creative works which include websites, scholarship, music, film, photography, literature, courseware, etc. CC are not really open source. You can visit the site to know more about it http://www.creativecommons.org

Features of CC are:

1. It allows the authors to share and redistribute their copyright work and make some uses of their work.
2. It also gives the author the liberty to decide the additional permissions of licensing and how they want their work to be used.
3. It allows licensors to redistribute the work but not for commercial use. If the work is used for commercial purposes then proper credit must be given.
4. It allows modification or copying of the work but only under CC License.

Apache: The Apache License is recognised by the Open Source Initiative as a popular and widely deployed license. Apache License version 2.0 rights can be applied to both copyrights and patents. Anyone who uses open source software licensed under Apache 2.0 must include original copyright notice, license copy, statement of any significant changes made to the original code.

- The licensor can copy, modify and distribute the covered software in source and/or binary forms
- All copies, modified or unmodified, are accompanied by a copy of the license
- Apache license doesn't require renewal. It can be used forever.
- Apache rights are granted irrespective of the geographical boundaries. It means the license is applicable in all countries.
- All notices of copyright, trademark and patent rights are reproduced accurately in distributed copies
- You can redistribute the code but with credits.
- This License does not grant permission to use trademarks
- Unlike GPL license, Software that uses any Apache-licensed component has no compulsion to release the modified version.

Apache web servers, Apache OpenOffice are licensed under Apache 2.0 License.

Cyber-crime

The word cyber means anything related to information technology (IT), computers and network and crime means an action considered as an offence and is punishable by law. So Cybercrime is the crime committed via the Internet and computer systems. Cyber crime is an unlawful act wherein the computer is either a tool or target or both . Cybercrime is not restricted to any geographical boundaries and is committed online. It affects the confidentiality, integrity and availability of data and computer systems. The person committing cybercrime can get unauthorised access to someone else's computer or accounts and can do things like identity theft, fraud, data stealing, data manipulation etc. Cybercrime has been on the rise for years. Few reasons which have given rise to cybercrime are greed to earn quick money, lack of awareness or knowledge among computer users, negligence, weak cybersecurity, easy access to computers etc.

Types of Cybercrime

Hacking

Hacking is a process where someone unknown gains access to your computer with the wrong intention of either deleting the data or stealing sensitive information. Skilled programmers who have good knowledge of machine code and computer operating systems are called hackers. Using their knowledge they can identify the flaw in the security system of the computer. It is very important to know that not all hackers hack the computer with wrong intentions. Hacking itself is not an illegal activity unless the hacker is compromising a system without the owner's permission. Today many companies and government agencies hire these skilled programmers to know the vulnerabilities in their system so that the security issue can be sorted and their system can work without threat of losing any sensitive information. There are three types of hackers named the white, hat grey hat and Black hat.

- **White hat** hackers are officially hired by the agencies so that the problem or the loopholes in the security system can be identified. White hat hackers are therefore called ethical hackers. So what this article happens to is completely legal and is not covered under cyber crime.
- **Black hat** hackers are the one which gets into security systems or computer networks by bypassing the protocols only with wrong intentions. The intention is to steal the sensitive information or money. Black hat hackers are cyber criminals as they crack the security system of the company. This process is called Cracking.
- **Grey hat** hackers are the one which we can say are between white hat and Black hat. This is because they get into the security system without the knowledge or permission of the owner. Usually, grey hat hackers will not exploit the found vulnerabilities. Their intent is to bring the weakness to the attention of the owners and of course to earn money.

Eavesdropping

It is stealing of information by unauthorized interception of a conversation as it is transmitted over a network by a computer, or phone. Special programs are developed by hackers to record parts of sensitive data communications from insecure networks. So, in eavesdropping, people are completely unaware that their communication is being intercepted and data is being stolen. Cell phones, computers, and laptops are first hacked and then used by the attackers to fabricate information according to their wishes. To avoid eavesdropping, you should

- Avoid public wi-fi networks.
- Keep your antivirus software updated.
- Use strong passwords.

Phishing and fraud emails:

Phishing is a cybercrime where attackers try to acquire personal information or data of people like username, password, and credit card details etc, by impersonating themselves as trusted entities. Fake sites are created which appear like the real website, which tempt people to give huge discounts and in return ask to fill forms with personal information. Phishing attacks are one of the most common types of cyber attacks which are conducted through electronic media, like emails and telephone calls. Phishing emails may try to trick you to download attachments such as word, pdf or zip files. Links on phishing emails could also lead you to a fake website and will be enough to download a virus on your computer.

You must be careful when you receive messages like

- confirm the personal information or
- click on a link to make payment or
- a message on government refund or
- free coupon
- Message saying that there is a problem with your account and asking you to reauthorise by verifying the personal information.

You should avoid clicking any unidentified link and any suspicious mail or message can be reported to www.cybercrime.gov.in to avoid any phishing attack.

Ransomware

There are some malicious softwares which are dangerous to your organisation to the extent that after gaining the access to the company's computers they target the company's database, file server and other applications so that the organisation is not able to access its own data. Ransom is then demanded to provide the access. The software used to take away the access and then demand for the ransom is called ransomware. So we can say that ransomware is an extortion software which locks the computer and demands money to unlock it. It is a growing threat by cybercriminals and inflicting significant damage and expenses for business and government organizations. In many cases, the victim must pay the money to cybercriminals because of the risk of losing access forever. Since malware attacks are often deployed by cyberthieves, paying the ransom doesn't ensure access will be restored.

Some of the tips by which you can protect yourself from ransomware are :

- Backup your data
- Secure your backups
- Use security software and keep it up to date.
- Use secure networks
- Practice safe surfing

Preventing cyber crime

Few measures you can take to prevent cyber crime are:

- Install a good antivirus software and keep it updated. You must also turn on the firewall.
- Never install pirated softwares
- Use strong passwords and avoid using the same passwords for different accounts. Also, keep on changing the password as often as possible.
- Try to avoid talking to strangers on social networking sites. You should not accept the friend request of the person you are not familiar with.
- You should not share any personal information publicly or on a social networking site. It can be easily misused.
- Avoid working on free Wi-Fi or whenever you use a public Wi-Fi network in a hotel or airport, using a VPN is always a good idea.
- Don't click on the links or attachments which you are not sure of or which are shared through online advertisements, spam mails or some unidentified posts. It can contain virus.
- It is always a good idea to log off your computer when you are not using it.
- If your computer is always connected, it increases the risk of being attacked by hackers and your data can be stolen. To go offline when you are not using the internet.
- Always keep a backup of your data.
- In case you work on someone else's computer you should make sure that your passwords are not auto saved. And when the work is done you should safely log out before leaving the machine.
- Whenever you do online transactions or e-banking make sure that the sites are trusted and secure.

The Government of India has developed a portal www.cybercrime.gov.in called National Cyber Crime Reporting Portal, where any person aggrieved of cyber crime can submit his complaint online.

Cyber safety

Today the internet has made things very easy and convenient for all of us but we should never ignore the risks with it which can have serious results. It is therefore important that whenever we are online we should follow safe practices and act in a responsible manner to minimise the online danger of Cyber crime.

The ability to use the ICT tools in a safe and responsible manner is called cyber safety. Cyber safety includes the following.

- We must avoid sharing our personal pictures.
- We must also avoid talking to strangers.
- We should keep strong passwords and should not share them with anyone.
- We must check the privacy settings of our social media account
- We must browse safely by not visiting unverified websites or opening unknown links

Identity protection

Identity theft is any kind of scam, or crime that results in the loss of personal information such as passwords, ID numbers, credit card numbers and are misused without your permission to commit fraud and other crimes. Thus, one needs to be careful while working online making sure that the sensitive and personal details are protected and are not misused. So, we must know how to be safe when surfing the web and follow certain guidelines. Protecting yourself from the online threat by following certain safe practices is called identity protection. Some of them are listed below:

- Never share your personal details on social networking websites.
- Never open suspicious emails.
- Keep scanning your computer from time to time and always keep your Firewall on. The antivirus should always be up to date.
- Your profile should always be private on the social networking site.
- You should not use simple and same passwords for different networking profiles. Your passwords should be a combination of letters, numbers and special characters and they must be updated on a regular basis.
- If you feel that your account is being misused or someone is posting messages on your behalf from your account, then you must report this matter either to your teacher or to your parents.

Confidentiality

Confidentiality ensures that data is protected from unauthorized users. The people with valid authorisation are only able to access the data. Thus avoiding getting it into the wrong hands by taking more stringent measures in terms of data security. The more sensitive the data, the higher the level of confidentiality. Therefore, all sensitive data should always be controlled and monitored. There are a number of measures that can be taken to assist with confidentiality including multi-factor authentication, strong passwords, encryption, segregation of data, and assigning users with appropriate user privilege levels.

Cyber bullying

Posting hurtful messages and commenting on a photo or a video posted by others is called cyber bullying. This includes sending text messages or email to hurt the sentiments of the other person. Cyber bullying happens when someone is targeted online specifically with the reason to make someone upset or to spoil its image. In cyber-bullying individuals are targeted. In cyber bullying, the cyberbullies post vicious things about a single person with a goal of shaming or intimidation.

Cyber trolling

Trolls have sadly become a "normal" part of internet life. People who partake in 'trolling' are referred to as 'trolls'. Trolling is recognised as deliberately inflicting hatred, racism or just simple provoking arguments between others. Trolls seek to rile online communities and attract attention to themselves. Whether they comment on blog posts or online news sites, they are looking to grab the attention of other visitors and disrupt discussion that would otherwise be about the page's content. So, they want to shift attention from the author's content and conversations about the content onto themselves. The more attention they get, in the form of comments directed at them, the happier the troll is.

Safely accessing web sites

The internet has brought revolution in our lives by making things comfortable for us from every perspective, like entertainment, elearning, easy access of information, flight booking, shopping, banking and carry out many other everyday tasks. However, there are a number of risks associated with going online. These result from either visiting malicious websites or inadvertent disclosure of personal information. Some of them are listed below:

Malware

Malware is a computer program designed to cause extensive damage to data and systems or to gain unauthorized access to a network. Malware can infect systems by being bundled with other programs or attached as macros to files. Malware include viruses, adware, spyware etc

Viruses

The word 'virus' stands for 'Vital Information Resource Under Siege'. A computer virus is a small software program that spreads from one computer to another and might corrupt or delete data. They are the most commonly-known form of malware and potentially the most destructive. A virus usually comes as an attachment in an email that holds a virus payload, or the part of the malware that performs the malicious action. Once the victim opens the file, the device is infected. Some of the examples are ILOVEYOU, Nimda, Stuxnet etc

Trojans

A Trojan horse, or Trojan, is a malicious software that looks legitimate but can take control of your computer. It is designed to damage, disrupt, steal, or in general inflict some other harmful action on your data or network. Once the Trojan malware is downloaded and activated, cyber criminals can spy on your activities, steal sensitive data and take full control of your computer. If you feel that your computer is running slow or it starts behaving strangely or there is a sudden increase in the popup then there could be a possibility that your computer might be affected by a trojan horse. Some of the examples of Trojans are Banking Trojans, ArcBombs, Clickers etc

Adware

Adware is a software that shows unwanted advertisements while you surf the net. Malicious adware can redirect you to the advertising sites to collect your information and can change the browser settings. Adware normally comes in software that you download from the internet – usually freeware or shareware – and it secretly installs itself onto your device without your knowledge. It keeps track of your browsing history and details like your location and preferences, which is further sold to the third party by the programmer to earn extra money. Examples are Fireball, Appearch, DollarRevenue, Gator etc

Simple steps to keep your Computer safe from Malware, Virus, Trojans, adwares:

- Keep Personal Information Professional and Limited
- Keep Your Privacy Settings On
- Be Careful What You Download
- Choose Strong and unique passwords
- Make Online Purchases From Secure Sites
- Be Careful What You Post
- Be Careful Who You Meet Online
- Keep Your Antivirus Program Up To Date
- Download files and applications from websites that you trust, such as official app stores.
- Don't click on links in unexpected and unknown messages.
- If you think a link looks suspicious then before you click, hover over that link to see the actual web address. If you do not recognise or trust the address, try searching for relevant key terms in a web browser.
- Be careful of offers that seem too good to be true.
- Don't agree to friend requests from people you don't know on social media networks.

E-waste management

Disposal of e-waste is an emerging global environmental and public health issue, as this waste has become the most rapidly growing segment. The waste arising from end-of-life electronic products such as computers and mobile phones, is one of the fastest growing waste streams in the world today. Discarded computers, televisions, fax machines, electric lamps, cell phones, audio equipment and batteries if improperly disposed can leach lead and other substances into soil and groundwater. Electronic equipment contains many hazardous metallic contaminants such as lead, cadmium, and beryllium and brominated flame-retardants which requires recycling in a scientific manner. Children are particularly vulnerable to lead poisoning – more so than adults because they absorb more lead from their environment and their nervous system and blood get affected. Many of these products can be reused, refurbished, or recycled in an environmentally sound manner so that they are less harmful to the ecosystem.

The mantra of ***"Reduce, Reuse, Recycle"*** applies in the case of e-waste too.

- You should try to **Reduce** your e-waste generation by taking good care of your products and maintaining them well so that you are able to use them for a longer duration.
- You should **Reuse** your electronic equipment by either donating or selling it to someone who can still use it.
- **Recycle** those products that cannot be repaired. Computer monitors, televisions and other electronic equipment should NOT be disposed of with regular garbage. There are companies and organisations which manage your electronics for recycling,

As a responsible student you can contribute in e-waste management in the following manner:

1. You can **donate your old electronic devices to NGOs** as they need basic devices to teach basic computer skills to young children and women from underprivileged backgrounds.
2. You can **donate to a college or school** in rural areas.
3. Since a number of electronics manufacturers are willing to buy back used products, **you can either Sell them back to manufacturers** or exchange them for new.
4. The safest way to dispose of e-waste is by giving it to a certified e-waste recycler as they also refurbish it to make new products.

It is important to make sure to format your electronic devices before disposing of them in a proper manner

Note: *IT Department, South DMC has developed and launched website https://ewaste.mcdservices.online for SDMC offices/ Citizens/ Markets/ RWA for submission of online request for disposal of e-waste-old/obsolete/unserviceable IT equipment. The e-waste will be collected on the basis of requests received through the online system."*

Indian Information Technology Act (IT Act)

The Information Technology Act, 2000 or ITA, 2000 or IT Act, was notified on October 17, 2000 and was passed in a budget session of parliament and signed by President K.R. Narayanan in 2000. It is the law that deals with cybercrime and electronic commerce in India.

The IT Act 2000 applies to companies that do business in India. This includes entities registered in India, outsource there, and maintain servers within the country's borders. The act covers all activity involving online exchanges and electronic documents. It covers the companies which are located and registered in India as well as those which aren't located in India but have their servers in India.

Following are the objectives of the Acts:

i. It grants legal recognition to all transactions done via electronic exchange of data or other electronic means of communication in place of the earlier paper-based method of communication.

ii. It gives legal recognition to digital signatures for the authentication of any information or matters requiring legal authentication

iii. It facilitate the electronic filing of documents with Government agencies and also departments

iv. It facilitate the electronic storage of data

v. It gives legal sanction and also facilitate the electronic transfer of funds between banks and financial institutions

vi. It grants legal recognition to bankers under the Evidence Act, 1891 and the Reserve Bank of India Act, 1934, for keeping the books of accounts in electronic form.

Technology & Society

Gender and disability issues while teaching and using computers

Today, technology has allowed people to shape the physical world and the world of knowledge to meet their needs and wants. The internet allows access to unlimited information and knowledge and provides a platform for economic, social and political participation. Digital skills could help transform our society for the better but only if they are not the preserve of a few: women and men from different backgrounds and with different experiences must be able to benefit from them. Currently, the digital skills gap is wider for older, less educated and poor women, and those coming from rural areas and developing countries. Research shows that female and male students in undergraduate computer science programs view computer culture differently and there is a huge difference in the ratio of girls:boys who opt for programming. School is often the first place where children are introduced to technology as well as learning the literacy and numeracy skills to make the most of the digital tools. But there are some of the common Gender issues faced while teaching and using computers:

1. The most common problem faced is lack of interest and motivation in children. The girls are not encouraged to choose career options which require technical skills.
2. Less opportunities given to girls.
3. Problems faced by those coming from rural areas or low economic backgrounds.
4. Lack of Role Models.

Gender equality is essential to ensure that both men and women can contribute fully to the betterment of society and the economy in general. The segregation of the two genders prevents us from reaching inclusive prosperity and equality, and this especially true of the gender digital divide. Compulsory education helps to eliminate the digital gender divide. Compulsory schooling is crucial to ensure that individuals gain the basic skills and competences needed for full participation in the society.

People with disabilities meet barriers of all types. However, technology is helping to lower many of these barriers. By using computing technology for tasks such as reading and writing documents, communicating with others, and searching for information on the Internet, students and employees with disabilities are capable of handling a wider range of activities independently. Some of the commonly faced disability issues (including physical and learning, both) while teaching and using computers are:

1. Physical disability like blindness, due to which sometimes children find it difficult to know about the right software and understand it on their own. There is special coaching to teach how to access information from the computer and there are specially trained teachers too. This causes limitation and restriction with those who are visually challenged and are not able to access the visual material present on the computer. Even teachers find it difficult to help such children if they are not properly trained.
2. Another important disability issue faced is learning disability which can be of various types. Children with learning disabilities need specialized training, personal attention and trained teachers to help them to cope up. Some of the learning disabilities are:
    a. Dyscalculia (which affects a person's ability to understand numbers)
    b. Dysgraphia (which affects a person's handwriting and motor skills)
    c. Dyslexia (which affects a person's reading and related language based skills)
    d. Non Verbal Learning Disabilities
    e. Oral /written language disorder
3. Another problem faced by the teachers and the student's is the unavailability of the teaching material and the proper hardware support system especially in rural areas due to lack of funds.

How technology has helped in overcoming disability issues in classrooms to make learning possible as well as effective

Assistive technologies, which includes softwares to help students overcome obstacles they face due to any learning disability.

a. Assistive technology (AT) can help people with learning disabilities or other cognitive challenges. For example, screen readers can improve the skill of reading. Screen reading software reads aloud whatever text is on the computer screen. This device is used by people with low or no vision. As the words are read aloud, they are highlighted on the screen. Few examples of the softwares are text-to-speech (Kurzweil 3000), speech-to-text (Dragon Naturally Speaking), word prediction capabilities (WordQ), and graphic organizers (Inspiration).

b. Laptop computers and tablet devices are beneficial for students with handwriting disabilities as they are able to take notes on a laptop or computerized device. Using a word processor can help students to complete work that is more organized and includes less spelling errors than handwritten work.

c. Students with writing skills disabilities can us softwares like Batorowicz, Missiuna, & Pollock-2012. Phonetic spelling software is designed to automatically convert the student's typing into the word that they intended to write.

d. The voice recognition systems (VRS) allow people to get the thoughts on paper without experiencing the challenges that can accompany handwriting or computer keyboarding such as letter drawing or "slow typing speed", respectively.

e. There are assistive technology keyboards which have altered appearances and easier functionalities than a typical keyboard. There are many computer keyboards for students with disabilities, each customized to meet the user's unique needs.

Today the digital transformation provides new avenues for the economic empowerment of women and can contribute to greater gender equality. The Internet, digital platforms, mobile phones and digital financial services offer "leapfrog" opportunities for all and can help bridge the divide by giving women the possibility to earn additional income, increase their employment opportunities, and access knowledge and general information. Some of the suggestions which can help to bridge the gap are:

1. More teachers should be trained to handle children with various disabilities
2. Specialized material and curriculum should be designed keeping in mind the students of all needs as students with different disabilities need different types of teaching aids/materials.
3. More special needs teachers should be hired in the school to help and motivate the students to excel in the field of Technology and set an example for others.
4. Extensive use of the latest technology should be introduced wherever possible. Most individuals who are blind use standard keyboards, however, Braille input devices are available. Braille key labels can assist with keyboard use. Most individuals who are blind use standard keyboards, however, Braille input devices are available. Braille key labels can assist with keyboard use.
5. Girls should be motivated by giving examples of female role models in the field of Technology so that more girls are inspired to get themselves inclined in computer science.

Summary

1. Digital footprint is the information shared by you or is about you available online.
2. Digital society is the society where everything is paperless and runs on digital technology.
3. The people who use digital tools on the internet are known as Netizens. It is a combination of two words, Internet and Citizens. Hence, Netizens are also known as digital citizens.
4. The rules we should follow when we are online are called net etiquettes. We must be very careful with what we post online. We must give credit to the source if we use someone's content.
5. The commonly used practices and technologies to protect data are Firewalls, data Encryption and Authentication.
6. Firewalls ensure that only authorized users are allowed to access or transfer data.
7. Data Encryption protects your data from unauthorized access even if data is stolen as the data can only be accessed with the right encryption key.
8. Authentication allows you to verify credentials and give access accordingly.
9. The rights which protect an individual or a company and prevent their original content and invention to be used by others without their permission are called Intellectual Property Rights.
10. Copyright is an intellectual property right which protects the literary and artistic creations of authors, artists, musicians etc.
11. A patent is an exclusive right granted for a new invention or discoveries.
12. A trademark includes a name, logo, word, or sign that differentiates goods from the goods of other enterprises.
13. Plagiarism means to copy or take ideas from someone else's work. Based on the type of copy, plagiarism is categorized as Ghost Writer, Photocopy, Potluck Paper, Self Stealer.
14. Open Source software is computer software which is available for people to use freely, to access and modify the source code and to distribute the modified version of the software.
15. GNU General Public License: It is one of the most popular open source licenses where any software that is written based on any GPL component must be released as open source.
16. Creative Commons licenses are for all kinds of creative works which include websites, scholarship, music, film, photography, literature, courseware, etc.
17. The Apache License is recognised by the Open Source Initiative as a popular and widely deployed license. Apache License version 2.0 rights can be applied to both copyrights and patents.
18. Cybercrime is the crime committed via the Internet and computer systems. Cyber crime is an unlawful act wherein the computer is either a tool or target or both.
19. Hacking is a process where someone unknown gains access to your computer with the wrong intention of either deleting the data or stealing sensitive information.
20. Eavesdropping is stealing of information by unauthorized interception of a conversation as it is transmitted over a network by a computer, or phone.
21. Phishing is a cybercrime where attackers try to acquire personal information or data of people like username, password, and credit card details etc, by impersonating themselves as trusted entities.

22. The software used to take away the access and then demand for the ransom is called ransomware.
23. We must install good antivirus software, prevent pirated softwares, use strong passwords, and prevent sharing personal information on social media platforms to prevent cyber crime.
24. Protecting yourself from the online threat by following certain safe practices is called identity protection.
25. Confidentiality ensures that data is protected from unauthorized users.
26. Posting hurtful messages and commenting on a photo or a video posted by others is called cyber bullying.
27. Trolling is recognised as deliberately inflicting hatred, racism or just simple provoking arguments between others.
28. Malware is a computer program designed to cause extensive damage to data and systems or to gain unauthorized access to a network.
29. A Trojan horse, or Trojan, is a malicious software that looks legitimate but can take control of your computer.
30. Adware is a software that shows unwanted advertisements while you surf the net.
31. The waste arising from end-of-life electronic products such as computers and mobile phones, is one of the fastest growing waste streams in the world today. This is called E-waste
32. IT Act grants legal recognition to all transactions done via electronic exchange of data or other electronic means of communication in place of the earlier paper-based method of communication.
33. Digital skills could help transform our society for the better.
34. Gender equality is essential to ensure that both men and women can contribute fully to the betterment of society and the economy in general.
35. Today the digital transformation provides new avenues for the economic empowerment of women and can contribute to greater gender equality.

Questions

1. Whenever pictures, videos, or comments are posted online they become a part of our:
   a. Digital Thumbprint
   b. Digital Footprint
   c. Digital data
   d. Digital setup
2. One of your friends has posted a video of you on the internet and you don't like it. You've asked him to take it down but they've said no because it's funny. What should you do?
   a. Keep asking your friend until they take it down
   b. Speak to your teacher or parents and tell why you don't like it and ask for help
   c. Leave it as you can't do anything else about it
   d. Post his video in return
3. You are guilty of plagiarism if you:
   a. You take reference from other's work for knowledge purposes.
   b. You take ideas from an online resource and create your own presentation.

c. You take reference from an online resource, create your project but mention it in acknowledgement.

d. Use the work of another and misrepresent it as your own.

4. Everything that you post online is saved for how long?

a. Always b. Few years c. One year d. Its never saved

5. You receive a mail from a branded clothing company saying that you have just won a lottery ticket of Rs 10 lakh as your mail was randomly chosen by the company. They need your credentials to verify. What should you do?

a. Never Click any link that appears in the message.

b. Never open any attachments in it

c. Immediately delete such mails.

d. All the above

The above case is the example of which attempt?

6. Select the strongest passwords from the given options:

a. tyT5#$9&uY b. great123 c. Googledevice d. 67temp67

7. What do you understand by Digital Footprint? What all is included in it?
8. Explain Plagiarism. What are the different types of plagiarisms?
9. If a stranger online asks you to send a picture of yours, what should you do and why?
10. Who all can see what you post online?
11. If you want only specific people to see your profile on social media, then what should you do?
12. One of your friends tells you that in an online gaming group, a person is making fun of him by calling him weird names. This online harassment is an example of _______________. What suggestion will you give to your friend?
13. A friend of yours wants to create an email account. He wants your suggestion on the password so that the account should be secured. What are the things you as a friend will suggest?
14. You created a password for your website. A friend of yours wants you to tell her the password. Will you tell her? Why?
15. "Whatever information available on the Internet is true and we can use or repost it".

How true is the above statement? Give reason/reasons.

16. If someone sends you a friend request online with a picture of your classmate, should you immediately accept it? Give reasons.
17. I installed an antivirus on my computer. After a month, I realized that my computer starts hanging and I am suspecting a virus in it? What could be the reason?
18. I'm online and I meet someone my age in a chat room. Is it OK to give him or her my address or phone number?
19. Mention a few online threats that you may encounter.
20. __________ are messages that try to trick you into providing sensitive information.

21. What are cookies?

22

Clicking ads and pop-ups like the one shown in this image could expose your computer to ___________.

23. You're working on a group project. When practicing your presentation, one person in your group says something that doesn't make sense to you. They say that the information is from an online article so it must be true. What should be your response? Will you reverify it?
24. Mention few etiquettes you should follow when you are online
25. Explain Intellectual Property rights. Name three important Intellectual Property rights.
26. a. GNU stands for ______________
    b. The license which covers works line websites, scholarship, music, film, photography, literature, courseware is __________
    c. _________ license doesn't require any renewal and is applicable in all countries.
    d. An example of an operating system under GPL is __________
    e. _________, _________ and __________ are the few types of cyber crime.
    f. Posting hurtful messages and commenting on a photo or a video posted by others is called __________
27. Hacking is always illegal? Do you agree with the statement?
28. Recently I went to a place where free wifi was available and I used it. Is my important data at risk? If it is stolen that it would be called as __________
29. Your parents wanted to do some online transactions and they were apprehensive about the risks while using netbanking. So they approached you and asked what precautions should be taken. What will you suggest?
30. Mention few measures to prevent cyber crime
31. Explain the following with an example:
    a. Trojan   b. Malware   c. Adware
32. Suggest a few ways to manage E-waste.
33. What is the IT Act? It is also called ITA 2000. Why?
34. Give few objectives of the IT Act.
35. What are the different types of disabilities which may cause hindrance while teaching?